COMMUNICATION AND INFORMATION SCIENCE

A series of monographs, treatises, and texts
Edited by
MELVIN J. VOIGT
University of California, San Diego

William C. Adams • Television Coverage of the Middle East
William C. Adams • Television Coverage of International Affairs
William C. Adams • Television Coverage of the 1980 Presidential Campaign
Alan Baughcum and Gerald Faulhaber • Telecommunications Access and Public Policy
Mary B. Cassata and Thomas Skill • Life on Daytime Television
Hewitt D. Crane • The New Social Marketplace
Rhonda J. Crane • The Politics of International Standards
Herbert S. Dordick, Helen G. Bradley, and Burt Nanus • The Emerging Network Marketplace
Glen Fisher • American Communication in a Global Society
Oscar H. Gandy, Jr. • Beyond Agenda Setting
Oscar H. Gandy, Jr., Paul Espinosa, and Janusz A. Ordover • Proceedings from the Tenth Annual Telecommunications Policy Research Conference
Edmund Glenn • Man and Mankind: Conflict and Communication Between Cultures
Gerald Goldhaber, Harry S. Dennis III, Gary M. Richetto, and Osmo A. Wiio • Information Strategies
Bradley S. Greenberg • Life on Television: Content Analyses of U.S. TV Drama
Bradley S. Greenberg, Michael Burgoon, Judee K. Burgoon, and Felipe Korzenny • Mexican Americans and the Mass Media
Cees J. Hamelink • Finance and Information: A Study of Converging Interests
Heather Hudson • When Telephones Reach the Village
Robert M. Landau, James H. Bair, and Jean Siegman • Emerging Office Systems
James Larson • Television's Window on the World
John Lawrence • The Electronic Scholar
John S. Lawrence and Bernard M. Timberg • Fair Use and Free Inquiry
Robert G. Meadow • Politics as Communication
William H. Melody, Liora R. Salter, and Paul Heyer • Culture, Communication, and Dependency:
Vincent Mosco • Broadcasting in the United States
Vincent Mosco • Policy Research in Telecommunications: Proceedings from the Eleventh Annual Telecommunications Policy Research Conference
Vincent Mosco • Pushbutton Fantasies
Kaarle Nordenstreng • The Mass Media Declaration of UNESCO
Kaarle Nordenstreng and Herbert I. Schiller • National Sovereignty and International Communication
Harry J. Otway and Malcolm Peltu • New Office Technology
Ithiel de Sola Pool • Forecasting the Telephone
Everett Rogers and Francis Balle • The Media Revolution in America and in Western Europe
Dan Schiller • Telematics and Government
Herbert I. Schiller • Information and the Crisis Economy
Herbert I. Schiller • Who Knows: Information in the Age of the Fortune 500
Jorge A. Schnitman • Film Industries in Latin America
Indu B. Singh • Telecommunications in the Year 2000
Jennifer Daryl Slack • Communication Technologies and Society
Dallas W. Smythe • Dependency Road
Sari Thomas • Studies in Mass Media and Technology, Volumes 1-3
Barry Truax • Acoustic Communication
Georgette Wang and Wimal Dissanayake • Continuity and Change in Communication Systems
Janet Wasko • Movies and Money

Modeling as Negotiating

Modeling as Negotiating

THE POLITICAL DYNAMICS OF COMPUTER MODELS IN THE POLICY PROCESS

William H. Dutton
University of Southern California

Kenneth L. Kraemer
University of California, Irvine

ABLEX PUBLISHING CORPORATION
NORWOOD, NEW JERSEY

Illustrations by Arthur Asa Berger.

This book is the product of a research project entitled "Fiscal Impact Budgeting Systems: A Behavioral Assessment," supported by a grant from the Division of Applied Research of the U.S. National Science Foundation (Grant No. DAR 7817606).

The views expressed herein are those of the researchers and should not be ascribed as views of the National Science Foundation.

Printed in the United States of America

Library of Congress Cataloging in Publication Data

Dutton, William H., 1947-
Modeling as negotiating.

(Communication and information science)
Bibliography: p.
1. Local finance—United States—Mathematical models.
2. Policy sciences—Mathematical models. I. Kraemer, Kenneth L. II. Title. III. Series.
HJ9145.D88 1984 361.6'1'0724 84-28429
ISBN 0-89391-261-1

Ablex Publishing Corporation
355 Chestnut Street
Norwood, New Jersey 07648

Contents

Acknowledgements

This book is a product of the Fiscal Impact Budgeting Systems Project (FIBS), carried out from 1978 to 1982. The project was supported by a grant from the National Science Foundation and administered by the Public Policy Research Organization at the University of California, Irvine. The purpose of the project was to conduct a behavioral survey that assessed the use and impacts of computer-based fiscal impact models in American local governments.

This project has greatly benefitted from the contributions of our colleagues, especially Martha Hollis, who should share whatever credit this manuscript may merit. Her contributions to the initial proposal and since then to a technical review of four fiscal impact models have complemented the behavioral analysis reported in this manuscript. Similarly, Dr. Susan Fallows conducted the case study of Anaheim, California, providing an example of insight, care and thoroughness that we have tried to match in our own field work.

This project could never have been completed without the cooperation and support of the model developers and practitioners, including: Donald Blumberg and Warren Suss of Decision Sciences Corporation; Sheldon Gans of Marshall, Kaplan, Gans and Kahn; Paul Tischler and Ali Montasser of Tischler, Montasser and Associates, Inc., and John Rau of Ultrasystems.

Dr. Debra Dunkle's consultation and support was essential to the statistical analyses presented in this study. Dr. Dunkle advised us on questionnaire design, and supervised the field survey, data reduction, and analysis. Without her help, these tasks would have been more difficult to complete.

Ms. Susan Komsky assisted in the design of the study's questionnaire and in the conduct of a series of telephone interviews prior to the field survey. Her predissertation work based on the field survey was suggestive of several lines of inquiry we pursued in later analyses.

The Public Policy Research Organization professional staff rendered essential support throughout the project. Every draft was routed to Doris McBride who organized the production of this manuscript from start to finish. Shirley Hoberman kept track of project expenditures. The PPRO secretarial staff, Rosa Garza, Cheryl Carey, Julie Takahashi, Sherry Merryman, Helen Sandoz and Mary Ann Tacha transcribed hours of interviews and typed dozens of manuscripts. Laurel Battaglia refined and clarified our prose.

Agnes Uy at the Annenberg School of Communications helped in typing the many draft manuscripts prepared at the University of Southern California.

Several colleagues reviewed this manuscript in whole or in part, including Martin Greenberger, Robert Meadow, Peter Monge, and Aaron Wildavsky. Their advice was of substantial value to the final version and we thank them. We are particularly grateful to Melvin Voigt and Walter Johnson at Ablex for help in shaping and expediting the published manuscript.

Finally, we wish to acknowledge the continuing support of our colleagues on the URBIS project, from which this project originally developed. Jim Danziger, John King, and Rob Kling are a continuing source of support through their criticism, advice, and individual contributions to social analyses of information technology.

Despite the substantial advice and help of so many people, the authors assume full responsibility for any errors or omissions that remain.

In any list, one item must appear first, one second, and so on. Such ordering is inevitable. The order in which the names of the authors of this book appear is a result of this necessity, and should in no way be taken to indicate primary or secondary roles in authorship.

Preface

In the course of writing *Modeling as Negotiating,* our views were transformed from marked skepticism to cautious optimism regarding the role of modeling in the policy process. Our early studies led us to believe that policy modeling was a highly partisan process used to support the legitimacy of decisions made on the basis of criteria far removed from the merits of the case. At a superficial level there was early support for this perspective in the literature as well as from our field observations of modeling.

Nevertheless, we eventually unraveled several general patterns of the modeling process that contradicted the view of modeling as primarily a partisan political process. For example, many participants in the process viewed it as a successful analytical exercise that qualitatively improved the process and outcome of decision making. At the same time, these participants knew that partisan political positions were influential in shaping the analyses. Also, modeling efforts that failed to incorporate influential participants, that excluded important groups or interests, tended to fail. Likewise, attempts to model reality in an extremely partisan fashion appeared unlikely to succeed. Most generally, modeling appeared to facilitate negotiation and consensus in the public policy process. In this respect, modeling was a political process, but one far more politically benign than we had anticipated. Moreover, modeling is more technically successful than we first believed on the basis of observing what we describe in this book as the labyrinthian process of implementing even a simple model into a complex policy process.

Still, our assessment of the role of modeling is tempered by the observation that while modeling might promote negotiation and consensus, these outcomes differentially affect the interests of various groups involved in the policy process. Most importantly, those groups excluded from the modeling process are unlikely to have their interests served by its outcome.

These discrepancies between our early expectations and later observations led us to an alternative perspective on the policy modeling process, which we call "consensus modeling." From this perspective, modeling is viewed as a tool for facilitating negotiation and, thereby, consensus in the policy making process. While we present this perspective in the introductory chapter of this book, its development actually followed the field work involved with this study. We hope this reverse chronological presentation provides the reader with a better conceptual lens from which to view the modeling process than we had when first exploring the complex relationships between analysis and politics in the policy process.

Our aim has been to formulate general perspectives on the politics of the modeling process. Nevertheless, we realize that our data are limited to a single case—the utilization of computer-based fiscal impact models in American cities. Notwithstanding this limitation, we believe this study merits broad attention because it is among the first to intensively examine the social and political dynamics of a similar class of models across a variety of organizations. In such a comparative case study, the variations in the modeling process across organizations are particulary informative about the role of personal, organizational, and historical factors, as opposed to the role of variations in the nature of the model *per se*. In addition, this focus permitted more in-depth research than might have been possible from a survey of a larger variety of models in organizations of different types.

There is a general tendency, with which we disagree, to dismiss the routine activities of the nearly 80,000 state and local government jurisdictions within the United States as less critical than dramatic actions of highly visible federal agencies and officials. Despite the glamour of the national elite and newsworthy events, our focus has been on the more mundane routines of politicians, bureaucrats, and technocrats within the thousands of governments affecting the daily lives of the public. Likewise, we have focused on a class of models that are neither glamourous nor necessarily sophisticated in their design and application. This is attractive from our point of view, for instead of becoming mired in explaining the entrails of a complex model, our presentation can focus on the social dynamics of organizations attempting to grapple with new technology in a highly charged political environment.

Most importantly, however, we believe that the perspectives developed in this study will withstand the careful scrutiny of other researchers looking at different models in different political and organizational settings. That is the process by which theories are developed and refined within a case study approach and we believe this is no less valid than more mainstream survey and experimental approaches to the development of theory in the social and behavioral sciences.

William H. Dutton

Kenneth L. Kraemer

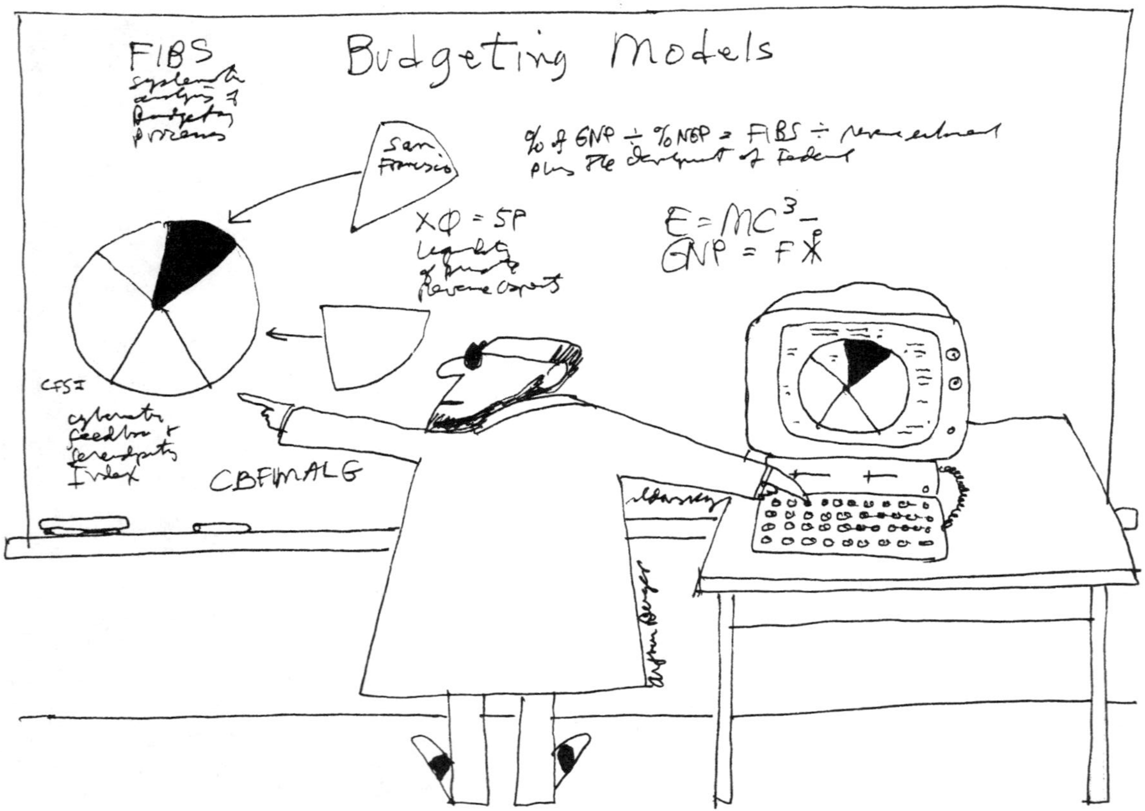
Budgeting Models
FIBS
San Francisco
XΦ = SP
E = MC³
CFSI
CBFIMALG

1. Models in the Information Society

Days after the publication of William Greider's (1981) 24 page *Atlantic Monthly* article, entitled "The Education of David Stockman," President Reagan's Director of the Office of Management and Budget made his now famous trip to the woodshed. At the meeting, Stockman offered President Reagan his resignation because of the national stir that had been created by the revelations in the "Stockman Papers."[1] Stockman's interview with Greider had undermined the legitimacy of the President's economic program, the centerpiece of the President's domestic policy. Comments that were attributed to Stockman suggested that the OMB director had systematically used computers and statistical analyses of the Office of Management and Budget to massage and manipulate taxing and spending statistics to support "Reaganomics," the supply side economics of the new administration. According to the article, early OMB analyses indicated that Reagan's proposed three year tax cuts combined with defense spending increases would create huge budget deficits of nearly $82 billion in 1982 and $116 billion in 1984. Stockman's reaction to these findings, which he felt were "absolutely shocking," was to alter the assumptions that underlay the OMB projections and revise the calculations in order to project a 1984 surplus if the Reagan budget plans were enacted.

In the wake of the Stockman Papers, the bulk of criticism leveled at David Stockman was relatively unconcerned with his manipulation of computer models and statistics to support the President's budget proposal. Instead, criticism focused on Stockman's "indiscretion" during his interviews with Greider (see, e.g., Segilman, 1981). Stockman's own early reaction to the article was to observe that his comments had been "off the record," not intended for publication. President Reagan's concerns reportedly focused on why his OMB director had been so open to a reporter and just how committed Stockman was to the President's economic program.

In the interviews, Stockman had suggested that "supply- side economics" was simply a euphemistic expression for the age old "trickle-down" economic policy. According to Stockman: "It's kind of hard to sell 'trickle down,' so the supply-side formula was the only way to get a tax policy that was really 'trickle-down.' . . . Kemp-Roth was always a Trojan horse to bring down the top grade."

The analysis of Stockman's interview given by *Time Magazine* also emphasized Stockman's indiscretion and apparent lack of faith in Reagan's policy. The writers of the *Time* article dismissed the massaging of OMB data with the following comment: "Feeding rosy data into calculations to get a desired result is hardly an innovation at OMB" (Magnuson, Beckworth, & Brew, 1981, p. 11). Another writer has made a "virtue" of Stockman's manipulation of the economic model in *Fortune*:

> All right, what did Stockman's duplicity consist of?
>
> *He changed the computer program.* As this event is introduced by Greider, the reader is encouraged to think that an intellectual swindle is taking place. The article first respectfully refers to "an OMB computer, programmed as a model of the nation's economic behavior"—language that will inhibit the reader from recalling the model's miserable batting average over the years. Then Greider tells you that this computer predicted huge deficits if the Reagan program went into effect. Whereupon Stockman "changed the OMB computer," so that it now spat out figures on economic growth and federal revenues more congenial to the Administration.
>
> Does this story demonstrate that the Reaganites were duplicitous? No, it doesn't, the story shows that they *believed* in their ideas. It would have been truly dishonest to rely on a computer model that failed to show the additional growth they were telling the country to expect after supply-side economic policies had been put in place. [Emphasis in the original article.] (Segilman, 1981, p.89)

In short, few people were surprised by the fact that OMB's statistics were manipulated to support Reagan's policy preferences. Rather, they were surprised by Stockman's indiscretion in revealing publicly what everyone suspected privately. In revealing inside information and expressing his personal doubts, Stockman had raised questions about his loyalty and value to Reagan's team.

The Stockman Syndrome: Old Wine in New Bottles?

The Stockman Papers are far from the first revelation of the partisan use of analysis in public policy making. Deceptions of a much broader scale were uncovered in the Pentagon Papers regarding official reports on the Vietnam War. But of possibly greater long-term impact than these notorious cases is the prospect of partisan use in the *routine* application of computer models, analyses, and forecasts by agencies of the over 80,000 government units in the United States.

Early studies of planning in American cities frequently highlight the political use of analysis. Floyd Hunter's study of Atlanta, Georgia, showed that "expert advice" was used only when it "fit" the relatively narrow interests of the policy makers (Hunter, 1956, p. 240). Alan Altschuler's (1965) case studies of planning in Minneapolis and St. Paul detailed the political obstacles to the use of rational planning analysis. Later studies on the use of computerized urban development models showed that these sophisticated models face political fates similar to simpler analyses. Edmund Fowler (1971) found that "the mathematics hid nonmathematical prejudices" (1971, p. 139) in the Massachusetts Department of Public Works utilization of land use and transportation forecasting models to support its freeway plans. Gary Brewer (1973) found that San Francisco's housing market model was used primarily as a tool for legitimizing rather than formulating policy. Howard and Janet Pack (1977a) found that use of urban development models actually increased the difficulty of reaching political consensus in policy making because the models make clear what there is to gain and lose, and by whom. Other studies by Greenberger, Crenson, and Crissey (1976) indicated that the political use of computer models extends far beyond the local arena to national economic models and "world models" of great public prominence.

Mason Gaffney (1978) has captured the thrust of these early studies of modeling by suggesting that some sophisticated computer models simply place "old wine in new bottles." Despite the rhetoric of reform and rational decision making that surrounds the introduction and use of these tools, it is merely "old style politics" that is manifested in these new technologies of the emerging information society. Or is it? Some have argued that computerized data and sophisticated models can bring new elements to public policy making that make a qualitative improvement in the outcome of the policy process (Greenberger, 1983; Keen & Morton, 1978; Kraemer, Dutton, & Northrop, 1981).

TECHNOLOGY AND POLICY MAKING

What's at Issue?

The Stockman case and similar controversies raise a significant issue about the role of modern information technology in American policy making.

Why is it not surprising that rosy data were fed into a computer model to get desired results? Why do senior public officials and senior members of the American press expect a model of the nation's economic behavior to be biased? Why is there so little concern over the fact that a computer model was manipulated to produce results consistent with Administration policy? Why did the Stockman revelations fail to raise a flurry of criticisms regarding such political use of analysis?

This is a fundamental issue about the utilization of new information technologies by policy analysts and bureaucrats within a liberal democratic society. It is not primarily an issue of the isolated indiscretion of a senior analyst/bureaucrat. The basic issue is that policy makers and the public apparently cannot expect policy analyses conducted with the aid of information technology to be objective, credible, and accurate. Indeed, the technology is expected to automate the partisan biases of politicians.

The irony of this situation is that it arises at a time when public agencies are increasingly reliant upon the use of sophisticated information technology for the conduct of policy analyses and forecasts. Information technology, which includes computers, telecommunications, management science models and mixtures of these technologies,[2] greatly extends the possibility for credible policy analyses. In fact, we are reminded that we are living in an "information society" where such tools are becoming increasingly valuable as a resource for improving the productivity of organizations and the quality of organizational decision making. How ironic it is then that the tools of the information society are generally expected to be used by policy analysts in misinforming the public and policy makers alike!

Policy Making in the "Information Society"

This ironic situation raises a broader issue concerning how evolving information technology will affect the governance of democratic societies. The increasing use of computer models for policy analysis at all levels in the American government is viewed by some critics as widening the knowledge gap between experts, on the one hand, and lay policy officials and the general public, on the other hand (Laudon, 1977; Schiller, 1981). This poses a fundamental conflict between democracy and technocracy; between involving broad constituencies in the policy making process, and concerning expertise and policy influence in the hands of a technical elite. This conflict is at the heart of what is problematic about the "information society"—a name used by several writers to refer to the increasing tendency of the U.S. economy and most developed nations' economies to move towards greater emphasis on information processing than on industrial production as a result of the triple revolution in computers, communications, and information (Bell, 1973, 1979; Nora & Minc, 1980; Porat, 1977; Williams, 1982). In the information society, not only is information processing a key economic activity, but information itself is a critical political resource of individual actors, groups and organizations (Danziger, Dutton, Kling, & Kraemer, 1982; Downs, 1967; Lowi, 1981). As a result, control of information, of the technology to generate it, and of the technical expertise to use it, is increasingly important in determining policy. But who controls information technology? And whose interests does it serve?

Debate on the locus of control over modeling is particularly controversial. Some scholars argue that technical experts—modelers—control this process (Greenberger et al., 1976) by dominating day-to-day decisions and technical actions. Other scholars indicate that political elites—politicians and bureaucrats—control the modeling process because they dominate the most critical features of adoption and utilization (Brewer, 1973). Debate also turns on the interests served by modeling. The proponents of modeling generally perceive the process to be nonpartisan in the sense that it provides "objective" information that is not biased to serve any particular special interest. Critics of modeling often suggest that models serve partisan interests—the self-interests of particular individuals or groups in the policy process.

Both of the dimensions shown in Table 1.1—locus of control and interests served—are in actuality continua rather than clear dichotomies. For example, politicians, bureaucrats and technocrats all share some control over models in the policy process. Yet the relative control of each of these actors is likely to vary such that one or the other of these categories is more descriptive of a particular distribution of control. Similarly, the degree to which the partisan or self-interests of politicians, bureaucrats, and technocrats are served is likely to vary on a broad continuum. But in any particular case, and over many cases, a "dominant" pattern can be discerned.

TABLE 1.1. Political Perspectives on Models

	Dominant Interests Served	
Dominant Locus of Control	**Partisan/ Self-Interest**	**Non-Partisan/ Pluralistic Interests**
Technical Experts	Technocratic perspective	Rational perspective
Political Elites	Partisan perspective	Consensual perspective

It is the intersection of these two dimensions of "control" and "interests served" that yields four perspectives on the modeling process. Each perspective maps quite well into the existing literature and research on the modeling process. Each is described next.

The rational perspective views models as "scientific" aids to policy making and analysis. From this perspective, the manifest role and explicit purpose for adopting models is to support decision making by analyzing the merits of alternative policy choices. Presumably, models are adopted to provide information to help solve problems of choice. A rational "problem-information-decision" sequence of decision making is implied. And, the eventual outcome of modeling is expected to conform to these explicit rational goals.

To conduct such analysis, technical experts are provided a great deal of autonomy in applying technical standards and in judging the merits of different policy options. Presumably, there are technically or scientifically appropriate theories embedded within the models and rules for operationalizing them for specific analyses. Thus, the quality of any particular analysis rests upon the ability of technical experts to apply these theories and rules independent of political guidance. And the outcome of this use of modeling is the provision of objective nonpartisan information, available to all, and portraying the relative impacts of alternative policies.

The information produced by modeling in any particular instance is not intended to "determine" policy choice but only to add to the larger base of information used by policy makers—mainly politicians and bureaucrats. Over time, however, the use of modeling *is* intended to increase the relative importance of science- and model-based information over other kinds of information in policy making. In order to achieve this effect, it is important that modeling be incorporated into the ongoing, routine functioning of the organization. Thus, from the rational perspective, "incorporation" is the most important stage in the modeling process. The introduction and local adaptation phases should be accomplished efficiently and quickly in order to facilitate incorporation and the continuing generation of model-based analyses. Examples of the rational perspective can be found in management science and modeling textbooks and in works by Anthony (1965), Hiltz and Turoff (1978), Simon (1960, 1971, 1973), Keen and Morton (1978), and Morton and Huff (1980).

The *technocratic perspective* (Table 1.1) views models as a complex technology controlled by the new priests of the information society and poorly understood by politicians, bureaucrats, or the public. From this perspective, the manifest role and explicit purpose of models is to promote and transfer the ideas of the model experts. The expert can embody an approach to problem solving in a computer model that greatly extends the reach and utilization of these ideas. The eventual outcome of modeling is expected to identify the most appropriate policy choices based on the rationale articulated by the model experts and built into the underlying logic of the model.

Such an approach implies a model of decision making that involves appeals to a recognized authority for expert advice and guidance. Decision-makers must scour the region or country for the proper authorities, who because of the rise of new analytical methods, might well be model experts. The experts are then expected to repeat the analyses by which they had gained their reputations, in a more or less predictable manner. Given such predetermination of model results, the influence of politicians and bureaucrats necessarily focuses on promoting or discrediting the experts and their models in order to affect the choice of experts and/or the perceived credibility of their results. Examples of the technocratic perspective are common in the practice of modeling (Boguslaw, 1965; Danzinger, 1979a, 1979b; Weizenbaum, 1976). And, not surprisingly, some of the most well-known modelers, such as Jay Forrester and Dennis Meadows, provide the best illustrations of such a perspective (see Greenberger, et al., 1976, for a description).

The *partisan perspective* of modeling contrasts most sharply with that of the rational perspective (Table 1.1). From the partisan perspective, models are tools of propaganda and persuasion of special interests in the policy process. They are adopted with the intention of legitimating choices that have already been arrived at by those whose control policy decisions—the dominant political coalition in an organization. Here, decision making follows a "decision-propaganda-conformity" sequence in contrast to the "problem-information-decision" sequence implied by the rational perspective. The consequence of partisan analysis is reinforcement of the interests of the dominant political coalition within the organization. Models are propaganda that provide support and legitimacy to the policy initiatives of those who control decision making.

For partisan analyses to be successfully conducted, modelers must be controlled by decision makers to insure that analyses support their interests. From this perspective, the most important phase of the modeling process might be introduction, when a choice is made to adopt a model that will support the position of the dominant coalition. However, the adaptation stage also is important especially when not guided and controlled by the initial adoption decision.

Examples of partisan analyses are the fuel for most critiques of the use of modeling in the policy process (Ascher, 1978; Benveniste, 1977; Brewer, 1973; Greenberger, et al., 1976). In many ways, David Stockman's reputed manipulation of models of the Office of Management and Budget to reinforce Reagan's tax cuts is suggestive of partisan analysis. OMB's analyses were simply used as a tool to legitimate "Reagonomics," a policy determined prior to and independent of the analyses. David Stockman was the political operative used to assure that technical experts supported the administration's interests in passing the President's budget proposals.

For the most part, the modeling literature has been written from one of these three alternative perspectives. Generally, modeling experts, decision science academics, and the advocates of modeling techniques describe modeling from a rational perspective. The textbooks, the professional societies, and the trade magazines speak from this viewpoint in prescribing the appropriate role of modelers and models. While the rational perspective is the most common *prescription* and is sometimes descriptive of reality, it deviates from most empirical accounts of the modeling process. Both journalistic and academic studies of the actual implementation and use of models have given rise to the technocratic and partisan perspectives as more accurate descriptions of the process, especially in highly unstructured, nonroutine, and more consequential policy decisions (Brewer, 1973; Dutton & Kraemer, 1977; Greenberger, et al., 1976; Greenberger, 1983; Kling, 1980; Kraemer & Dutton, 1979).

Consequently, there is growing skepticism over the value of modeling in policy arenas where there are sharp differences of opinions and interests. Unfortunately, few interesting policy choices are not characterized by such differences of opinions. Moreover, policy analyses—from any perspective—are inherently political in that significant policy choices inevitably affect who gets what, when, and how (Lindblom, 1980). To more fully understand the political dimensions of modeling, therefore, this book examines the use of a particular class of models in American local government. And on the basis of this analysis, a new perspective on the politics of modeling—consensual modeling— is suggested as an alternative view of the role of modeling in the policy process.

The *consensual perspective* of modeling differs significantly from the more prevalent conceptualizations described above. From the consensual perspective, models are primarily tools for negotiation, bargaining, and interactive decision making among the representatives of conflicting interests and opinions in the policy process. However, negotiation is not the manifest or explicit aim of those involved in the modeling process. In fact, the manifest purposes for adopting and utilizing models tend to be multiple and shifting over the life-cycle of the modeling process. That is, different participants in the modeling process have varied objectives and these objectives change as participants change and as policy issues evolve.

Modelers are not isolated and independent within such a process nor are they simply the instruments of politicians. Rather, they pursue the modeling process with indirect guidance, consulting broadly among the array of participants that represent different interests involved in the policy choice. Modelers attempt to anticipate the reactions of various groups and interests to the technical choices they make in order that their choices are viewed as correct and that the product of their efforts are accepted. By anticipating and reacting to a diverse array of interests, modelers are constantly involved in a process of negotiating and resolving conflicts over a variety of factors, including the state-of-nature (how participants define reality), the alternative policy choices, the outcomes of these alternatives, and the criteria for evaluating these choices.

From the consensual perspective, the most critical stage of the modeling process is that of adaptation.It is primarily during the adaptation phase that modelers can adjust models to take into account the competing beliefs and interests of various participants. However, the introduction of models is important also, since adoption itself is indicative of agreement over modeling as a process by which to negotiate and bargain.

METHODS AND DATA

This formulation of the consensual modeling perspective is empirically grounded in the politics surrounding the implementation of fiscal impact models in American local governments. Fiscal impact models are mathematical models designed to calculate the fiscal impacts both of alternative development plans and of the probable impacts of intergovernmental and local policies on these plans. Such plans and policies might include a planned unit development, a major rezoning, a shopping center development, a freeway, a new tax rate, a Proposition-13–type tax limitation, or a new intergovernmental revenue source. Fiscal impact models can be used to answer "what if" questions about such plans and policies; that is, the models can be used to calculate the costs and revenues that result from various development and environmental possibilities.

A fiscal impact or cost-revenue analysis is a "projection of the direct, current, public costs and revenues associated with residential or nonresidential growth to the local jurisdiction(s) in which growth is taking place" (Burchell & Listokin, 1978). Traditionally, fiscal impact analysis omits a wide array of costs and benefits commonly associated with urban development, including many such secondary effects of development as the alteration of neighboring property values; economic impacts on developers, renters, and homeowners and on private, commercial, and industrial enterprises; impacts on the revenues and expenditures of other government jurisdictions; and a host of social, political, and environmental effects. In short, fiscal impact analysis provides a *partial* assessment of development effects. Even so, such analysis is far from simple, requiring scores of simplifying assumptions and sophisticated estimating techniques to deal with the complexity and uncertainty of the real world. Such analysis also requires many numerical calculations to capture the costs and benefits arising from growth-induced change.

While fiscal impact analysis is manageable with manual methods, it is constrained in several respects. Many cost-revenue analyses require hundreds of calculations. Not surprisingly, therefore, one of the major problems of manual analysis is the prevalence of arithmetical errors. Moreover, given the interdependence of calculations, the cumulative errors of manual calculation are often enormous. Computers, on the other hand, eliminate these calculation problems. Moreover, computers allow analysts to calculate the revenues and expenditures associated with a large number of development alternatives, to introduce far more decision variables, and to vary many more assumptions than would be feasible using manual processing. Thus, in principle, they improve both the quantity and the quality of information available to allow for informed decision making. And they increase both the speed and the ease with which such sophisticated analysis can be done.

Theoretically, such cost-revenue models are introduced into city and county governments to improve the ability of policy makers and planners to determine the fiscal profitability of urban development and, coincidentally, to improve the ability of urban managers to develop land use plans in a rational way. (For a more technical description of these models, see Appendix.) To the extent that the adaptation of fiscal impact models in specific local governments results in these improvements, we would expect that they would subsequently become incorporated by the government and routinely used. Consequently, we asked two broad questions about these models in our study: (a) Who controls how these models are used by the major actors—politicians, bureaucrats, professionals and technocrats? and (b) Whose interests are served by the use of models? The answers to these questions are developed from our analyses in subsequent chapters and used to generate the consensual perspective on the role of models in the policy making process.

As a case study of a limited class of models in a special governmental setting, this book explores the politics of modeling by using a mix of qualitative and quantitative methods. Four case studies of local governments that have implemented computer-based fiscal impact models constitute the main qualitative effort. Each case study is organized according to three stages involved in model implementation (introduction, adaptation, incorporation), and each examines the technology, its social setting, and the use and impact of the models. Each case study also focuses on some unique theme of importance to the implementation process, such as the influence of the environment of the modeling effort, or the political uses of the model.

Although implementation of these models usually occurred over several years, we were able to study the implementation process by the presence of extensive documentation, including records of city clerks, tape recordings and videotapes of council meetings, reports of economic consultants on the models, studies and analyses by planning staff who used the models, and manuals for both model-operators and model-users. In addition, we have relied extensively upon the perceptions of major actors involved during implementation, including city council members, city administrators, planning and budget staff, economic consultants, citizen participants, and the model developers.

There are approximately ten versions of computer-based fiscal impact models available in the United States, some of which have been "packaged" for transfer to more than one government body (Appendix). In order to illustrate the variations among available models, especially the packaged models, four fiscal impact systems are examined in this study: the Fiscal Impact Analysis System (FIAS), the Local Government Fiscal Impact Model (FIM), the Fiscal Impact System for Communities (FISCOM), and the Municipal Impact Evaluation System (MUNIES). The selection of "packaged" models for study was dictated by both theoretical and practical concerns. From a theoretical standpoint, we wanted to study "implementation" separate from the "development" of models. When a model is developed in-house, it frequently is difficult to separate the development and implementation phases. And, from a practical standpoint, we wanted our research to be relevant to the most frequently occuring situation—a situation in which a model is transferred-in from another government body or from a private supplier.

Table 1.2 lists the four systems and selected sites where they have been installed. Each of these systems can be adapted to local peculiarities by the developers in consultation with users. Most of the companies marketing the systems "tailor" them in order to increase their usefulness to particular users. Such "tailoring" illustrates an important feature of policy models generally, and those studied here in particular—namely, that they are nonstandard. The prototypical descriptions utilized in this study should not be allowed to obscure the diversity of these models. For example, some models are proprietary and others are not; some embed econometric models and some do not.

The quantitative analysis in this study is based upon a 1980 field survey of all known (as of 1980) local governments that were users of four specific fiscal impact models: FIAS, FIM, FISCOM, and MUNIES. The population of these local governments numbered 21. Within each government, we surveyed both the principal analyst who was responsible for the model and several model users. The latter included elected officials, managers, planners, budget and finance officers and, on occasion, citizens who had participated in a model's implementation or use. The survey is

TABLE 1.2. Four Fiscal Impact Systems

	FIAS	FIM	FISCOM	MUNIES
System Name	Fiscal Impact Analysis System	Fiscal Impact Model	Fiscal Impact System for Communities	Municipal Impact Evaluation System
Marketed by	Decision Sciences Corp., Jenkintown, PA	Ultrasystems Inc., Irvine, CA	Marshall, Kaplan, Gans and Kahn, San Francisco, CA	Tischler, Montasser and Associates, Inc., Washington, D.C.
Selected List of Sites Where Installed [a]	Ottawa, Canada	Anaheim, CA	Irvine, CA	San Diego, CA
	Orange County, CA	San Jose, CA	Rancho Cucamonga, CA	Greece, NY
	SEMCOG, MI (including Detroit)	San Juan Capistrano, CA		Metro-Washington, DC, Council of Governments (COG)
	Tulsa, OK	Huntington Beach, CA		

[a]The above mentioned sites where systems have been installed is *not* a comprehensive listing; named sites are merely illustrative.

based on self-administered, mail questionnaires, completed by over 80 percent of the respondents surveyed in the cities and counties that have implemented any one of the four fiscal impact models. A total of 125 users participated in the study by completing self-administered questionnaires and/or being personally interviewed. The focus of the quantitative analysis using these data is both descriptive and explanatory. That is, the survey sought both to describe the nature and extent of model use and to explain the relative success or failure of different modeling efforts.

THE CASE FOR CONSENSUS MODELING

The consensual perspective *emerged* from our study of fiscal impact modeling in local governments. We did not begin with it. Rather, the consensual perspective was formulated from instances of the successful use of computer-based fiscal impact modeling. Here, success is not equated with technical elegance or abstract criteria of rationality. Rather, it simply means that the participants overwhelmingly viewed the process as successful. Indeed, the perspective of consensual modeling developed late in our efforts as a means of making sense of a process that many participants viewed as successful, but for which the more common perspectives of rational, technocratic and partisan modeling were inadequate.

Modeling as Negotiating

The consensual perspective is appealing and useful on several grounds. First, models have attributes that more or less facilitate negotiation and bargaining (Table 1.3). Among these attributes are the tendency for models to focus conflict away from the individuals and from the positions of parties involved in policy conflicts to the facts, options, and implications of the debate and to the process of modeling. Second, the use of models provides a bargaining process that contestants might agree to for resolving disagreements. Third, by its very nature, the modeling process provides bargaining options and formulates them as alternatives. And finally, models often explicitly provide criteria for weighing alternatives that might be accepted by contestants in the policy process. In short, by deflecting conflict away from individuals and positions, and by providing a process, options, and criteria for resolving disagreements, modeling provides ingredients found important to successful negotiating strategy (Fisher & Ury, 1981).

The modeling process not only embeds certain features of successful negotiations, it also is empirically suggestive of a negotiating process. In fact, it is only by viewing modeling as negotiating that our findings re-

TABLE 1.3. Modeling as a Negotiating Strategy

Characteristic of Successful Negotiating Strategy[a]	Characteristics of Consensual Modeling
A. Convince parties to a conflict to negotiate.	A. Bring representatives of relevant interests and parties into the modeling process.
B. Agree on a process for resolving conflict not an outcome.	B. Obtain agreement to modeling as an appropriate process for informing and possibly reaching decision.
C. "Separate people from the problem."	C. Focus on reaching consensus over appropriate model, data, and assumptions rather than debating positions on broader issue. The model is meant to inform.
D. "Focus on interests not positions."	D. Define concrete options and a range of options that reflect all parties' interests.
E. "Invent options for mutual gain."	E. Iterate through the options and analysis; sequentially narrow choice toward options which provide for mutual gain to relevant interests and parties.
F. "Insist on objective criteria."	F. Obtain agreement on criteria for choice in advance of analysis with the model; analyze consequences of options on agreed criteria, i.e., fiscal impact.

[a]Adapted from Fisher and Ury (1981).

garding the implementation of computer-based fiscal impact models appear as reasonable expectations rather than organizational pathologies. For example, the final report or final analysis generated as the product of modeling studies tends to be far less important than the various decisions and compromises and preliminary analyses that preceded it. The final report is anti-climactic, which reflects the negotiated compromises that had been ongoing throughout the adaptation process. Likewise what appears as a mismanaged, exceptionally long, and rather labyrinthian implementation process is functional to negotiation by ensuring that analyses sufficiently reflect the diverse views of participants with interests and influence in the policy process. In part, it is the influential role of models that necessitates that they are negotiated to accommodate the variety of groups and interests concerned over policy choices. Thus, what is perceived from a rational perspective to be an inefficient and "political" implementation process might be viewed, from a consensual perspective, as an efficient and effective negotiating process.

THE CONDITIONS SUPPORTING CONSENSUAL MODELING

While the consensual perspective is attractive both as an intellectual perspective on modeling and as a means of organizing the empirical findings that are reported below, the appropriateness of this perspective, or any other perspective, appears to be contingent upon certain features of the political context and the technology.

The Political Context of Consensus Modeling

Certain features of the social and political setting appear to require and/or facilitate consensus modeling. First, is the extent to which policy problems are relatively unstructured. More unstructured problems appear to drive toward consensus modeling. In the case of modeling the costs and revenues of urban development, problems are often poorly structured. The local government that sets out to model the cost and benefits of alternative strategies for urban growth is faced with a series of unknowns. There is seldom precise information even on the current "state-of-nature"—current housing, population, industry, and commerce. Also, the relationship of these factors to governmental costs and revenues is likely to be incomplete and imprecise. The alternative public policy options are uncertain. Other factors such as the broader regional and national economy, housing market, prevailing interest rates, and industrial location and expansion decisions are as important if not more important than public policies in shaping urban development. Finally, the problems are relatively unstructured in that no well-defined criteria exists for assessing alternative policies. Criteria range from impacts on a community's economic base to local government fiscal impacts to broad social and environmental impacts on the community. Given such highly unstructured problems, models appear to provide a process for specifying the state-of-nature, alternatives, and the consequences of alternatives, as well as providing criteria for assessment.

A second feature of the social context, the degree of conflict over policy, also might contribute to the process of consensus modeling. Controversy over growth policy tended to characterize the local governments that adopted fiscal impact models (Chapter 6). It also characterized the four intensive case studies (Chapters 2–5). For example, Tulsa's politicians adopted a model while involved in a continuing controversy over planned growth versus laissez-faire development. In San Diego, controversy pivoted around the partisans of no-growth, managed growth, and pro-growth positions. In the context of controversy over policy positions, modeling appears to divert attention from the positions of community contestants to more concrete assumptions and criteria for modeling alternative urban development scenarios.

Technology and Consensus Modeling

In addition to the foregoing features of the political context, it might be that the most appropriate perspective on modeling is dependent upon specific features of the technology. Some models might be more amenable to rational analyses. For example, certain cash-flow models might be well enough specified that there is little conflict over the appropriate modeling assumptions and relationships. Other models could be so deterministic of results that conform to partisan political positions that their use inevitably evolves into a partisan analysis. This is the case, for example, with Arthur Laffer's model of the relationships between tax rates and governmental revenues; the model almost inevitably endorses policy for the reduction of tax rates. Although less deterministic, other models might be so identified with the policy positions of their creators that use of the model degenerates into little more than a technocratic process, or into another form of partisan analysis. For example, while Jay Forrester's "systems dynamics" is a highly flexible modeling approach, his controversial history of using systems dynamics to endorse environmental policy supportive of limits to growth tends to behaviorally predetermine future uses.

In fact, many of the most well-known models and modelers have largely shaped current images of the modeling process. However, these well-known cases might be systematically different from the more routine modeling activities of relatively anonymous modelers in thousands of organizations. The most celebrated cases of modeling might even be well-known because they differ markedly from the more common patterns of modeling across most organizations. In short, there might be fundamental differences between *celebrity* versus *institutional* modeling.[3] We believe that the consensual perspective is appropriate for understanding institutional modeling even though it varies from classic examples of celebrity modeling.

Our analysis revealed several features of models that appear to facilitate consensus modeling. First is the simplicity of models. Fiscal impact models are conceptually simple: they are accounting or bookkeeping models that project governmental costs and governmental revenues over a one- to twenty-year planning horizon. As a consequence of this simplicity, fiscal impact models are easy to understand at the broad conceptual level. Moreover, at this broad level there is likely to be a widespread agreement on the value of the models' embedded fiscal criteria to the evaluation of policy alternatives. Even though scholars have argued that such fiscal criteria bias local government land-use decisions toward exclusionary zoning policies, most local government officials and citizens feel that fiscal criteria are appropriate; and they cannot agree on other possible criteria.

A second feature of models conducive to consensus modeling is their implementation flexibility. Fiscal impact models are extremely flexible. The specific assumptions, relationships, and operations utilized to calculate costs and revenues are largely unspecified by the models until the modelers implement them in collaboration with representatives of local governments. Such flexibility permits the models to be readily adapted to various local concerns over how costs and revenues are calculated.

The third feature conducive to consensus modeling is comprehensibility. A problematic feature of fiscal impact models is that they tend to incorporate so many variables, time periods, and assumptions that their operation can become extremely complicated over time. Thus, the models can become relatively incomprehensible to all but the most informed and involved participants in the modeling process.[4] Most people understand the cost and revenue concept of such models, but not all the concrete assumptions, data, and relationships that determine their results.[5]

The Consensus Modeling Process

The modeling literature as well as our field work supports the utility of viewing modeling as a three stage process involving introduction, adaptation, and incorporation. But our studies of model implementation (Chapters 2–5) demonstrate that movement through these stages is more labryinthian than linear. Within a number of cities, the implementation of models involved so many twists and turns, iterations and reiterations, that the process belied usual linear characterizations. For example, Tulsa adopted a fiscal impact model that had been developed by outside consultants and used in other cities. The consultants spent one year redeveloping the model before transferring it to Tulsa. While the consultants were adapting the model for Tulsa, the city's planners developed their own models. Both the original and local models were then utilized and, subsequently, rejected (Chapter 4). In Anaheim, a more or less cyclical process emerged as each new proposal for development launched a new cycle of adapting and using a model that had become incorporated into the city's planning processes (Chapter 5).

Implementation is labyrinthian also in the sense that there are multiple participants and multiple points at which the implementation process might fail. Implementation is not simply an activity of modelers. Fiscal impact modeling consultants are joined by in-house analysts from finance, budgeting, and planning and in-house computing personnel. These technocrats are joined by a variety of bureaucrats responsible for monitoring the implementation process, coordinating the activities of various departments, linking the modeling effort to the general planning process, and facilitating various stages of the modeling process, such as marshalling input data from various operating departments and agencies. Modelers and bureaucrats are joined by a heterogenous group of politicians including elected officials, various advisory groups, appointed officials and the representatives of community groups and interests, including the media, developers, and homeowners. Given this multiplicity of actors, the implementation process tends to be characterized by multiple and shifting agendas, reflecting a pluralistic array of participants, whose involvement shifts over time. These goals and agendas of the principal actors are critical to most modeling efforts.

Modeling Impacts

An empirical examination of modeling suggests that while models have a multitude of impacts on the decision-making process, these impacts tend to be marginal in their effects on any particular decision and, more generally, on decision making as a process (also see Brewer, 1973; Greenberger, et al. 1976). Many of the specific impacts are discussed in Chapter 7. But certain impacts of modeling, considered as a group, appear to have a broad role in conflict resolution and consensus building—a pattern that underscores the relevance of the consensual perspective. Conflict resolution and consensus building evolve from the role of modeling in structuring problems, informing and involving participants, setting agenda, and legitimating decisions as well as nondecisions.

The use of models tends to help analysts and policy makers to structure problems by necessitating working definitions of future conditions, development alternatives, consequences of the alternatives, and criteria for assessing the alternatives. This is a substantial structure that models *can* impose on policy problems and, in reality, models are used much more simply. Usually, only *some* future conditions, alternatives, consequences and criteria are considered rather than a comprehensive set. This narrowing reduces the scope of conflict and allows the participants to concentrate on finding bases for consensus. An important part of finding a basis for consensus is the role of computer models in informing participants about practical constraints and marginal differences regarding policy alternatives (Brewer, 1973). For example, in San Diego, the modeling process informed participants about the practical limits to how much growth the City of San Diego could feasibly manage; and in Tulsa, final analyses of alternative growth strategies suggested that there were only marginal differences in the oveall fiscal impacts of competing growth scenarios. In each case, this information was unknown or unexpected, prior to the modeling effort. When it became known, it helped build consensus by eliminating certain issues from future discussion.

In addition to informing participants, modeling provides a means of involving contestants in policy disputes and securing their commitment to such consensus. Modelers tend to actively anticipate the reactions of participants, to develop formal structures such as user committees to test their reactions to recommendations, and to consult broadly to assure that their recommendations are sensitive to the full array of interests concerned. In addition, many participants are involved in developing or at least reviewing the assumptions and in providing the input data for the models.

In structuring problems, models often shape what issues people think about; that is, models set the issues agenda (Chapters 2 and 7). For example, fiscal impact models focus attention and debate on fiscal issues as opposed to a variety of other socioeconomic issues in community development. If the cities in our study had adopted models focused on estimating the impacts of development on the community's economic base and on the generation of jobs, or on social and economic integration, or on air and water quality, public discussion and debate might have been different indeed. But, the choice of fiscal impact models rather than these others focused the participant's discussion and debate.

Modeling often promotes consensus over the outcomes of analyses by producing unambiguous forecasts that constrain the interpretations of the results. For example, by forecasting the dollar and cent differences between alternative development options, there are few conclusions people can reasonably draw regarding the most fiscally profitable alternative given acceptance of the modeling assumptions. This is in marked contrast to ambiguous forecasts whose interpretation is typically left to the highest political authorities.

The Implications of Consensual Modeling

These impacts of modeling illustrate several broad political implications of the modeling process. The first, which has already been suggested, is that modeling tends to facilitate conflict resolution and consensus building in policy making. This conclusion is in contrast to previous research that found that modeling increases the difficulty of reaching political consensus by making clear who gets what (Pack & Pack, 1977a).

Nearly all of the specific impacts of modeling discussed above can be linked to the general function of conflict resolution. Modeling tends to separate groups and their positions from the policy problem. Modeling focuses participants on becoming more informed about the objective state of policy problems, and more involved in helping structure problems that involve concrete data. Modeling provides a more common agenda of issues for the participants. By creating a process for resolving conflicts, it also constrains the scope of conflicts by shaping the issues and contestants that are involved in policy discussions. By legitimating decisions and non-decisions alike, models also promote consensus among the broader public concerned with the policy issues.

These impacts of modeling in policy making are not necessarily benign in their outcomes and, therefore, point to a second political implication of modeling. In the process of helping to resolve conflict and build consensus, models almost inevitably bias the outcomes of policy making. Models are not apolitical in their impacts. Because models are tools for negotiation and bargaining among various contestants in the policy process, their structure, their forecasts, and their policy implications will all tend to support and legitimate the interests of those most influential in the modeling process against those left out of the modeling process.

More broadly, the impacts of modeling suggest a third political implication: modeling can and does have important implications for the nature of policy making processes. If viewed from an historical perspective, any particular model analysis is only one of scores of studies done over years in the evolution of public policies within various jurisdictions. Thus, any particular analysis tends to have a marginal impact on the character and outcome of the policy making process. But the incorporation of modeling as an on-going feature of decision making *does* impact the policy process. Modeling introduces micro-level changes that shape the framework of policy debate, the criteria for choice, the extent to which model results will be binding on the participants, and the limits of negotiation and compromise over policy outcomes. Once accepted and institutionalized as part of the policy process, these features of modeling change the way in which policy debates are carried out and, thereby, fundamentally change the nature of policy making and policy outcomes in the longer run.

In summary, models can be influential in the policy process by structuring problems, informing and involving participants, setting agenda, and legitimating decisions and nondecisions. As such, models can serve as tools for facilitating conflict resolution and consensus. In doing so, models are not neutral tools. Rather, they are political tools of negotiation that will tend to support and reinforce the interests of those involved in the modeling process over those left out of that process.

Such a potentially powerful technology is seldom left in the hands of the modelers—the technical experts. Quite the contrary. Model implementation is virtually a labyrinthian process that must be sensitively negotiated by the modelers who anticipate the reactions of multiple participants with sometimes shifting and conflicting agendas. The multiple points at which the process can be blocked, delayed, or defeated tends to force responsiveness on the part of the modelers and other participants. In this way, policy modeling tends to become a process of negotiation and bargaining. Rather than pathological, such a labyrinthian political process is functional to conflict resolution.

This overview is consistent with what we have labeled as a consensual perspective on the modeling process. This perspective seems to provide a more satisfactory interpretation of our field studies of the modeling process than alternative perspectives that tend to dominate the modeling literature. Yet, consensual modeling is contingent on several aspects of the technology and political context. Conceptually simple and operationally flexible models might facilitate consensus modeling while more conceptually complex and more deterministic models, for example, might lead to either technocratic or partisan modeling. Also, political environments characterized by conflict over poorly structured issues might be more congenial to consensus modeling. Finally, "institutional" modeling is more likely to be characterized by consensus modeling than are dramatic and more unique cases of "celebrity" modeling.

It might be that models play a far more powerful role in politics and policy than suggested by traditional perspectives on the modeling process. Models do more than inform. And, models seem to play a more useful political role in policy making than simply legitimating past decisions. Models might well serve as tools of negotiation and bargaining and thereby contribute to conflict resolution and consensus in policy making processes. For example, from the perspective of consensus modeling, Stockman's manipulation of computer forecasts was clearly a partisan act, but it was only one episode in a process that is continuous and that is being repeatedly revised in the context of political debate over economic policies and forecasts. Such forecasts are informing discussions of economic problems and policies and might share some responsibility for the evolving consensus over the impacts of alternative public policies on the U. S. economy.

OUTLINE OF THIS BOOK

This chapter has presented the general framework and the major theoretical perspective of the modeling process that has emerged from our analysis. Later chapters will describe the politics of model implementation and the role of models, information, and technical experts in the policy process that have lead to these conclusions.

Chapters 2 through 5 present intensive case histories of the implementation and use of fiscal impact models in four U.S. cities: Irvine, California; Tulsa, Oklahoma; San Diego and Anaheim, California. Each case study is suggestive of several themes. The themes that emerge from each case study guide the presentation and emphasis of each chapter. In this way, the cases illustrate the unique experiences of each city, but highlight the general importance of the relationships between the political setting and the modeling process.

Chapters 6 and 7 take a more comparative view based on analyses of the field survey data. Various themes of model implementation and impacts are explored to examine the generalizability of ideas generated by the cases themselves and by the literature on models in the policy process.

The final chapter returns to some of the broader questions that provoked the study. This chapter generalizes beyond the limited data of this study to discuss the implications of the findings for a more general understanding of the politics of modeling. Moreover, the descriptive findings form a basis for several normative observations on how the modeling process might be better approached from the perspective of consensus modeling.

NOTES

1. The "Stockman Papers" was the term coined by the editors of *The New Republic* (December 2, 1981, p. 5), as an explicit parallel to the Pentagon Papers.
2. This definition of information technology as having three components--computers, telecommunications and management science techniques--was first formulated by Thomas Whisler (1967). The increasing linkage among these components is illustrated by the coining of new words such as "compunications" (Oettinger, 1971) to symbolize their joining.
3. We are indebted to Martin Greenberger for suggesting this distinction.
4. Fiscal impact models vary in complexity. The more complex systems use sophisticated econometric techniques, including regression. Still, in a variety of circumstances, all of the models tend to be less comprehensible as time progresses and models evolve. Partly, this is a consequence of the amount and variety of input data that these models can accommodate. By accommodating many assumptions, data elements, and relationships, the actual outputs of the models become less comprehensible to those without a direct role in implementation.
5. The broader modeling process can also become incomprehensible due to the complexity and dynamism of modeling within local governments. The broad process includes procedures for dealing with interdepartmental relationships; the coming and going of model analysts, politicians, and various

bureaucrats; changes in computer hardware and software; as well as changes in the policy environment with the ebb and flow of movements for rent control, restrictive zoning, and economic development. The modeling effort can create a fairly complex life history over several months to several years of the implementation process.

In many respects, these changes during the adaptation process reflected more macro-level changes in the political environment. This was best illustrated in Tulsa, where shifts in the political coalition controlling the Mayor's office had major impacts on the bureaucratic and organizational politics of the implementation process. Yet, the dramatic changes in the political environment were important to other cities including Irvine and San Diego (Dutton, 1981, 1982b; Kraemer, 1981).

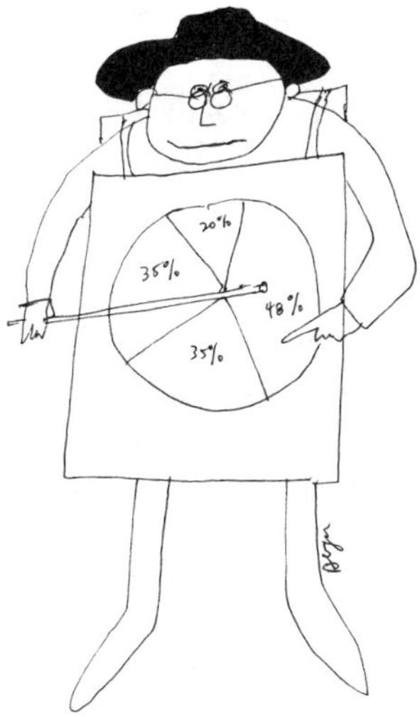

2.
Models as a Negotiating Tool

More than any case in our study, the City of Irvine's use of fiscal impact modeling provides a classic illustration of the use of models as a negotiating tool. This case is presented first, therefore, both for what it reveals about consensus modeling and for what it reveals as a foreground to the other cases. Most participants in Irvine's modeling process viewed it as a successful analytical exercise that qualitatively improved decision making processes. Although partisan political positions were influential in shaping the conduct and outcomes of the analyses, no one position was decisive. The modeling process incorporated a wide range of influential participants and their positions. Modeling deflected the partisans away from rigid positions favoring growth or no-growth to discussion and negotiation about the overall size of the community and the rate of community growth. Thus, in the end, the modeling process was perceived to have made a qualitative improvement in both the confidence of participants about information important to policy debates and in the likelihood of a negotiated consensus over how to view the policy environment and policy choices.

METAMORPHOSIS OF A LAND BARONY

Two great tracts of open land lie between the greater Los Angeles region and the San Diego region in Southern California. One is Camp Pendleton, the 195–square-mile reserve of the U.S. Marine Corps in the northern end of San Diego County; the other is the 130–square-mile Irvine Ranch. The Irvine Ranch is owned almost entirely by the Irvine Company (TIC), which has been characterized by David Curry as:

> a modern feudal barony; rich in lands, a patron of the arts, benevolent to its serfs so long as they regularly remit their rents, and often imperious in its dealings with other baronies, such as Orange County and the University of California. (Curry, 1970, p. 18)

The Company's chief enterprise, until about 20 years ago, was a mixture of intensive agriculture on its prime lands and cattle-raising on its hillier sections.[1] The shift in emphasis from ranching to development began in 1959 when the Regents of the University of California tentatively approved an Irvine Ranch site for a new campus,[2] selected from among 21 sites examined for the University by the consulting firm of Pereira and Luckman.[3] TIC and the University then jointly retained William L. Pereira and Associates to develop master plans for the university and surrounding area.[4] Following completion of these plans, the entire ranch was divided for planning purposes into three sections: a 55–square-mile southern or coastal area around the university, for initial development; a 31–square-mile central area, primarily agricultural land; and a 44–square mile northern area, primarily mountains and foothills. Master plans were then prepared for each of these areas (Table 2.1).

Of the southern area, 16 square miles or 10,000 acres were to constitute a university-oriented community of 100,000 people. These and other conditions were made a part of a 1960 agreement between the University's Board of Regents and TIC which provided for: the donation of 1,000 acres of land for a new university; purchase of an additional 500 acres of land

TABLE 2.1. Sequence of Master Planning for the Irvine Ranch[a]

Area	Acreage	Cumulative Acres	Year	Prepared by
UCI Campus Plan	1,500	1,500	(1960)	Consultant
University Community Plan	10,000	10,000[b]	(1960)	Consultant
Southern Sector (South Irvine Ranch)	34,100	34,087	(1964)	Consultant
Central Area General Plan	32,400	66,800	(1970)	TIC
Lomas Ridge-Addition	11,000	77,000	(1972)	TIC
Northern Sector-Additon	14,900	92,628	(1973)	TIC
Composite General Plan Review and Update	92,628	92,628	(1973)	TIC

[a]*Source:* Griffen (1974, p. 39)
[b]UCI and adjacent areas.

by the University for faculty and staff housing; and "no significant departure, without the mutual consent of the parties" from the land-use plan designed by Pereira (William L. Pereira & Associates, 1960).

A general plan for development of the southern Irvine Ranch, based on Pereira's report and including the university community, was approved by the Orange County Planning Commission and Board of Supervisors in 1964. Construction subsequently proceeded fairly rapidly in this section and by 1970, the resident population was 20,000 with employment of 30,000. The jobs were chiefly in shopping and commercial areas, in the university (which sported an enrollment of 5,000 students), and in the industrial complex near the Orange County Airport, where over 280 firms were located. The residential development stressed planned villages, usually with single-family dwellings or town houses on small lots. These areas generally were well-shielded from commercial developments and traffic arteries. Commonly-owned open space and recreational facilities were provided within each major development, often winding in a linear fashion about the buildings.

In 1970, however, the scope and scale of development was changed dramatically when TIC announced plans for the City of Irvine, the "largest planned city on the North American Continent." Basically, the plan called for extending development into the Central Ranch or agricultural section. The urbanized area would be 85 square miles, and by the year 2000, population would be 430,000. The city would consist of 40 individual residential villages connected by landscaped "environmental corridors" that would also include regional parks, secondary schools, commercial and industrial centers, and bicycle, pedestrian and equestrian trails. The residential developments would be similar to those already built on the Ranch.

TIC's plans also proposed separate incorporation of parts of the Irvine Ranch by the city, as opposed to continued administration by Orange County government. Formulation of this proposal was spurred by the attempts of surrounding cities to annex industrial developments and other portions of the ranch in spite of their earlier assurances that such annexations would not be sought.[5] Other factors also spurred the proposal. As David Curry noted:

> incorporation or annexation of parts of the Irvine ranch would transfer planning control of the affected areas from the county planning commission to a city planning agency; they would almost certainly constitute a charter for complete urban development of such areas; and they would probably present the Irvine Company with a more permissive government environment for pursuing its own development plans, independent of broader county or regional, social and environmental considerations. (Curry, 1970, p.29)

BIRTH OF A NEW CITY

As each village on the ranch was developed, TIC created Community Associations to own and maintain the open space and physical facilities (swimming pools, tennis courts, community halls, etc.) provided by the developer. Each association had its own officers and board of directors who made decisions about how the residents' mandatory association fees would be used for operating and maintaining the facilities, and when the fees would be increased to meet rising costs. These associations were thus quasi-governmental bodies. By the same token, although prohibited from overt political action by law, the associations were, in fact, quasi-political bodies by virtue of their interaction with the residents and their resource allocation authority within each village. Their officers, in particular, constituted an informal elite of community leaders.

By 1970, there were 30 Community Associations in existence around the University. At the initiation of TIC, and with its technical and administrative support, the leaders of these associations formed the Council of Communities of Irvine (CCI) to consider alternative forms of governance for the new city, including TIC's incorporation proposal, annexation to other cities, or non-incorporation. There was never much doubt that separate incorporation would top CCI's agenda.

Just three months later, in September 1970, CCI applied to the Orange County Local Agency Formation Commission (LAFCO) for incorporation of the City of Irvine.[6] The application proposed that the new city's boundaries incorporate all of the 85 square miles planned for urban development by the Irvine Company, and TIC staff contributed maps and related justification materials.

One month later, CCI resubmitted its application to LAFCO with *new* boundaries for the city. This application reduced the area requested for incorporation by over two-thirds (from 85 to 27 square miles), leaving out a great deal of the agricultural land in the central sector of the Ranch. A number of reasons were given for this quick change. One offered by Lyndol Young, attorney for one of the principal landowners, Joan Irvine Smith, was that "the Irvine Company was anxious to get the incorporation proposal approved before the installation in January [1971] of a board of supervisors that is no longer 'under the control of the Irvine Company.'"[7] A related reason was the prospect of strong opposition from adjoining cities[8] that had expected to annex portions of the Ranch; a smaller incorporation area would weaken their case before LAFCO. A third reason was the prospect of strong opposition from area residents to the large city incorporation; it was expected that the request for incorporation of a much smaller city would draw less opposition, thereby increasing the likelihood of LAFCO's approval. Still another reason was the prospect that the Irvine

Company might have to pay additional city taxes if the central-sector agricultural land were included within the proposed city boundaries.[9]

The agricultural lands were an important fiscal and land-use policy issue. The Irvine Company had placed nearly all of the central sector (and other lands) into agricultural preserve for 10 years and obtained substantial property tax reductions as a result. According to California law, such agricultural preserves might serve one of two objectives: (a) discouragement of premature and unnecessary conversion of agricultural land to urban uses; or (6) permanent preservation of agricultural lands for their public value as open space. Since it was the announced intention of the Irvine Company to develop all of the agricultural lands within the central sector by the year 2000, it is clear that preservation of these lands was intended primarily to serve the former rather than the latter objective, and to reduce taxes.[10] This plan was not without opposition; the agricultural preserves were to become a major issue in future council elections and land-use planning for the new City of Irvine, as the residents divided into political factions made up of the various neighborhood groups. Some groups, exemplified by the Irvine Tomorrow Association of Communities, wanted to preserve agricultural and public open space, provide park and recreation amenities and offer housing for low income people. Other groups, symbolized by CCI, wanted the intensive urban development of the Irvine Company master plan as a means of enhancing their real estate investments and providing a sufficiently broad market for various public and private urban services.

CCI's request for incorportion with the reduced city boundaries was approved by LAFCO in February 1971. Subsequently, steps were taken to elect a city council and start a city government. The first council meeting took place in December 1971.[11] It became apparent immediatley that the members of the new city council were split 3:2 into Irvine Tomorrow and CCI supporters, respectively.[12] Three of the people elected to the council—William Fishbach, Gabrielle Pryor, and Henry Quigley—had run on a platform aimed at achieving independence from TIC's development plans and a high quality of life within Irvine (e.g., provision of parks, open space, riding trails, etc.); the other two—John Burton and E. Ray Quigley—had run as supporters of the Irvine Company master plan. As a means of bringing this issue to a head, the new city officials began their own general planning program using the year 2000 as the planning horizon.

Creation of a New Master Plan

When the city incorporated, it inherited the master plan that previously had been approved by the Orange County Board of Supervisors—essentially TIC's master plan. City officials therefore began their own planning process and hired the Los Angeles consulting firm of Wilsey and Ham to assist them. As with many other activities in the new city, the council directed that the master planning effort be conducted with extensive citizen participation. In addition to numerous groups representing the residential villages and commercial/industrial interests, the council created a special Citizen's Advisory Committee (CAC) with individual members nominated by each council member.[13] It was the council's intention that this group be given special attention in the planning process because it represented both individual council members and significant portions of their constituencies. There were numerous meetings with the CAC and other citizen groups during the planning process, but when Wilsey and Ham presented their preliminary general plan report, the CAC roundly criticized the firm for its inadequate consideration of their recommendations. On November 13, 1973, Juanita Moe, speaking for the combined Citizens Advisory Committees, indicated to the council that the CAC was:

> deeply distressed that many of our recommendations have been ignored, or in the case of Agricultural Preserves, given lip service only. To formalize these concerns, we are turning over to you petitions signed by a majority of the committee members. Concerns include:
>
> 1. Loss of prime agricultural lands to urbanization, particularly the prime soils in the Central Irvine area . . . 81 percent of citizen respondents (to a questionnaire circulated by the CAC) felt maintaining agriculture within the city was important enough to support special tax measures, yet Wilsey and Ham stated . . . that Agricultural Preserves "will not be included directly in the Plan considered for adoption." Citizens vigorously object on the grounds that, as a practical matter, once the city has committed land to other than agricultural uses, it will be lost forever.
> 2. Rapid industrialization without the means to meet all the housing needs.
> 3. Increased energy demands in a time of energy shortage.
> 4. Costs of hillside development.
> 5. Increased air pollution in a critical air shed.
> 6. Spiraling public costs—(Studies show economies of scale for cities between 25,000 to 250,000 inhabitants. But at 250,000, per capita costs and taxes start to go up and rise faster and faster as the cities get larger and larger.) *Basic to all these problems is the question of an optimum population level. The medial level suggested by citizen input was 200,000.* [Emphasis added.][14]

Despite extensive subsequent discussions, it soon became clear that neither the council nor the citizens could agree upon a single future for the new city. Consequently, the council instructed the consultant firm to prepare a general plan which allowed three different options for future development. All of these options were similar up to the 1980 point; but they

TABLE 2.2. Summary of Irvine General Plan Options

Option	Population	Description
1	354,000	The so-called moderate growth alternative.
2	450,000	The maximum growth alternative, basically similar to the Irvine Company's plan for the "largest planned city on the North American Continent."
3	171,000	The low growth alternative, which assumed that a major portion of the existing agricultural land would be permanently maintained in that status.
4A	221,000	Preliminary version of "new Option 4."
4B	245,000	The alternative finally selected for the General Plan for the City of Irvine.

varied greatly in terms of the rate of development assumed through the year 2000 (Table 2.2).

By 1975, the practical difficulties, the uncertainty, and the questionable legality posed by operating under three general plan options became too much for the city planners and top staff. Consequently, the city manager pressed the council to choose a single general plan option—either one of the original three options or a new option involving some combination of these three. The council agreed and in August, 1975 put into motion planning studies for what would come to be known as General Plan Amendment #4, or GPA #4.[15] They further decided that choice among the options should be based on their *comparative fiscal impact*.[16]

The reason that fiscal impact was given such importance was that the city, being new, had a limited tax base. It also had one of the highest property tax rates among the cities in Orange County. Consequently, the question of fiscal impact was paramount in the minds of citizens and political officials alike. Moreover, fiscal impact was a central feature in the arguments of opposing community groups. The opponents of low growth continually used fiscal impact considerations in arguing against proposals for open space, parks, and low-income housing. For example, opponents argued that adoption of plans for park and open space usage would keep land off the tax rolls. Such land uses would further generate city expenses for purchasing the land, maintaining the land and facilities, and operating recreational programs—all without any offsetting revenues. In contrast, they argued, rapid development of commercial, industrial and residential land uses would increase the tax base of the city and, eventually, provide sufficient monies to finance parks, open space, and other amenities desired by the community. The low-growth advocates countered that this "trickle-down'' theory of financing amenities would not work and that, even if it did, the best open space land would be allocated to other uses by the time funds were available to purchase it. Debates on other issues such as provision of low-income housing were more acrimonious. City officials felt that the only way to settle such competing claims was with some sort of ''objective'' comparison of alternative development plans. Costs and revenues related to different plans seemed an appropriate basis for such comparison.

Introduction of the Irvine "Economic" Model[17]

As might be expected, the task of determining the fiscal impact of the general plan options was assigned by the council to the city's planners located in the Community Development Department. None of the planners had previous experience with conducting fiscal analyses. Mel Roop, a senior planner, had attended a seminar in San Francisco where he had heard about fiscal impact models and thought they might constitute the needed tool for the analysis. Since the expertise with such models rested mainly with consultant firms, the planners issued a request for proposals (RFP) for a model that could be used for fiscal analysis of the general plan options.

The RFP called for development of a computerized fiscal impact model that would afford guidance for measuring the economic impacts of the various land-use options in the general plan. The consultant was to: include capital costs as well as operating costs in the model; have all of the assumptions in the model approved by the city staff and a citizen's advisory committee; analyze the city's three land-use options in terms of their cost and revenue implications for the government and their tax implications for citizens; and, provide a general economic analysis of the surrounding Orange County.

The principal actors in the decision to adopt a fiscal impact model were many, and their objectives divergent. The city council wanted to know the short- and long-run implications of the general plan options. The city staff supported the basic notion of a computerized model in the hope of eventually obtaining a computer for the city which would house the fiscal model and perform many housekeeping functions such as accounting, payroll, and record keeping. Some citizens supported the model because they were concerned with the adequacy of the city's future tax base to support quality schools; some because they were concerned with the already high tax rate and wanted to have development proposals carefully scrutinized; and some because they thought the model might make explicit the city's extraordinarily high capital costs associated with growth such as that implied by TIC's master plan. Finally, TIC itself supported the model because company officials felt that it would confirm their position on development and might thereby expedite the adoption of their master plan.

Although divergent, the objectives of these actors coalesced remarkably well around the need for a fiscal impact model, owing primarily to the strategies pursued by the two council members who took the lead in advocating model adoption to the rest of the council and to the city staff. Even these two had dissimilar reasons for supporting the model: Gabrielle Pryor wanted a tool for forecasting the fiscal impacts of development as an aid to decision making; John Burton was interested in the computer technology used to implement the models and in "the technological possibilities of computerizing the entire city." Pryor and Burton also had a joint interest in finding a tool that would help to resolve their conflicting viewpoints, acrimonious debates, and futuristic speculations about how the Irvine Company development plans would affect the tax rate, open space, low cost housing, housing appreciation, and quality of life, among other things for Irvine citizens. They thought the model might be a means of facilitating compromise by objectively forecasting fiscal impacts.

Consequently, they joined forces to convince other council members of the need for a fiscal impact model. Pryor and Burton, knowing that the issues of concern to themselves were insufficient to motivate the other members to support the model, appealed to what had now become the council's common concern: countering the plans, models, and sizeable planning staff of the Irvine Company.[18] As Pryor indicated, "this was an extremely sensitive issue to the council because, from the very beginning of the city, the council and city staff had been out-gunned by the Irvine Company's planners, models and data, and they were getting fed up. They wanted to be able to equal if not exceed the Company's expertise and the economic model [fiscal impact model] looked like a way to do it (Pryor, February 1980, interview).

Burton and Pryor were aided in their efforts by two economists, Charles Hugey and William Littlefield, both members of the CAC. The economists were "turned loose to become very vocal before the council about the need for an economic model" (Pryor, February 1980, interview). As citizens, these economists were concerned about overcrowding in the schools and about providing a sufficient physical infrastructure (e.g., streets and highways, storm drains, water and sewage facilities, parks, recreation facilities). They felt the model would make explicit the city's capital costs associated with growth. And this information, in turn, would provide a basis for obtaining public funds, or coercing the developer to build the facilities, or discouraging growth.

The two council members also were aided in their efforts by the city manager and the Administrative Services staff. The manager wanted a single general plan and viewed the model as a tool for aiding choice among the options. The manager and the Administrative Services staff also wanted a computer that would serve the financial and administrative operations of the city. They saw the model, which the council wanted, as another possible application justifying an in-house new computer system. Consequently, they lent their support to these council members.

The council unanimously decided on October 14, 1975, to adopt a computerized fiscal impact model and to allocate up to $20,000 for a consultant to develop such a model.[19] The three council members who had not actively supported the model acquiesced with little understanding of either computer models or computer technology.[20] They were responding primarily to the overwhelming support for the model.

A total of 12 proposals was received from various planning and economic consulting firms. The very fact that a dozen firms bid for the Irvine model contract reinforced the council's and staff's perception that adequate modeling technology existed. However, in the end, only three proposals were considered technically competitive.[21] The proposal from Marshal, Kaplan, Gans and Kahn (MKGK) was the winner. Not only was the MKGK bid considered technically superior to the other proposals, but the firm seemed to understand best both what the council wanted and how to communicate it effectively. In the words of Pryor:

> We felt they would not just talk in complicated economic terms—some economists are just unbelievable when talking to city councils—but would make their points clear to us, and then we could translate it to the community, which is an important thing when you are sitting on the city council. So we chose them (Pryor, February 1980, inteview)

The council approved the contract with MKGK in February 1976, and directed that the Citizen's Advisory Committee, which had been established to provide citizen input to the general plan amendment process, oversee the model's implementation.

The very adoption of the model had a powerful political effect. Previously, debate and conflict had characterized city council meetings in the initial deliberations regarding GPA #4, as Burton and Pryor argued extensively over the relative costs of open space and housing densities. No one could predict the future fiscal impact on the city and its citizens of decisions which had to be made in the present. Adopting the model permitted a temporary suspension of long-range development decisions until the model was completed, and resulted in a suspension of the competition and conflict which such decision making generated between Burton and Pryor, releasing them (and the rest of the council) to attend to other matters. Moreover, by directing the city staff and citizens to oversee the model adaptation process, the council essentially shifted responsibility from itself to the city staff with input from the CAC.

Adaptation of the Model for Evaluating General Plan Options

The principal actors in model adaptation were essentially the same as those involved in model adoption, with the addition of the consultants and the CAC. Most of the council's involvement with the actual transfer of the model, however, was through delegated authority—the city staff and the CAC were to be the real participants and were required to report back periodically to the council. In addition, the council assigned two of its own members, John Burton and William Vardoulis, to the CAC. The CAC and the city staff focused attention on the consultant firm MKGK.

The Consultant and the Model

MKGK had had previous experience with fiscal impact analysis. The firm had used a generalized corporate cash-flow model (the "Big-Red" model built by the national accounting firm, Kenneth Leventhal Company) to assess the public and private capital costs of development.[22] But they had never used a model to estimate the public operating and maintenance costs or public revenues associated with private development: the Irvine contract represented a major adaptation effort for the company.

The key person at MKGK responsible for developing the Irvine model was Peter Bass, an economist. His first major task was to totally restructure the model to include government costs and revenues. But the most difficult and time-consuming task was developing the data and assumptions for the model. Bass worked for three months with the Administrative Services staff, with various planners in the Community Development Department and with planners in the Irvine Company in order to generate land use, service cost, and revenue base data for the analysis. Cooperation was remarkably good.[23] Bass worked with all major department heads in the city to generate development standards (e.g., the number of park acres to be provided per 1,000 people) and to develop cost and revenue "functions" associated with population, land use and other development conditions. The total set of assumptions was reviewed five or six times by all of the participants. Bass also worked with the CAC that had been created by the council to monitor the model's adaptation to the city and, eventually, to "sign-off" on all assumptions incorporated into the model.

Use of the Model

These approved assumptions and data[24] were then fed into Bass's modification of the Leventhal computer model to perform the necessary calculations on an annual basis through the year 2000, and to produce 11 different summary tables for each of the three general plan options.[25] Each option was evaluated using four different assumptions of geographic area because the boundaries of the city were still open for discussion.[26] Thus, a single general plan evaluation consisted of 12 model runs (3 options × 4 boundary alternatives); evaluation of all three alternatives therefore required 36 model runs.

Midway Report on the Model Results

MKGK made two such major evaluations using the model.[27] The first was midway through the project in the summer of 1977, for a presentation to the Irvine City Council; the second was in the fall of that same year, to produce data for the final report. At the time of the midway report, the Irvine Company Board of Directors was engaged in a major internal struggle over ownership and control of the company. The Irvine Foundation, a nonprofit tax-exempt private foundation and the majority shareholder in the company, was forced by federal tax law (which Joan Irvine Smith helped to get adopted) to dispose of its interests in TIC. Bidding for the company was fierce with two major groups vying for ownership and control: Mobil Oil Corporation and a consortium of developers headed by Alfred Taubman. The ultimate bid of $500 million was higher than either company officials or Irvine residents had expected. Among the residents, moreover, the bid generated fears, fed by local newspaper stories, that the new owners would have to begin rapacious development of the Ranch in order to handle interest payments on the money borrowed to purchase the company and in order to make an adequate return on their investment.

The struggle for ownership and the bidding war heightened concerns of Irvine residents and the council about general plan Option #2, which followed the Company's 1970 master plan and called for an ultimate population of 450,000—the largest among the options (see Table 2.2). In addition, MKGK's midway run showed that Option #2 was the least financially favorable for the city and for the Irvine School District. These factors provided the basis for the council's determination that Option #2 should be eliminated from further consideration. The council then instructed the planners to come up with a new Option #4, which would fall between the two remaining options.

This was an extremely significant decision.[28] It not only reduced by 100,000 people the upper range population that would be considered for the City of Irvine, but it effectively set the eventual population somewhere between Options 1 and 3 (see Table 2.2) since the most likely option would be some sort of middle-ground compromise. As it turned out, Option 4 represented a built-out population of 221,000:

Boundary Assumption	Option 3	"New" Option 4	Option 1	Discontinued Option 2
City, Sphere, and Coast	171,000	221,000	354,000	450,000

This midway report convinced the council of the model's utility. Although none of them understood how the model worked, its results confirmed the fiscal wisdom of the general plan option toward which city officials and the community were moving as a compromise choice, namely the middle-ground Option 4, and consequently they were satisfied with the model. Although the March council meeting where the model and findings were presented was anticlimactic from a substantive standpoint, it was dramatic from another standpoint. An important event during this meeting was a demonstration by Sheldon Gans of MKGK of how the model could be used by the council to answer their own questions. Gans brought a computer terminal connected by telephone to a time-sharing computer located in Kansas City into the council chambers and demonstrated the model's ability to produce results by changing a few of the inputs. Initially, someone elsewhere in city hall was trying to dial out on the same telephone line used by Gans, and this prevented good electrical connections which in turn produced chaotic numbers. This simple incident reinforced the stereotype of the "fallibility" of computers which everyone noted in good humor. After the problem was corrected, the demonstration proceeded and, according to one of the council members:

> John and I (asked) . . . him if he could then plug in a certain number of acres of apartment units and he said yes. We said 26 units to the acre and we plugged that in—which is pretty dense. As I recall those were the only two variables we gave him . . . We might have given him a price per unit . . . Back came the tax rate that those dwellings would necessitate. It was all pretty convincing. (Pryor, February 1980, interview)

This demonstration crystallized the acceptance of the Irvine model and was a key event in its implementation. "Seeing is believing," and the council members now had seen a sample of how their commissioned product could be used both now and in the future. The model's demonstrated flexibility furthered the idea of getting "local control" over the model so that the council and staff could "play" with it themselves.

Consequently, the council directed the city staff to take the steps required to "assume control of the model" and to operate the model without the consultant's assistance.[29] The council unanimously approved two service contracts to facilitate that effort[30]—one for computer time-sharing services so the city staff could operate the model in-house and the other for the use of the parent model in which Irvine's economic model was embedded.[31] Since the city lacked any data-processing or computer personnel, the model builders encouraged the city to hire someone with such skills to be custodian of the model. A computer specialist, Alex Wilk, was hired by the city and training in model operation was provided for him by MKGK. This selection of the first city computer specialist was a milestone because it planted the seeds not only for further fiscal impact model development, but also for further computing development within the city.

The Consultant's Final Report

MKGK's second major evaluation of the three general plan options was compiled in a report titled *Fiscal and Economic Analysis of General Plan Options* (MKGK, Novemer 15, 1976), and, subsequently (March 31, 1977), a presentation on the report was given by Sheldon Gans to city officials at a joint meeting of the City Council, Community Services Commission, Planning Commission, and Transportation Commission. The report and presentation indicated three important findings:

1. Option 4 was the most favorable option, especially when city and school taxes were viewed in combination.
2. All options presented a tradeoff between population size and open space area. The larger the population, the greater the total taxes would have to be, because the taxes required to support school expenditures were six times as much as those required to support other city expenditures. The larger the open space area, the greater the city expenditures required for maintenance. By keeping its population relatively low, the city could pay for some of its desired open space and at the same time taxpayers could be spared some of the tax burden that would be required for additional school expenditures. (Peabody, May 1980, interview)
3. A maximum spread of 11 percent in combined city and school taxes existed at the end of development between the least and most expensive options and boundary conditions studied. In relative dollar terms, this amounted to an annual average tax differential of $93/year on a house valued at $60,000 in 1976.

The latter finding was the most significant of all. As stated by MKGK in their report, the importance of this finding was that "the [fiscal] differences among any of the alternatives were clearly not so large as to justify [their] constituting the sole or even the major reason for choosing one plan option and boundary condition over another. Quality of life, environmental, social and other factors need to be considered'' (MKGK, 1976, p. S–41).

From the standpoint of quality of life, the major difference among the options centered in assumptions about the character of residential development and open space preservation. Option 1 assumed the highest residential densities and the least amount of retained open space (Table 2.3). Option 3 assumed the lowest residential densities and the greatest amount of open space. Option 4 fell between these options. In subsequent council discussions, which were spread over several months, it became clear that Option 1 was politically infeasible because it failed to preserve the character of development extant on the Ranch. Option 3 was considered economically infeasible by the pro-development majority because it set aside too much public and private undeveloped open space. The council debate was considerable concerning whether the city ever would be able to purchase, or to get TIC to donate, the 23,000 acres of public, undeveloped open space assumed by the option. The Council also debated whether it would be able to (or should even try to) convince TIC to retain the 8,500 acres of private undeveloped open space assumed under the option. Unable to agree, they sought the middle-ground position of Option 4. Unlike 1, Option 4 emphasized single-family detached housing while also decreasing the acreage devoted to attached housing and apartments. Although the public, undeveloped open space was about the same in both options, Option 4 assumed almost twice as much private, undeveloped open space (Table 2.3). The critical difference between Options 1 and 4 here was that Option 4 assumed that an area of the central sector Ranch designated as Village 14 and charted by TIC for development would not be developed. Rather, it would be retained for agricultural uses permanently.

TABLE 2.3. Comparison of GPA Options at Build-Out in the Year 2000[a]

City, Sphere & Coastal Boundaries	Option 1	Option 3	Option 4
Selected Land Use (Acres)[b]			
Residential			
Single family detached	17288	7711	18216
Single family attached	3769	1921	3470
Apartments	1601	737	925
Public undeveloped open space	10056	23022	11706
Private undeveloped open space	3855	8586	6755

[a]*Source:* MKGK (1976, p. S–10, Exhibit 5)

[b]Although commercial and industrial acreages varied with each option, they are not considered relevant for this comparison and, therefore, have not been included.

Training of City Staff to Use the Model

The presentation of MKGK's final report ended the consultant's involvement with the economic model except for training city staff to use it. It took only a few weeks to train city people to be able to operate the model on the Kansas City time-sharing service. A variety of people were trained in operation of the model: council members (Burton and Vardoulis), planning commissioners, CAC members, and city staff. But the task of using the model fell largely to the city's planners, financial analysts, and computer expert. Once the model was accessible to the city staff, it was used periodically to provide information in response to specific questions asked by the council, commissioners and staff. Usually, these questions had to do with minor adjustments in land-use patterns, population, or development phasing with respect to Option 4.

Adoption of the General Plan Amendment #4

The net effect of the foregoing adjustments to Option 4 was to increase the amount of residential land while decreasing the open space (including space set aside for agriculture), to increase the commercial acreage to support the new residential uses and, by extension, to increase the built-out population of Option 4 to 245,000. Although the council negotiated intensely over these adjustments, the die was cast and on September 15, 1977, the council selected Option 4 as the General Plan for the City of Irvine.

The model played an important role in the general plan decision. As expressed by Eddy Peabody, the former planning director:

> I think that some council members placed greater importance on the model than others. For example, the final general plan option was approved on a three to two vote. For the three individuals [Burton, Vardoulis, Sills] who voted for Option 4, fiscal impact was an important consideration. The other two councilmembers [Pryor and Gaido] felt there were other things besides economics that you make land use decisions on. Their concern was more with agriculture and open space preservation.[32]

Moreover, the model was used in policy argument among the supporters of Option 4. On the evening of the final vote on GPA #4, Council member John Burton and Mayor William Vardoulis debated the wording of a proposed council resolution that would tie approval of the GPA #4 land-use plan for Village 14 to future development of the Irvine Industrial Center-East and the future annexation of the northern area. Burton wanted to substitute the phrase "may be dependent" for the phrase "shall be dependent," arguing that there were many contingencies that later might result in the need to change the land-use plan for that village and so there was no need to tie that development specifically to Irvine Industrial Complex (ICC)-East and annexation of the northern area. Vardoulis, who had drafted the resolution, responded as follows:

> I totally disagree. I think it shall be dependent in both cases because it is dependent. The economic study shows that it is very dependent on what happens in ICC-East and what happens with the northern sphere. I'm not saying that, in fact, no development can occur in Village 14 if, for example, all of the property comprising IIO-East is traded to the Marine Corps. This does not mean that Village 14 cannot proceed and be developed and must be left in permanent open space or agriculture. What it means is that the whole land use plan [for Village 14] has to be re-evaluated. I want it to be perfectly clear that development of Village 14 is dependent on these two items [annexation of the northern sphere and development of IIC-East]. *I think that came out loud and clear in the economic study and I don't want that to be lost.*[33] *[Emphasis is added.]*

Despite its contribution to debate, the model was not the critical factor in the selection of Option 4. The key factor was the overwhelming community opinion that the city should not be allowed to grow to half a million people as originally projected in the Irvine Company's master plan. Neither TIC, the council, nor any other decision maker could ignore public opinion. For example, Ray Watson, former President of TIC, said:

> The number of half a million just kept eroding by the pragmatics of politics more than anything else. It was just so overwhelming at that time. The city was just starting out, and 500,000 population was just too huge. The number just became politically intolerable. (Watson, March 1980, interview)

Here, the model's contribution lay in supporting community opinion and providing an objective basis for negotiating the final land-use and population configuration. When participants actually used the model to clarify decision consequences in the refinement of general plan Option 4, it was as a means of influencing choices at the margins (such as raising or lowering residential densities and commercial acreage).

The model also had important political impacts. Earlier, it had supported the position of the low-growth council majority by showing that TIC master plan Option 2 was the most expensive option. Thus, it added a temporary political edge to that majority. It also set the outside feasible population limits within which negotiations about the ultimate population would take place among the council, and between the council and TIC. Again, this was a strategic advantage to the low-growth majority on the council. Moreover, while the model never reduced decisions to purely technical criteria, it played a role in facilitating compromises among members of the council and between the council and TIC. For example, Council member Pryor indicated that:

> The model made it much more difficult to take an extreme position. You couldn't say you wanted all open space because somebody would say let's see how much that'll cost. Nobody ever thought about that before. I mean open spaces are supposed to be free. So it made it very hard to go to that extreme.
>
> It also made it difficult for the Irvine Company to come in and say they needed to develop the city immediately because it's cheaper than dragging it out. You could say let's see about that and we would tell the planning department to scope that one out. What would happen was that your range of alternatives would get narrower and narrower and you would have to pick the one that was the most economically and fiscally appealing to your constituents at that time. (Pryor, February 1980, interview)

During the process of reading the final decision on Option 4, however, the model was also used to support the position of the pro-growth majority which had come to power in the city of 1976. Just prior to the final vote, the pro-growth majority presented the following economic and political arguments for including the Village 14 area for urban development rather than permanently retaining it for agriculture or open space:

> *Vardoulis*
> First of all, we did an economic study. We looked at development under Option 4—the plan that's before us. We found that the lowest cost was Option 4. Second, we are not fooling the public [by keeping land in agriculture preserves]. [We] like the concept of having agriculture for as long as [we] possibly can have it. But if we were to turn around and say we are not going to sell any development in that area [Village 14], what would happen is that area probably would be developed in somebody else's jurisdiction. For example, the coastal area went to Newport Beach. The Irvine Company—they may deny this— but I think they lobbied very heavily to have that area go to Newport Beach. I can see the same type of thing happening in the northern sphere and then we would not have any control over what happens. If we were to turn around and tax the Company, I don't think they'd let us annex it [nothern sphere] and would annex it to somebody else[34]
>
> *Sills*
> I think that if we were not to show [Village 14] on the general plan as marked for future development we would not be living up to our responsibility to the community and to the people who will live here. I think it goes without saying that the area will eventually be developed and now is the time for us to start our planning and put it on the map so that we know that we are going to have some element of control over it. . . . The more we try to

> make this city with all kinds of agricultural areas, the more we're really trying to build homes like on the tenth or eighteenth hole at Burning Tree [an expensive development] and if we continue to do that every home in this community is going to cost $250,000. There won't be a place for the $20,000 to $25,000 a year person to live. So I have to reconcile the dispute in my own mind by saying let's develop.[35]
>
> *Burton*
> I have heard the phrase "tax break" for about the tenth time tonight and I think it raises a philosophical difference between conservative and liberal. There is no such thing as a tax break to a corporation because the tax is always passed on to the consumer. The corporation doesn't pay the tax. We do. And whenever we start chastizing corporations because they're making huge millions because of tax breaks, because they have tax loopholes, all we're doing in that case is saying let's raise the price of housing a little more if we're going to impose greater and greater taxes on the developer or the voter. And that's what we're talking about and it's a very philosophical difference. It's not illogical on our part. It's not irresponsible. It's very simply that some of us feel that perhaps we ought to keep taxes a little lower, perhaps we ought to tax a little less and perhaps we ought to spend a little less.[36]

In her final response to the other members of the council, Pryor said:

> When we say that we will be developing an area in ten years there are certain things that are going to happen. There are certain public expenditures that have to be moved in preparation for that development. You have just said that we will be developing that land [Village 14] some time after the next ten years. I'm saying to you that you had better start preparing for that development in a way that is cost-effective. You're not doing that if you don't charge property taxes that will pay for a fair share of that development. I can assure you that the citizens of this city pay a heck of a lot more in property taxes per acre than the Irvine Company does in its agricultural areas. I don't think it's fair to have us subsidizing future development on lands that are now agricultural preserves, but that's exactly what's going to happen.[37]

Incorporation and Subsequent Use of the Model

The general satisfaction of the council and staff with the role of the model in the adoption of a single option for the general plan assured incorporation of the model into the local government. Even when the council membership changed (in late 1976 and again in 1978), continuity of support for the model was maintained. The key role in maintaining council support for the model was played by the city staff, which was able to influence the new council members, as indicated by Pryor:

> They (Council members Sills, Vardoulis, and Gaido) were new and they had just come on and they didn't trust John or me necessarily. What you do in that case is get the staff to recommend to them the appropriate positions. They were doing what the staff recommended at that point, and *the staff was behind what had gone on before*. (Pryor, February 1980, interview) [Emphasis is added.]

The new council members were willing to accept the recommendations of the city staff because they expected the staff to be neutral regarding use of the model and to serve their interests at least equally with those of the holdover council members. Moreover, the new council *needed* the city staff to explain the model to them, to train them in its use, and to review its use.

Conversion of the Model to the City's Computer

Nowhere is the continued support for the model better symbolized than in a June 1978 vote of the city council, post-Proposition 13, when the following considerations favored scrapping the model: the model had fallen into disuse after the general plan debates were over since the decision it was meant to inform had been made; the data and assumptions were now two years old and it would require considerable staff effort to update them to reflect the current conditions;[38] the model was considered difficult to access and use since it had not been designed for continuous use, but for episodic use such as for the general plan evaluations; the model still was available only via remote time-sharing; and planned future uses of the model required its adaptation to operate at the village level rather than only on a citywide basis—a difficult conceptual problem and an even more difficult problem of data collection and data handling. This set of conditions confronted the city with the prospect of considerable expenditure on the model at a time when post-Proposition 13 pressures seemed to call for "canning the model and putting all of the available planners to work at the counter processing builder's applications so that development would be speeded up and city revenues increased." A motion to do precisely this was proposed before the council, but it failed.[39] Rather than scrap the model, the council reaffirmed its support for it and approved an extensive work program for converting it to the city's own in-house minicomputer, updating the land-use and cost data for the model, and adjusting the model assumptions to include "new parameters such as Proposition 13, its associated legislation, and the systems development change."[40]

The MKGK model was converted to the city's computer and most of the data and assumptions were updated during a 14-week study period beginning in July 1978. The conversion was not aimed at changing the model itself (i.e., the relationships in the model). Rather, it was aimed primarily at changing the data structure and data handling to facilitate day-to-day use. For example, the model's file structure was changed from a single large data base to seven files; the binary coded input/output was changed to conversational language (i.e., English-like statements); input of data and assumptions was made an on-line procedure; and the operation and use of the model was made interactive.

Routinization of the Model

In December 1978, the city council officially made the updating of data and assumptions for the model an annual process. Administrative responsibility for the model was shared between the administrative services and community development departments, with the former responsible for support services and the latter responsible for model use. Custody of the model was placed in the hands of three staff people: the computer specialist for the model software; a budget analyst for the cost data; and a planner for the land-use, community standards, and other planning data and assumptions.

In those areas where the outcomes of model use were routine, the council assigned control to city staff. Two such areas were growth management and budget making.[41] During use of the model for evaluating general plan options, the council and city staff had learned that the model provided a useful tool for negotiating with TIC over the amount and timing of specific developments in the city. The model could be used to indicate what population and land-use mix would balance government costs and revenues given expected tax rates; and thus, for example, approval of residential densities in a particular development could be held hostage to provision of those commercial activities which would provide the needed sales taxes; or, approval of residential densities could be held hostage to maintaining hilltops and canyons as permanently open space.

Model use for budget making was undertaken in a similar way. Essentially, the model was run for the coming year to determine the overall level of government spending "required" by existing and planned development, and "possible" with expected revenues. This level of expenditure was then proportioned out to the individual departments as a proposed ceiling on their budgets.

Specific model uses for these purposes typically do not involve political controversy. Situations requiring council intervention can be handled by a council agreement to assign one or two of their members to staff study teams. Consequently, these model uses and decisions are, to a high degree, routinized. However, the council retains control over all other uses either directly by requiring approval for model runs, or indirectly by setting priorities for computer use which effectively shut out other uses. Moreover, the council retains control over the model's assumptions and decision rules by requiring a formal procedure and, ultimately, their approval for changes.

The political uses of the model during incorporation appear to be similar to those during adaptation. The council, in particular, used the model to: negotiate with TIC by indicating precisely when population or development changes necessitated public facilities and then requiring the developer to provide them in exchange for plan approval; legitimize decisions made on other grounds by pointing to how the model supports the council's position; gain support for their position by observing that their position relies on objective computer output and technical criteria; and confuse public discussion and debate by complex and technical discussion of the model assumptions or results.

However, the political impacts of the model during incorporation in Irvine are different from those during adaptation, primarily because in the meantime the dominant coalition on the council changed from a low-growth to a pro-growth orientation. Whereas the early low-growth coalitions used the model to keep population around 220,000, the subsequent pro-growth coalitions have slowly but surely edged the built-out population of the city upward to 245,000. This has been done by using the model in setting land uses and population densities when considering specific developments as part of growth management. Development in the city usually proceeds on a village-by-village basis. Thus, when TIC seeks to bring a new village into existence, it must negotiate with the city over the quantity and timing of public and private facilities for the village and for other aspects of the larger city (services, facilities, circulation, sewage, storm drainage, etc.) affected by the village. The council uses the fiscal impact model to determine when various facilities will be needed and whether overall city revenues will be sufficient to build, operate and maintain them.

In this way, the model has provided a political tool for extracting concessions from TIC and for demonstrating the reasonableness of what is extracted. And, as one observer says, "when problems arise with a particular development, the developer usually ends up paying for resolving the problems." The cost/benefit calculus for the developer is that of delayed decision versus a more costly development project. Since development costs can be passed on to future buyers or commercial, industrial or residential space, the choice is usually clear—the developer agrees to pay for resolving the problems just to get the development approval. But the developer also gets something in exchange, usually higher density or more commercial area set aside or more time to bring commercial activities on-line.

TIC seems to have accepted the Irvine "Economic" Model as a suitable basis for these negotiations. At least, Company officials have not openly criticized it, nor have they advocated an alternative. Moreover, TIC has consistently taken a strong interest in the model. TIC has not only provided land-use data based on its five-year development plans, but has participated in the modeling program by reviewing the reports based on the model, conducting an in-house critique of the model and, most recently, commissioning a critique by the consultant firm of Peat, Marwick and Mitchell.

The former Planning Director thinks that some of the model's findings influenced the timing and sequence of TIC's development, although not necessarily to the city's advantage:

> I can't recall it being used, at least while I was there, as a tool to beat the Irvine Company over the head, for example. However, the Irvine Company took a real interest in participation in the whole program and I think they got some answers for their own corporate planning purposes out of it. And it helped them develop their own strategies of how to deal with the city. That was very apparent to me.
>
> Their corporate plan was a five-year program that said when they were going to build and where and how much. In the case of Village 10, I think the model had something to do with their decision to delay it somewhat. We had done a separate model run on Village 10 after the general plan evaluation was done. It showed a positive result because there was a lot of commercial development in that area. I think that may have influenced their decision to finish up what they were doing in the other villages [on the grounds that Village 10 would eventually produce net revenues for the city] (Peabody, May 1980 interview)

Regarding a special model run for the Irvine Regional Center, Peabody said:

> We also made a special run on the impact of the regional center. That run was an important consideration in the city pushing the heck out of the Irvine Company to get going [on development of the regional center.] It didn't do any good, but. . . . (Peabody, May 1980; interview)

Thus, TIC probably supports the model's use in part because it can use the results to its own strategic advantage,[42] or ignore the results when it feels it necessary. Perhaps the most important reason for supporting the model's use is that it is better than the most likely alternatives—namely, requiring the Company to pay for all public facilities, or slowing down the rate of development until public monies can be found to pay for needed facilities. And the model might provide a quantitative and seemingly objective basis for negotiations that TIC planners and managers can, in turn, use to justify their decisions to the company's Board of Directors.

The model also appears to have had an impact on bureaucratic politics. The dominant coalition on the council has succeeded in limiting use of the model to those areas where the outcomes are predictable and has obtained the support of the city manager, computer staff, and planners in delaying or denying other uses on the grounds of priority need for administrative uses of the computer. For example, one Planning Commissioner commented about the problems of gaining access to the model:

> What I find fascinating is the internal politics about why you can't use the model when you want to use it. They've set up an economy, a token economy, for the computer, which is that there is only so much computer time available for non-operational functions. So the different department staffs come in and bid for that time, and the Planning Department's use of the computer time for modeling is a low priority. And, computer time for the planning staff to be running the model for the Planning Commission is an even lower priority. So when you ask questions that could be answered by the model, they say we won't be able to run it because we've run out of our tokens to buy time.
>
> The reason this came about is that I was saying that we should have fiscal impacts on everything we do. I asked for a fiscal impact analysis on Irvine Town Center; I asked for it on all projects. The Planning Department staff got very concerned because I spent all of this time talking about fiscal impacts at the Planning Commission meetings. Also, the Planning Commissioners who were representatives of the pro-growth faction knew it was going to be embarrassing in many cases if the cost-benefit ratios were made public. So they simply got to their persons on the City Council and said, don't let the model be run without your permission. So, finally, the City Council came down and said that in order to get a model run, you have to get City Council approval of any run. But, the public justification, which is that the city would go broke if we ran the model as much as we want, is a lot of bunk.

Finally, the model has peformed the political function of showing the citizens of Irvine that the council does not simply bow to the wishes of TIC. Few citizens are able to monitor the council's actions closely enough to know whether the sum of its actions represent capitulation or not. However, the existence and continued use of the model and the exactions that come out of it *convey the impression to citizens that the council does not capitulate*. So long as there is no easy way to determine the actual state of affairs and the council majority can point to the use of the model in their deliberations, they effectively ignore minority claims of a sell-out to TIC.

NOTES

1. The Irvine Ranch was originally part of three Mexican land grants: the Rancho Santiago de Santa Ana, the Rancho San Joaquin, and Rancho Lomas de Santiago. By 1870, a partnership of James Irvine, Benjamin and Thomas

Flint, and Llewelyn Bixby had acquired 110,000 acres of these three ranches for raising sheep. In 1876, James Irvine bought out the other partners and acquired sole title. James Irvine II assumed control of the Ranch in 1893, after the death of his father, and brought in agriculture as the dominant activity. Much of the land was leased to tenant farmers and the rest was farmed directly by the Irvine company. By 1895, the Ranch had 31,000 acres of barley under cultivation, together with large amounts of potatoes, wheat, corn, and beans. After the turn of the century, agricultural production was further diversified with the introduction of citrus, sugar beets, artichokes, peas, and other crops. During the early 1900s, in order to drill wells and construct catch basins and reservoirs needed to provide water for irrigation, TIC began to sell off parcels for residential development, which eventually became portions of Newport Beach and Laguna Beach. Beginning in the 1930s, the Irvine Company began to develop portions of its land for urban uses, primarily in the coastal areas around Newport Bay. Rather than sell this property outright, the company chose to develop it on a leasehold basis. The leasehold policy continued until 1967, when the company began to experience opposition to the leasehold system from potential buyers of housing. In the late 1950s, TIC began receiving offers from developers interested in buying portions of the Ranch, but decided to retain the land and restructure the company to carry out its own process of land planning and development.

2. Although urban development was carried out by TIC during the 1950s, no other single factor influenced urbanization of the Irvine Ranch as much as the decision by the UC Board of Regents to build a new university there. The impetus for the decision came not from the Regents, however, but from TIC, which offered to donate 1,000 acres for the new campus if the Regents would locate it on the Ranch. Company officials felt that a new campus on the Ranch would create a major focus for urban development in the same way that the UCLA campus had done for the Janss Corporation and Westwood some 30 years earlier. As a means of attracting the new campus to the Ranch, TIC offered to donate land and engaged William L. Pereira to design plans for a university community of 100,000 people on 10,000 acres around the campus. Pereira's plans portrayed a community similar to classic university communities in Europe, such as Oxford and Cambridge, which have a high degree of physical and social integration of town and gown (see Gilbert, 1961). Pereira's concept fired the imaginations of University officials, state officials, and local government officials in the area, thereby generating a great deal of support for the final decision to locate the new campus on the Irvine Ranch.

Although not commonly recognized as such, Pereira's plan for the university community also was instrumental in TIC decision making about urban development on the Ranch. There was considerable disagreement within the company about whether to actively pursue urban development over agricultural operations and, subsequently, how to pursue urban development. Nathaniel M. Griffen describes the effect of Pereira's plan on TIC as follows:

> Pereira's 1960 plan for the Irvine campus of the University of California was the turning point in the thinking of the Irvine Company with re-

spect to future development. He first introduced the concept of a satellite new community as opposed to an extension of the suburbanization which occupied the northern half of Orange County (Griffin, 1974, p. 16).

3. The groundwork for the Regent's decision had been laid by the architectural firm of Pereira and Luckman, who had been hired in 1958 by the Regents to do a site selection study for an Orange County campus of the University of California. The Regents had decided to build three new campuses in California, one of which was to be located in Orange County because of projected population growth in the area. (The other campuses were to be built in the San Diego and Santa Cruz areas.) Twenty-one different sites in Orange County were studied in a report that emphasized the need to locate the new campus in an area that would allow it to grow within an expanding university community (Pereira & Luckman, 1958). Such a university-community concept required that the campus be located within a relatively undeveloped area. It also required the resources for development. The Irvine Company indicated that it was willing to meet the requirements and offered the land to the Regents to cinch the deal. Thus the Ranch was ultimately chosen by the Regents because it seemed to represent a unique opportunity to develop a new city that would grow in concert with and complement the new university.
4. William L. Pereira, who did the site selection study with Luckman, later became the chief architect for both the Irvine Campus and the Irvine Company's development of the Ranch. Studies for the new campus and the new university city were begun in 1959 and completed in 1960 by Pereira, who had split off from Luckman and formed his own company (William L. Pereira & Associates, 1959, 1960). The studies by Pereira painted an attractive picture of what such a new university community might be like, and along with the earlier site selection study and TIC's donated land, helped to sell the Regents on the Irvine site. The studies also helped to justify the Regents' decision to the public and to competing large landowners who had hoped to attract the new campus to their sites.
5. Several annexation proposals were made that disturbed both TIC and Irvine area residents and helped to touch off the incorporation effort. The City of Newport Beach attempted (and later succeeded) to annex a portion of the Irvine Industrial Complex-West. The City of Santa Ana attempted (and failed) to annex a 938 acre section of the Industrial Complex, and tied up incorporation for a year and a half through a series of petitions and lawsuits. The basis of the suits was a 1963 TIC agreement that Santa Ana could one day annex the 938-acre section. But when TIC changed its plans and enlarged the size of its university centered community from 10,000 acres to 53,000 acres, it recommended that a new city government, encompassing almost the entire Industrial Complex, be created; and it abrogated its previous agreement with the City of Santa Ana. Both the Local Agency Formation Commission and the California courts denied Santa Ana's petitions. See Burby and Weiss (1976, p.159).
6. Local Agency Formation Commissions (LAFCOs) exist throughout Cali-

fornia and were established to review all proposals for city incorporations, annexations, and boundary modifications. The five-member board of each LAFCO is comprised of elected officials, appointed by the Board of Supervisors, from cities within each county.

7. Such forthright comment by the counsel for a member of the Board of Directors seems surprising. However, during the period in question, Joan Irvine was frequently at odds with the policy positions of the Board majority and revealed "insider" information and suspicions.

8. The cities adjoining the Irvine Ranch were Newport Beach, Laguna Beach, Costa Mesa, Santa Ana, Tustin, and Orange. Officials in these cities had been led to believe that they might annex portions of the Ranch. For example, Pereira's 1960 study of the university community showed "spheres of influence" which euphemistically designated areas of the Ranch that might be annexed by adjoining cities. However, TIC officials had hoped to forestall annexations until their plans were complete and boundaries were determined for the new City of Irvine.

9. TIC could have eventually applied to the new City of Irvine to keep the central sector and other portions of the Ranch in agricultural preserve. However, this would have been risky because residents of the new city might not have approved the application. Many of the area residents wanted to maintain in perpetuity the rural character of the Ranch as they had found it. Consequently, they might not have agreed to allow TIC to place the land in preserve status at lower taxes knowing that it would later be converted to urban development when market absorption of the land made such conversion profitable for TIC. Moreover, the residents might have permanently zoned the land for agricultural and open space uses.

10. The Williamson Act (or the California Land Conservation Act of 1965) provides for contracts or agreements to be made between landowners and county boards of supervisors for designated property to be placed in agricultural preserves for ten years. In return, such lands are assessed for property taxation according to their value in agricultural use rather than according to their development potential. The agreement automatically renews itself each year for a period of ten years and limits the use of the land to agriculture and related activities.

    In January 1969, the Orange County Board of Supervisors had agreed to place 49,000 acres of Irvine Company land, including most of the central sector, into such preserves. This agreement reduced TIC's annual property tax bill by $1.5 million in 1970, with considerable reductions in subsequent years as well. Each year, TIC reviews its long-range development plan in order to identify areas it will want to develop ten years into the future. It then files a notice of nonrenewal with the County indicating which portions it wants to withdraw from the agricultural preserve. Once TIC exercises its right of nonrenewal on a parcel, that land is available for development ten years later. During that period, the taxes are raised year by year from an agricultural rate to its full value for urban development.

11. The Orange County Board of Supervisors approved the boundaries and set incorporation and council elections for December 1971. At that time, in-

corporation was approved by a vote of 3,214 to 1,560 and a five-person council was elected.

12. The first meeting of the city council was held on December 29, 1971. William Fishbach was elected mayor, and a voting pattern was established that would hold throughout the life of this council—John Burton and E. Ray Quigley against Fishbach, Gabrielle Pryor and Henry Quigley. UCI student surveys of council meetings indicate that of the council votes that were not unanimous, two-thirds were split in this manner (Irvine Student Coalition, undated).

13. In January 1973, the city council created six advisory committees to work with the planning consultant. See Irvine City Council, "Press Release," January 2, 1973.

14. See statement by Juanita Moe for the Combined Citizens Advisory Committees to the Irvine City Council, November 13, 1973. The 200,000 median population figure mentioned by Juanita Moe is important because of what it symbolized for citizens. Basically, the CAC was saying that such a built out population represented a compromise among a whole set of concerns ranging from quality of life, to city economics and preservation of open space. Although the importance of this figure was frequently discounted in contemporary discussions among the city's planners and public officials, it was very important to the citizens and the CAC. Moreover, as will be seen later, the General Plan option ultimately adopted by the city council was very close to the 200,000 population figure. Thus, the figure had great symbolic, practical, and historical importance.

15. Minutes of Irvine City Council Meeting, October 28, 1975. This meeting merely ratified a consensus among the council. In August, 1975, the council had asked its planning staff to indicate the tasks, procedures, time frame, and cost involved in a process to select one general plan option. The council discussed various staff reports on the requirements of such a planning program at several subsequent meetings. They also discussed at considerable length the problems of operating under three general plan options. It is clear from the meetings that the council was in agreement on the need to at least *try* to select a single option. Moreover, at each meeting they issued various staff directives and approved various efforts to secure consultant assistance in the process. Interestingly, some members of the council thought the process could be completed in *two* months. As it turned out, GPA #4 was adopted 19 months after the process began. See: Memorandum from Mel Roop, Senior Planner to City Manager regarding "Program for selecting one general plan option," August 8, 1975; Memorandum from Claudette Donatella, Assistant Director of Planning to City Manager regarding "Program for selection of one general plan option," October 10, 1975; Memorandum from Claudette Donatella, Assistant Director of Planning to City Council regarding "General plan amendment for the selection of one option, "October 24, 1975; Minutes of Irvine City Council Meetings for August 4, August 16, October 4, October 14, and October 28, 1975.

16. The fiscal impact model was one of four consulting studies for which the city contracted (the others being for urban design, environmental impact, and transportation) as part of its GPA #4. The aim was to develop a single

land-use plan whose purpose, according to the Director of Community Development, was to ensure the following:

> Consistency between the city's plan and the plans of other agencies.
> The ability to answer citizens of Irvine as to development policies for underdeveloped land with more accuracy and detail.
> The ability to create one comprehensive capital improvement plan.
> The ability to implement a complete transformation plan.
> The direction for further study on fiscal policy/economic impact and growth management.
> (General Plan Amendment No. 4 Workbook, City of Irvine Department of Community Development, May 3, 1977.)

17. The so-called "Irvine Economic Model" is not really a model of the economy of the City of Irvine as the title might suggest. Rather, it is a model that calculates government revenues and expenditures for a given development plan, compares total revenues to total expenditures, and indicates the net fiscal loss or gain to the city. Thus, it is a fiscal impact model. For some unknown reason, city officials prefer to call it an economic model even though some of them know better.

18. Although John Burton and Henry Quigley had run on a platform in favor of TIC's master plan, they maintained that they were independent of the Company and that they supported TIC's master plan because it made economic sense. In order to maintain political credibility, it is likely that they had to disagree periodically with TIC to symbolize their independence. Their support of improved planning capability for the city can be viewed as a way of indicating that independence without disapproving specific development plans of the Company.

19. Irvine City Council Minutes, October 14, 1975; and City of Irvine, "Request for Proposal—Economic Impact Analysis." Irvine, CA: October 1, 1975.

20. Speaking about the various council members' understanding of the model, one commissioner, who is an economist and planner, said:

> I don't think any of them knew then or know now how it works. They sit there and try to understand it. They understand something of the language. They pick up on the symbolism of it. They may even learn to turn the computer on and do a couple of things like that. But, in terms of really understanding what's happening inside that model, they don't know. They still don't realize that I can sit down with this little sheet of paper and do the exact same thing in 20 minutes that the model does in 90 seconds.

21. The three top proposals were by Ashley Economic Services of Laguna Beach, Economic Research Associates of Los Angeles and Marshal Kaplan, Gans and Kahn of San Francisco. All three proposals were within the $20,000 limitation set for the project, but the proposals varied as to the scope of services provided. See Ashley Economic Services, "A proposal for fiscal and economic impact studies." South Laguna, CA: November 10, 1975; MKGK, letter to City of Irvine Planning Department and attached Proposal. San Francisco, CA. November 7, 1975; and Economic Research Associates, Los Angeles, CA: November 1975.

22. The Leventhal model had originally been developed for assisting private developers in determining the economic feasibility of new town development. MKGK had used the model for Kaiser Engineers of Oakland, California to assess the capital costs associated with building Kairparowitts New Town, a new community associated with the development of a coal mine and power plant in southeastern Utah. They also had applied the model to analyze capital costs of development for Ciudad Guayana, and a new industrial city in Venezuela.

23. There were several reasons for the high degree of cooperation. None of the parties had the data required by the model, yet all were interested in seeing it assembled. Moreover, each of the major parties at interest controlled a unique portion of the required data so it could not be assembled unless they cooperated. Finally, all parties felt that the model would support their position on development, or at least would indicate more precisely where major points of negotiation might exist. Thus, no one party appeared to have more to gain or lose than another. The city had cost and revenue data; the company had the land-use data. Standards for service and assumptions about future development phasing had to be agreed to by the city and the company if either was to believe in the results of the model.

24. These assumptions and data involved: the amount of land by type of use that would be brought into developed status each year to the year 2000; the capital, operating and maintenance costs associated with public physical facilities; the standards for provision of public facilities (e.g., the amount of land devoted to parks and open spaces per 1,000 people in the community) which would "trigger" capital expenditures at different population levels; the operating costs associated with the provision of public services such as police, fire, education, libraries, and planning; and the revenue factors associated with land uses, population, public service fees, and state or federal subventions.

25. Not all of the tables represented model outputs. Rather, some were simply summaries of the data that had been input to the model. The 11 summary tables were as follows:

Table 1 Development of city by land-use type by period (acreages)
Table 2 Cumulative development of city by land-use type by period (acreages)
Table 3 Cumulative population and housing units in city by land-use type
Table 4 City annual capital expenditures by item type
Table 5 Cumulative city capital expenditures by item type
Table 6 City periodic maintenance costs
Table 7 City periodic operating costs
Table 8 City annual general fund revenues
Table 9 City cumulative assessed value by land-use type
Table 10 Financing of city capital improvement projects by period
Table 11 City fiscal impact summary

Table 11 was the "bottom line" because it indicated the "implied" property tax rate per $100 assessed value; that is, the tax rate that would be required to meet the excess of expenditures over revenues for any particular development period (MKGK, 1976).

26. These geographical areas included: (a) the present city area, (b) the city and its sphere of influence (most likely next area of incorporation), (c) the city, sphere of influence, and coastal region (possible future area of incorporation), and (d) the Irvine Unified School District area. The latter was included because the council wanted to know the fiscal impact of general plan options on the school district as well as on the city since citizens would be faced with the *total* tax burden and, ultimately, might hold the council responsible for it. The council had no formal control over the District since it was an independent governmental body with its own elected officials.

27. Before the general plan options were run, MKGK used a two-year historical data base to make sample runs of the model and the results were compared with actual city budgets for the same period to assess the model's historical reasonableness. Since the model was built on historical budget data, this does not constitute a substitute test for the model's validity.

28. Two years earlier, in November, 1975, when the council polled itself for their preference for one of the general plan options, Council members West, Burton, Anthony, and Henry Quigley had indicated preference for Option 1 although both Anthony and West had indicated they wanted to decrease the built out population and increase the open space provisions of the plan. Council member Pryor had indicated preference for Option 3, but would increase the built out population and housing available for lower income families. Now, a new council (Burton, Pryor, William Vardoulis, David Sills, and Mary Ann Gaido) was departing further from TIC master plan. In letters written to the City Manager, each of the council members had indicated his or her preference for one of the general plan options. Council member Burton included a caveat in his letter which was a prediction of subsequent events. He indicated that whatever option was agreed upon then by the council, the final choice of an option would be significantly affected by "the results of the Urban Design Implementation Plan, the Economic Study, and the DEOCCS study." See: memorandum from Councilman John H. Burton to City Council and City Manager regarding "Single Land Use Option," November 6, 1975; Memorandum from Councilman Robert J. West to the City Manager regarding "Single Land Use Option," November 5, 1975; Memorandum from Mayor Anthony to City Manager regarding "Selection of One Land Use Option for our General Plan," November 4, 1975; Memorandum from Mayor Pro Tem Henry Quigley to City Manager regarding "Single Land Use Option General Plan," November 3, 1975; Memorandum from Councilwoman Gabrielle G. Pryor to City Council and City Manager regarding "General Plan Option—Single Land Use Option," November 5, 1975.

29. Irvine City Council Minutes, October 13, 1976. This action was in response to a Memorandum from the Director of Community Development to the City Council regarding "Continued Use of the Economic Model by City Staff," October 1, 1976.

30. Irvine City Council Minutes, December 14, 1976.

31. The time-sharing contract was with the United Computing System, Inc., of Kansas City, which had the Leventhal model on-line on a Control Data computer.

32. As it turned out, this was only a theoretical savings. It assumed that current and future residents would be willing to trade avoided school taxes for increased city taxes and to devote these to the purchase of open space rather than having the avoided school taxes in their own pockets. There was some basis for this assumption. The CAC had indicated in November of 1973 that 81 percent of the respondents to a citizen survey felt that maintaining agriculture within the city was important enough to support special tax measures on citizens to purchase permanent open space (see earlier section on "Creation of a New Master Plan."). It is unclear why the council didn't act on the basis of this widespread support; perhaps it didn't believe the CAC survey; perhaps citizen support for additional tax measures had eroded by 1977, when the consultant's final report was considered. Whatever the reason, it appears that the council might have lost a real opportunity, as California's Proposition 13, passed in 1978, dramatically changed the city's ability to enact new tax measures.

33. Edited quotation from tape recording of the Irvine City Council Meeting, September 15, 1977.

34. Edited quotation from tape recording of the Irvine City Council Meeting, September 15, 1977.

35. Edited quotation from tape recording of the Irvine City Council Meeting, September 15, 1977.

36. Edited quotation from tape recording of the Irvine City Council Meeting, September 15, 1977.

37. Edited quotation from tape recording of the Irvine City Council Meeting, September 15, 1977.

38. A review of the economic model's history, assumptions and report formats is contained in a staff report on the "Economic Model" dated May 16, 1979, and presented to the Planning Commission by the Directors of Community Development and Administrative Services for a Planning Commission Study Session on May 24, 1979.

39. It is interesting to note that although the model was "saved" in the battle over faster permit processing, the planning director was not. One commissioner described the situation this way:

> You've got Vardoulis [a council member] and the Irvine Company who want to make our planning department simply a permit-issuing group. You walk in the front door with a proposal at 8:00 a.m. in the morning and you walk out with a permit at 5:00 p.m. What they've done is fire the old planning director because he wasn't doing enough. Nothing was said publicly, but the internal debate was that the processing of permits was taking too long and he [the former planning director] was not managing the Planning Department. He was too much of a planner and not enough of a manager. Then, they hired a guy who's not a planner, but an administrator. What he really is, is their boy. Now everything just flies through there.

40. The updated model assumptions were subsequently presented to the council for approval at a meeting on September 26, 1978. See staff report to the city council from the Director of Administrative Services and the Director of Community Development regarding "Updated Economic Model Assumptions," September 22, 1978. See also the 1979 staff report cited earlier which indicated the council's directives to the planning staff for revision of the model.

41. There have been several other uses of the model that were not investigated in depth in this study. These include:

1. Evaluation of land-use alternatives as part of the IIC-West 15th Amendment Study.
2. Analysis of the impact of Proposition 13.
3. Analysis of the potential effect of a two-year injunction on development for a housing lawsuit.
4. Support of the city's lobbying efforts against two pieces of legislation in state government.
5. Evaluation of the fiscal impact of delaying the opening of Irvine Regional Center.

These formal studies, and many informal uses of the model, provide ample testimony that the innovation has been incorporated into the government's operations and decision-making processes. For a review of the above studies and a recent status report on the model, see: Memorandum from the Director of Community Development and the Director of Administrative Services to the City Council regarding "Fiscal Impact (Economic) Model Assessment," June 17, 1980. It is interesting to note that this memorandum is the first time that an official document of the City of Irvine recognized that the model was a fiscal impact model and not an economic model. Moreover, the memorandum goes to considerable length to explain this fact to the council and to point out valid and invalid model uses.

42. Several features of the Irvine model are different from most other fiscal impact models. First, land-use data and projections are very reliable compared to other places. A single developer, the Irvine Company, controls the rate and kind of land-use that is brought into development and makes its plans based upon its own corporate cash flow model. The company then supplies its internal projections to the city's planners each year, and the city uses these estimates as model inputs. This procedure not only increases the likelihood that the estimates will be more accurate, it also makes the process of estimating land-use, housing and population easy in comparison to most other cities where many developers are involved.

In the Irvine case, there might be some tendency for the developer to exaggerate the amount of development projected in order to look good in the city's model forecasts. That is, the company can make its development proposals look fiscally profitable by indicating that commercial land-uses will be brought on-line earlier and in larger acreages than actually intended. Since considerable time elapses between the time when the forecasts are made and the time when the city is able to monitor the company's actual performance, this could be an effective short-term strategy. In the long run, however, it might not be effective if it were to stimulate opposition to the company's development plans.

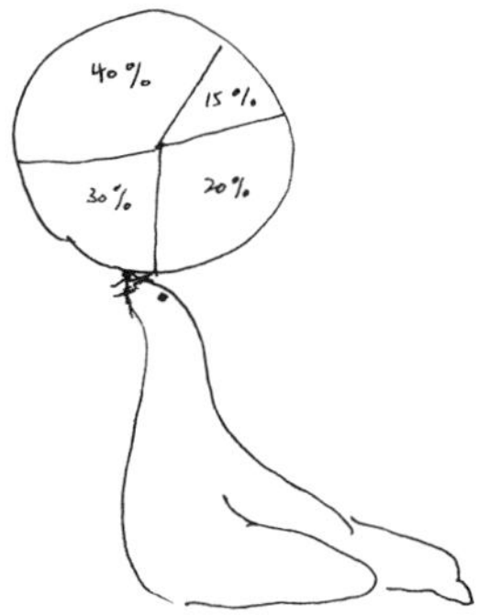

3.
Negotiating Decisions and Non-decisions

The use of a fiscal impact model to analyze the City of San Diego's growth management plan illustrates the way in which modeling can refocus conflict away from positions in a policy debate to the assumptions and process of modeling and thereby facilitate negotiation and compromise. But, the case also illustrates the fact that modeling is a two-edged sword.

On the one hand, modeling helped to resolve differences of opinion and interest among contestants in the debate over revision of San Diego's general land-use plan. Modeling appeared to have an instrumental, albeit marginal, role in narrowing and resolving differences between the Mayor's support of a "growth management" plan calling for greater in-fill of already developed areas and the real estate and builders' opposition to growth management, calling instead for a more laissez-faire approach to urban development.

On the other hand, modeling tended to reinforce the interests of those involved in the modeling process against those left out of that process. For example, participants in the modeling process structured the analysis to support the early development of a controversial new community, called "North City West," regardless which of several alternative land-use plans were judged to be most fiscally profitable. In this way, modeling aided the decision over growth management, but reinforced the decision to build North City West—a nondecision to those left out of a modeling process.

NORTH CITY WEST

On October 22, 1979, the San Diego City Council voted 6–2 to approve the first phase of a housing development generally known as "North City

West,'' an area of approximately 4,000 acres located in the northwest of the City of San Diego, California, just east of the small coastal city of Del Mar. The first-phase plan provided for the development of 400 acres in the Carmel Valley portion of North City West to include about 2,000 housing units and about 5,000 residents. The Carmel Valley phase was roughly in the middle of North City West and was the first of nine neighborhoods to be developed over a period of 20 years. Envisioned as a ''city within a city,'' North City West is expected to house 40,000 people and to absorb about 13 percent of all city growth up to 1995.

Starting in the 1950s, the historical process leading to the City Council's decision of October 22 was a complex blend of politics, planning, and analysis that defies straightforward interpretation. North City West was many things to many people: it was at once a planner's dream, an environmentalist's nightmare, a speculator's windfall, a citizen's solution to the housing shortage, and a politician's path to higher office. It was one of the most controversial development plans in San Diego's history. Early on, the plans to develop North City West emerged in a pro-growth context facilitated by a laissez-faire attitude on the part of government officials. When North City West development became a public issue, it was first raised by planners who actively promoted a development plan that later would be honored by a national planning organization. But the completed plans faced the economic recession of 1974 and a new political environment shaped by public concern over rapid growth, inadequate public facilities, the ascendance of environmental awareness, and the election of a mayor committed to fiscal conservatism and revitalization of the central city. Subsequently, North City West development had to await the completion of a city-wide growth management plan and a financing plan for North City West. Once the principles of growth management and financing were established, the city joined with developers to implement plans for North City West.

Four historical periods capture the central themes in the North City West chain of events: laissez-faire development (1950–1970); planning (1970–1973); growth management (1974–1978); and implementation (1978–1980).

LAISSEZ-FAIRE DEVELOPMENT (1950–1970)

During the 1950s and 1960s, officials of the City of San Diego actively promoted development to diversify and revitalize a locally depressed economy (Hafter, 1976). This promotion took the form of the establishment of an Industrial Development Corporation, a laissez-faire approach toward developers, and the adoption of the city's original ''Progress Guide and

General Plan'' on July 20, 1967 (City of San Diego, 1967). The plan envisioned the urbanization of much undeveloped land in San Diego (including a large proportion of the North City West area) prior to 1985.

PLANNING (1970–1973)

According to one planning official, developers placed little credence in the general plan document. It covered 350 square miles. Given its scale, North City West would appear the size of a postage stamp on a standard ''center-fold'' planning map of the city. All the same, planners were receiving numerous rezoning applications from developers who were taking the 1967 General Plan and going directly into applications to rezone property, often asking for variances from the plan. In this context, the planning professionals began to lobby the city's appointed planning commission for more planning staff and more information from developers.

ASD Corporation submitted the first proposal for developing a small portion of North City West in late 1969. ASD followed all procedures and submitted a plan in conformance to the General Plan. This first North City West proposal was approved routinely. Early in 1970, the ASD proposal was joined by proposals from at least three other developers. Concurrently, hearings were being held on city contributions for providing utilities to the North City West area.

This development push in North City West, along with continuing development throughout the city, created a difficult workload for the planning department. The public began to express concern over the pace of development. Concern was heightened when a planning department intern published an article highly critical of the city for sanctioning massive and unplanned growth and advocated a comprehensive master plan for the entire North City West area (Zovanyi, 1970). Thus, planning for North City West was becoming an issue when, in August of 1970, the city council approved ASD Corporation's specific plan for developing 700 acres of the westerly Carmel Valley portion of North City West. Opposition voiced by citizen and planning groups raised the issue of planning for North City West as a whole. In response, the planning commission ordered a one-year building moratorium in that area. In the months following the moratorium, the planning commission recommended funding for the preparation of a plan for North City West and scheduled a workshop to coordinate their efforts with the council.

The joint planning commission and council workshop was held in early October. The workshops resolved that the planning commission's moratorim would be lifted, but that the council would stop processing Carmel Valley permits until a ''master plan'' for a ''city within a city'' was devised. Over the following months, a model planning process was followed through a lengthy series of reports, policies, and plans to guide the development of North City West.

This planning process proceeded rather smoothly up to the 1971 elections. In the November elections, two-term Republican State Assemblyman Peter Barton Wilson was elected Mayor. Pete Wilson, a Yale-educated lawyer, had been elected to the California Assembly from the 76th District of San Diego in 1966. In the Assembly, he served as both Republican whip and a member of the taxation and environmental committees. His mayoral platform stressed city control over development and his reputation was that of a fiscal conservative (having sponsored property tax relief measures), an advocate of controlled growth, and an opponent of North City West (Hogan, 1980).

In retrospect, the 1971 election marked a transition in San Diego politics. The former Mayor, Frank Curran, backed by banker-industrialist C. Arnholt Smith, was the traditional political broker, contrasting with Wilson, a model of the reform mayor. North City West was first proposed in the Curran era, when shirt-sleeved developers who could frame a house were dealing with a city administration cloaked in the tradition of old-style politics and plagued by accusations of bribery and corruption. North City West was finally approved in the Wilson era, when developer representatives in three-piece suits who had never framed a house formally negotiated with a reform government utilizing sophisticated analytical tools.

Despite the election of a mayor reputedly opposed to North City West, planning continued along the same lines that were set by the previous administration. Funds were approved by the city and county for an environmental study of North City West. An economic analysis also was conducted, and it showed that development would generally have positive economic impacts; fiscal impacts were not part of the analysis. And, in January 1972, the city council amended the 1967 general plan to accommodate urbanization of the remaining North City West area. Reports, preliminary plans, and workshops continued as did construction of the infrastructure to support the area's development. As late as 1973, when public debate arose over North City West, the debate focused on the boundary lines, rather than on the wisdom of development *per se*.

In the background, however, a reassessment of North City West was underway. In the summer of 1972, Wilson's administration made efforts to assess the costs and revenues of North City West development. In July, the new, less growth-oriented council adopted a policy requiring a total cost-revenue analysis prior to development. Then, in January 1973, the planning commission requested the city's Community Development Department to complete a cost-revenue analysis of North City West.

However, the city bureaucracy seemed to move on its own inertia, irrespective of Wilson's efforts to reassess the fiscal impacts of the development. City planners unveiled their concept of North City West in September, before a cost-revenue analysis was completed. One month later a two-page environmental impact report on the plan was prepared and, in November, still without the fiscal impact information, the planning commission adopted the "North City West Community Plan" at a public hearing at which little opposition was voiced.

GROWTH MANAGEMENT (1974–1978)

The failure of the Community Development Department to complete a cost-revenue analysis was frustrating to Wilson. The department reported to the City Manager who reported to the entire council. So, Wilson went around the bureaucracy and hired Michael Babunakis, a former state legislative analyst with expertise in cost-revenue studies.

In February 1974, Wilson was able to gather the support of enough council members to postpone action on North City West until Babunakis could conduct a fiscal impact analysis and planners could gather more information to address project boundary issues. The council voted unanimously to postpone a final decision, scheduling a conference for April 17–23 to receive reports on the fiscal impacts of North City West.

At the April 17 conference, Mayor Wilson seemed to have gained control over the city bureaucracy. At least, there appeared to be orchestrated opposition to North City West. Babunakis reported that the city's projected growth could occur without North City West, a development that would detract from downtown redevelopment and contribute to urban sprawl. The City Manager presented an economic report suggesting that North City West would require increased local property taxes in order to finance schools. The Planning Director spoke in favor of developing North City West, but said he had serious reservations about development "at this time." Finally, Mayor Wilson proposed (by letter) that a method be found to have North City West pay its own way for schools and other public facilities. On the same day, the Del Mar City Council voted unanimously to send a letter protesting development of North City West to the San Diego City Council. Two days later a public hearing on the North City West plan was rescheduled to May 2. Ironically, on the day of the postponement, the planning director accepted an award from the California Chapter of the American Institute of Planners, presented to the City Planning Department in recognition of the North City West plan.

At the May 2 meeting, the plan was put up for adoption by the City Council. The council voted unanimously to table the plan, and invoked policies requiring that development undergo a comprehensive cost-revenue analysis and be phased with projected growth. Thus, the council appeared to agree with Wilson that although the North City West plan was excellent, development was premature until vacant land closer to the central city was developed. But the council was not unanimous in its agreement with Wilson; plan supporters had voted with opponents only after reaching a critical compromise in which they were assured that North City West would receive top priority once an overall development time-table for the city was prepared.[1]

Following this decision, North City West proponents reorganized. Council member Lee Hubbard, Wilson's chief competition for the Mayor's Office, a cement contractor, and chair of the Council's Transportation and Land Use Committee, took a lead in speeding up the development. In September, he sunk more city resources into North City West, leading his committee to approve a water main for part of the area. Other supporters began to organize, forming a North City West Property Owners Association (NCWPOA), composed of about 162 landowners, for the purpose of seeking tax relief and speeding council approval of development plans. Eventually, and despite Wilson's objections on fiscal grounds, supporters of North City West were able to obtain a critical swing vote on the council, and to adopt the "North City West Community Plan" and the accompanying Environmental Impact Report on February 27, 1975. However, approval was conditional on all public facilities costs being paid by the property owners.

The Growth Management Strategy

In 1974, several members of the city council and Mayor Wilson had attended a conference in Texas where Professor Robert H. Freilich from the School of Law at the University of Missouri, Kansas City, was a featured speaker. Freilich had been legal council for Ramapo in New York and presented a case study on that community's "growth management" efforts. The relevance of growth management to the goal of slowing urban sprawl in San Diego was clear to Wilson, who subsequently invited Freilich to an informal meeting with the city council to discuss growth management and the problems of San Diego. By this time, the city was in the process of updating its 1967 General Plan. Also, a city task force had concluded that creation of a growth strategy for the city and region was of the highest priority. Apparently, Wilson hoped to develop a model growth management policy with the revised General Plan for the city.

In the spring of 1975, the city retained the consulting services of Freilich to advise the city on the preparation of a growth management program. Freilich suggested that the city develop alternative growth scenarios (current trends versus managed growth) and evaluate four components of these alternative growth plans: planning, legal, economic, and fiscal impacts.

Soon after retaining Freilich, the planning department and city manager were puzzling over how to do a fiscal impact analysis of growth management. Babunakis provided a push for their efforts by drafting a questionnaire (reviewed and revised by the planning department) to find out which other cities were doing fiscal impact analyses and how they were conducting them. Responses to this questionnaire provided a basis for a letter to various fiscal impact consultants and model builders, soliciting their interest in doing the fiscal analysis of San Diego's growth management plan and inviting them to a briefing.

These solicitations generated a list of consultants that was passed on to the city's Comprehensive Management Program (CMP) to assist in selecting a consultant for the fiscal evaluation of the Growth Management Plan. CMP was a sub-unit of the city's Financial Management Department, developed and supported in 1974 with funding from the U.S. Department of Housing and Urban Development under Comprehensive Management Financing. CMP was chosen to conduct the fiscal analysis process because of its mandate to develop management improvements, which involved it in a six-year program of developing statistical data, econometric modeling, and fiscal forecasting techniques. CMP also was presumed to have the most in-house technical expertise in fiscal analysis.

However, CMP analysts were reluctant to become involved with the fiscal analysis effort, as they had a poor, almost hostile, relationship with the planning department, which had primary responsibility for the growth management plan. Despite these reservations, CMP took the lead role in evaluating the fiscal impacts of alternative growth management scenarios.

CMP sent out a request for proposal (RFP) for the fiscal impact analysis, and evaluated all responses to the RFP jointly with the planning department and Babunakis. The evaluations gave high priority to proposals from firms that had already developed a fiscal impact model on the grounds that a developed model would help speed the analysis. The evaluations yielded three top candidates, with the Municipal Impact Evaluation System (MUNIES) being most preferred by the planners, and the Fiscal Impact Analysis System (FIAS) being most preferred by the CMP analysts.[2] MUNIES, marketed by the consulting firm of Tischler, Montasser, and Associates, Inc., (TMA) was chosen. MUNIES seems to have been preferred by the planners because it had a track record. It also appears that the planners were more in tune with the MUNIES consultants, who had somewhat more experience with planners and planning departments (in contrast to the FIAS consultants).

Different interpretations of the selection process emerged depending largely upon the observer's position on growth management issues. Supporters of growth management argue that the MUNIES model became known through the Babunakis questionnaire and was chosen through an impartial selection process. Opponents of growth management, of Freilich, and of the MUNIES analysis, argue that Freilich initiated contacts with the MUNIES firm and biased the selection. According to one participant, "A lot of people will attribute MUNIES coming in, and Tischler, Montasser, and Associates, Inc. coming in, to Freilich. They think they're Freilich's boys but that's not true."

It is clear that neither the MUNIES model nor any other model would have been adopted if Wilson had not pushed for growth management or if Freilich had not needed a fiscal analysis to back up a growth management plan. However, Wilson appears never to have been involved directly in the choice of the model consultants. And, while Babunakis and Freilich pushed sophisticated analytical techniques, they also had no role in the choice of the specific model consultant. This role seemed to devolve upon the technical experts within the planning department and the Comprehensive Management Program, with the planners' preference prevailing.

North City West Continues

As CMP went about analyzing the fiscal impacts of growth management in order to revise the 1967 General Plan, North City West financing issues continued to emerge. The city council directed the planning director, city manager, and city attorney to cooperate with the NCWPOA in preparation of the first precise plan (City of San Diego, 1975), a financing program for capital facilities, and a master EIR for the precise plan area. The council also accepted a $5,000 offer from NCWPOA to hire municipal financing consultants to develop financing provisions for the plan. Mayor Wilson opposed the latter action, arguing that, even if the land-owners provided all public facilities, it would still cost the city more to provide police, fire, and trash collection services than the land would produce in property taxes, and, specifically, $2.5 million per year more than to furnish the same services in already urbanized areas.

Wilson's support on the council was not improved by the 1975 city elections. Despite the fact that Wilson was reelected by a large margin, having defeated Council member Hubbard in the primaries, the elections led to an over-all conservative, pro-development shift on the council with the election of four new Republicans. Growth itself was not a major public issue in the elections. The platforms of the pro-development council members stressed law and order and fiscal concerns.

North City West and Growth Management

The months following the election were devoted to planning. In July of 1976, a little over a year after he was retained, Freilich submitted a description of the proposed Growth Management Strategy to the city council, entitled "A Growth Management Program for San Diego." Freilich proposed a five-tier concept. Tier III was composed of "developing areas" and included North City West. Tier III objectives were for "supporting additional investment . . . to allow growth of areas already served by capital facilities." Tier IV land, to be held in reserve, was described as "presently vacant and zoned predominantly for agriculture." These tier descriptions were received with little controversy. (Years later these tiers were collapsed to three and labeled "urbanized," "urbanizing," and "future urbanizing" areas with North City West included within the urbanizing areas.)

A task force, composed of city staff and private sector people including members of the Chamber of Commerce and the Construction Industries Federation, hammered out the basic growth management work program, which later served as the basis for conducting several studies. These were a housing study (completed later by a Denver firm), economic studies of income and employment (later conducted by Economic Research Associates of San Diego), an environmental study that included transportation impacts (later done by Copley International of San Diego), and a fiscal impact study (to be done by city staff utilizing the MUNIES model).

The MUNIES Analysis

The MUNIES analysis took over a year to complete, and involved two major phases. The first phase involved the generation of population forecasts and land-use data for the alternative development scenarios. It was conducted by the planning department and involved two important political decisions, which might or might not have been made intentionally to influence the outcome of the analysis.

The first decision was to incude North City West in every growth scenario. Initially, in developing the land-use and population totals for urban sprawl and managed growth scenarios, planners presented a variety of alternatives in a series of workshops. In all but one scenario for managed growth, North City West was planned for inclusion in Tier III "developing areas." This single exception did not go unnoticed by the major North City West proponent, Council member Hubbard, who attended the planning workshops. According to one participant, Hubbard argued that any exclusion of North City West from Tier III was contrary to established plans and agreements. The planner presenting the alternatives indicated that its exclusion was an inadvertent error that would be corrected; from then on, every alternative growth scenario for San Diego would entail the early development of North City West.[3]

The second political decision was to construct growth scenarios that represented the extremes of growth management and urban sprawl. Analytically, this strategy was reasonable because the forecasts were only meant to be rough estimates based on many simplifying assumptions. Politically, this strategy proved to be a poor choice because the extreme cases were subsequently considered unrealistic by city decision makers.

CMP analysts influenced the development of land-use scenarios by the planning department. Initially, the land-use differences between the two scenarios were rather small and the CMP analysts told planning, "hey, look, we want you guys to know that there isn't going to be much of a difference in the outcomes from these scenarios." They explained that the model was a linear program driven solely by the service demands generated by a land-use base.[4] If there is only an inch's worth of difference in demand bases there is only going to be an inch's worth of difference in the fiscal impacts. Shortly after that discussion the planning department returned with another set of land-use data. This set yielded a $200 million difference between managed growth and urban sprawl scenarios and led to the accusation that the planning department was stacking the deck in favor of managed growh.

The second phase of fiscal analysis involved the use of the MUNIES model and was conducted by CMP with the help of the consultants. According to the CMP analysts, the land-use data supplied by planning determined the outcomes of the fiscal analysis. However, several CMP decisions were made in the implementation of the MUNIES model that importantly affected the outcome of the fiscal analysis.

First, the analysts attempted to construct an analysis that was both comprehensive and very detailed, against the advice of the consultants who sought a more simplified analysis. When San Diego purchased the MUNIES program, the model had been applied only once in a manner similar to the way in which the city wanted to apply it. Montgomery County, Maryland, had evaluated alternative growth scenarios for the county with the jurisdiction divided into four geographical areas. For the most part, it had been used to analyze the fiscal impacts of individual developments, such as a new planned unit development. In contrast, CMP was directed to do a financial analysis for the entire city making distinctions among Tiers I through V. In actuality they limited their analysis to Tiers I through III because Tiers IV and V would not be developed prior to 1985. Therefore, CMP had to distinguish between the costs and revenues by each Tier, type of dwelling unit (single versus multiple), type of land use (commercial, industrial, or residential), and for city schools as well as the general-purpose government. And each of the marginal costs and revenues attributable to growth had to be generated for two alternative growth strategies, continued "urban sprawl" versus "managed growth" or in-fill. Consultants sought simplicity to lessen the difficulty of consulting the data base and of specifying the many assumptions and parameters of the fiscal impact model. The CMP analysts pushed complexity because they desired a high level of accuracy and sophistication in their forecasts. The cost of this complexity was considerable delay in the analysis. It became a massive undertaking, absorbing two to three person-years of staff time.

Second, the CMP analysts made important assumptions that affected the outcomes of the analysis. An example concerned the development of assumptions for estimating the costs of police services. Previous studies of police service costs found that the greater the population density, the higher the crime rate and the greater the number of calls for service; therefore, the greater the cost for police services. By this logic, the Mayor's growth management plan calling for in-fill would increase police costs by increasing population densities. On the one hand, the analysts knew that urban redevelopment projects, such as San Diego's major downtown redevelopment project called the Marina, would place higher income groups in the downtown area. Thus, the historical relationship between population density and crime rates might be invalid. However, CMP stuck with the thrust of previous studies and the police department's analyses and used population density as a primary predictor of crime rates, calls for service, and police costs. According to one of the analysts, "so, in the first study we used density and got blown out of the water by the mayor. Police costs were much higher under a densified management approach than under sprawl. . . . Eventually, on the second study, we just looked at it on a per capita basis. For the most part, these costs just netted out."

Given constant aggregate population forecasts for both scenarios and a major reliance on per capita cost multipliers, the final fiscal impact analysis would forecast much the same fiscal impacts for managed growth as for sprawl. The major differences that did occur resulted from the costs of building more new schools if urban sprawl patterns dominated. In part, this finding was influenced by modeling assumptions. Historical data suggest that single-family homes generate more pupils per capita than multifamily dwelling units. Because growth management meant a larger proportion of multi-family units, the managed growth scenario generated fewer students and reduced costs for schools.

On February 15, 1977, about two years after Freilich was retained, the City of San Diego and Tishler, Montasser, and Associates, Inc. (1977) submitted the MUNIES fiscal impact analysis of growth management alternatives for San Diego.[5] The analysis strongly supported Mayor Wilson's policy preferences. The report indicated that, given the city's projected growth in population, controlled growth was far more profitable to the city than urban sprawl. In fact, the two scenarios revealed cumulative potential savings over a twenty-year period of $221 million from growth management as opposed to urban sprawl. This result was immediately challenged by growth supporters. Private developers argued that growth management would not save such huge sums and that the planning department had constructed scenarios that represented unrealistic boundary conditions. For example, their vacant land inventory included much undevelopable open space (e.g., federal or state lands and steep hillsides).

In essence, a number of people accused the planning department of stacking the deck in favor of Mayor Wilson's growth management plan. Some people implied that the department was an arm of the Mayor, that growth management was the Mayor's program, and so the planning department did what they could to make the Mayor look good. There is no evidence to suggest that the planning department was directed to slant the analysis in any way, but the interviews suggest that planners probably anticipated the reactions of the Mayor when they constructed the analysis.

In May, as a result of the controversy raised over the analysis, the council scheduled a series of workshops to revise and agree on new land-use projections and a new fiscal impact analysis of growth management. The planning department was to create more realistic land-use projections for the two scenarios.

The Growth Management Consensus

While fiscal impact analyses were being revised, there was a developing consensus that Mayor Wilson's growth management plan would be acceptable largely because it favored fiscal conservatism while also seeking to accommodate expected growth rates, rather than limit them. This stirred opponents of North City West who began to realize that approval of growth management also meant approval of North City West. City reports and rumors that things would start happening in North City West began to circulate in the fall of 1977. These rumors spurred coastal residents to organize the Coalition for Responsible Planning (CRP), which would seek to delay or block North City West development over the next three years. The Coalition for Responsible Planning was formed in April of 1976, to oppose North City West and to support "responsible planning" throughout the region. With a well-financed campaign, CRP threw several wrenches into the machinery. In June, Council member Morrow was persuaded to change his mind on North City West, and the plan was voted down in a 5–4 decision. Yet Hubbard said, "when things are logical and sensible, they have a way of resurfacing." And so it did.

Shortly after this reversal, Wilson began to lose builder and developer support, and to receive growing criticism of his growth management program. Then out of the debate emerged growing consolidation of support both for Mayor Wilson's Growth Management Plan, and for moving ahead on North City West.

The Second MUNIES Report

The revised MUNIES fiscal impact analysis of growth management alternatives was published in late July 1978 with little fanfare and no controversy (Economic Research and Analysis Program, 1978). The analysis supported greater in-fill (growth management) with more conservative cost differentials than in the original analysis. What differentials remained could be explained largely by the greater costs of building schools if current trends continued.

The relationship of growth management to North City West was evident to both sides. One developer noted during a personal interview that the growth management plan said the "North City West community planning area *should* be urbanized." And the Coalition for Responsible Planning organized a campaign and demonstration for the February 26 council meeting on the growth management plan. CRP feared that approval of the plan would allow the start of North City West construction. CRP argued that North City West was mostly vacant, zoned agricultural, and located 10 miles from the urban periphery, and therefore fit the Tier IV category of land to be held in urban reserve (CRP, 1977).

IMPLEMENTATION (1978–1980)

Immediately after the fiscal impact report was completed, the "Carmel Valley: Precise Plan" was submitted on August 25, 1978 by city planning staff to the planning commission for review by the North City West Community Planning Organization. On the 31st, the planning commission recommended adoption of the Carmel Valley Precise Plan, the accompanying EIR, and the Design Element. The commission approved the Precise Plan and Design Element for Carmel Valley despite strong objections of some North City West residents and CRP representatives. On November 3, Mayor Wilson said that North City West was "the next contiguous area in the city to be developed." He did not commit himself to vote for the project, but said, "we have done an awful lot of in-filling."

Not only had in-fill proceeded, but the fiscal impacts of North City West suddenly grew more profitable since the Babunakis study. On December 12, a fiscal impact report on the Carmel Valley Neighborhood was completed for the NCWPOA (Foster and Weddell, 1978). The report indicated that operating costs would be more than covered by revenues generated from the very beginning of the project. The city relied on out-of-house analyses of North City West fiscal impacts and appeared to have forgotten the earlier study by Babunakis.

On the heels of this fiscal analysis, the planning commission recommended adoption of the North City West Planned District Ordinance on January 4, 1979, with the exception of the financing element. Five days later the Transportation and Land Use Committee accepted a North City West financing plan concept, and directed the City Manager to explore alternative methods of financing school facilities and to investigate the probable impacts on the City of Del Mar for a later report on the committee.

By some accounts, Wilson had moved from opposing to stalling to pushing North City West. A *Los Angeles Times* article suggested that Wilson had threatened San Diego County with sanctions if it challenged the construction of North City West (Smollar, 1979). The article reported that the city might reconsider its pledge of a $1 million contribution to a new office building the county planned for downtown redevelopment. Wilson spokespersons denied any such sanctions. County planners did challenge North City West, saying that it would result in overcrowding of neighboring schools, congested freeways, and damage to agricultural lands. Except for the county, the City of Del Mar, and the CRP, most agencies fell in line behind North City West. On February 20, the State Coastal Commission approved the issue-identification and segmentation phase of the city's Local Coastal Program for North City West. On February 23, the City Manager's office suggested that developers and, ultimately, new residents would pay the full costs of school construction—1972 million—and set about reaching a compromise with the affected school districts. On February 26, a *San Diego Union* editorial on North City West emphasized that the area should be developed to accommodate projected growth and suggested a plan to resolve the school facility financing issue.

On the same day, Wilson's growth management plan was formally and unanimously ratified by the city council allowing for the immediate development of North City West. By this time, growth management was a non-issue. In part, this was because Lee Hubbard was no longer on the council. Also, there had been the series of compromises with respect to the land-use data, growth management, and the early development of North City West. Nearly every segment of the development community seemed to realize that some form of growth management would be adopted.

This was because the public in general in San Diego was concerned over growth. While the growth management plan was built on forecasts assuming unrestricted growth, the plan was argued as a means to accommodate that growth in the most qualitatively desirable and fiscally prudent manner. Finally, the popularity of Mayor Wilson was so substantial that both developers and construction interests realized that they had to get along with Wilson and that, to do so, they had to build within some growth management framework.

All the same, approval of growth management at this time was not simply a political coincidence; it had been planned over two years before. That is, February of 1979 was scheduled for council approval of the growth management plan. The schedule was contained in a PERT (Program Evaluation Review Technique) chart developed by Freilich prior to August 1977.

However, the growth management-North City West connection was resurrected over the Tier designation of North City West once again; this time by the county's Integrated Planning Office (IPO) (1979). IPO indicated that while the city's growth management plan was generally compatible with county plans, the county would have designated North City West as a "Future Urban Development Area," not as an area for near-term development. This complaint seemed to stir little concern.

After February 26, Wilson, the council, and city administration joined developers in implementing the Carmel Valley plan. A variety of issues continued to arise over the financing of schools and the impacts of North City West on unincorporated areas and the City of Del Mar. But now it was the City of San Diego and developers versus the school districts, San Diego County, and Del Mar.

More studies were conducted. In June, the County Board of Supervisors committed $7,500 to study the impacts of North City West on unincorporated areas. Wilson unsuccessfully offered to have the city do the study for the county, for the city was required to conduct such a study anyway under the California Environmental Quality Act. Also in June, the county and CRP argued that the forthcoming environmental impact report on North City West would be deficient (biased in favor of North City West), but still would show increased demands for county public services. The same month, the City of Del Mar maintained that their study of the impacts of NCW on Del Mar (which they refused to release), conducted by the consulting firm of Williams-Kuebelbeck and Associates, found that the development would result in a major increase in visitors to Del Mar's beaches. To enforce these objections, Del Mar initiated a lawsuit.

In September, even more study results were reported. On the 5th, the county's study, conducted by Criterion, Inc., found the main impact of North City West on North County residents to be congestion of parks and beaches, with other impacts being minor. Two weeks later, Del Mar's financial consultants argued their finding that development of North City West would have substantially adverse fiscal impacts on the city. On the same day, before the project's final hearing, the final environmental impact report on North City West was issued by Regional Environmental Consultants (1979). According to the EIR, "The proposed self-contained community could mitigate the project's growth-inducing aspects." Negative impacts on traffic conditions and sewage capacity purportedly could be offset.

On September 25, a memo to the city council from Deputy City Manager John Fowler (1979) countered Del Mar's still unpublished fiscal impact report with San Diego's own fiscal impact study (Financial Management Department, 1979). San Diego's study found that any costs Del Mar incurred from North City West would be more than offset by increased sales tax revenues.

On September 27, a "final" council hearing was held on the Carmel Valley Precise Plan, the North City West Planned District Ordinance, and the Design Element. City staff recommended adoption of each document. However, the council voted a continuance of two weeks for review of the Del Mar fiscal impact report. Then on October 22, 1979 the city council approved development of Carmel Valley.

Much remained to be resolved after the October decision, including: Del Mar lawsuits based on the *Livermore* case (Associated Homebuilders vs. Livermore, 1961); lawsuits based on conflicts of interests; approval of a final subdivision map; approval of a special assessment district to pay for public facilities; an acceptable plan for financing schools; and a solution to the problem of spoiling the Los Peñasquitos lagoon and estuary. Still, the November elections left North City West development in good standing. Mayor Pete Wilson had regained the support of developers and was reelected by an overwhelming majority. While an opponent of North City West replaced a supporter on the council, the balance of the council had not been altered, and major capital facilities were either installed or programmed.

NOTES

1. From a political perspective, delay of North City West seems to have been a victory for Wilson's effort to slow sprawl and revitalize the central areas of the city. From an economic perspective, the delay was part of a general economic recession, what was later called the "deep freeze" of 1974 and

1975. One North City West developer said that during this period, " . . . it didn't really matter what City Hall did. We couldn't get any money to build anything and nobody could buy it if we did. . . . Everything was turned off."

2. The CMP analysts, and a Ph.D. economist in particular, preferred FIAS because they believed that the model's econometrics components made it a more sophisticated tool for fiscal impact analysis.
3. Some planners remember no political direction on this issue and claim that early development of North City West was simply the most reasonable strategy given its topography, location, and other features.
4. MUNIES does not have to be a "linear" program driven solely by the service demands generated by a land-use data base. It simply was implemented in that way in San Diego.
5. Prior to the publication of the growth management report, the report and San Diego data were sent to Tisher, Montasser, and Associates, Inc. The model developers reanalyzed some of the data, prepared some additional runs, and did some additional comparisons that San Diego originally had not prepared. They also drafted the final report.

4.

Refusing to Negotiate, Refusing to Model

Modeling can not serve as a tool for negotiation and bargaining if major contestants in a conflict refuse to involve themselves in the modeling process. That is exactly the problem that leads to the failure of planners to successfully utilize a model to analyze alternative planning scenarios for the development of Tulsa, Oklahoma.

Planning and modeling began in Tulsa under Mayor LaFortune, a liberal Republican mayor committed to guiding growth back toward the older areas of the city. The costs and benefits of this "balanced growth" strategy were to be compared with alternative development scenarios, including continued urban sprawl, with the aid of a computer-based fiscal analysis as one of several analytical efforts. However, shortly after the decision was made to model alternative planning scenarios, a new conservative Republican mayor, Jim Inhofe, was elected.

The new administration was not only opposed to "balanced growth," it was opposed, in many aspects, to governmental involvement in general land-use planning. Not wishing to discourage private development, the new administration quickly downgraded the growth guidance effort and isolated the modeling process within the metropolitan planning agency. While the new administration ignored the modeling effort, planners and analysts successfully transferred a fiscal impact model to Tulsa and continued the implementation process in the hope of resurrecting growth planning at a later date. Eventually, analysts did present the results of a fiscal analysis of alternative growth scenarios to an uninterested city commission, which then recommended the discontinuation of the modeling effort. Soon afterward,the model, modelers, and planning agency were scrapped, reassigned to other agencies, and disbanded, respectively.

Clearly, this case[1] suggests that if powerful contestants are not successfully incorporated in the modeling process, modeling might well fail to provide a tool to facilitate negotiation and consensus.

THE SETTING

Tulsa, Oklahoma is emerging as a major city of the Southwest. Despite the socioeconomic diversity that accompanies a city of over 360,000 people, Tulsa politics is shaped by a cowboy heritage of individualism and self-reliance together with the importance of oil in the local economy. One facet of Tulsa politics shaped by this heritage is an anti-planning tradition. "People don't want anyone telling them what they can and cannot do," says a local official, especially "outsiders," "consultants," or "Easterners." Another echoes, "It's a very conservative community. The oil industry is very important and they're very upset about restrictions and windfall profit taxes and all those kinds of things. And in general, people have a fairly anti-government stance." It is an environment in which the freedom of the entrepreneur is so valued that planning is occasionally denounced as an "un-American" activity.

Tulsa's distrust of a powerful government is reflected in the city's charter, adopted by the electorate in 1908, one year after Oklahoma became a state. Tulsa's charter established a mayor-commission form of government that is still intact today, a hybrid of the commission form originated by municipal reformers, which left Tulsa's government structurally fragmented, but very "democratic."

In contrast to the traditional reform model of non-partisanship, elections in Tulsa are partisan. The majority of voters in Tulsa County are registered Democrats, but, historically, Republicans have registered Democratic to have a role in state primary elections where the Democrats have held a dominant position. Partisan politics in Tulsa itself is competitive, although Republicans have generally enjoyed the stronger position.

Given a structurally fragmented government, an anti-government culture, weakly organized but competitive local parties, and a flourishing oil industry, influence in Tulsa politics and society gravitated to the city's burgeoning economic elite. Although at times divided, this economic elite continued to dominate Tulsa politics through the 1970s. This setting led also to efforts to informally overcome the legal fragmentation of authority. In fact, an effort to centralize government operations has been a continuing theme of Tulsa politics.

THE EMERGENCE OF PLANNING ISSUES

Comprehensive land-use planning for the Tulsa area began in the early 1950s (Robertson, 1980). A report by the City Planning Commission (1953) advocated long-range land-use planning, emphasizing citizen participation in the development of plans. Also in 1953, Tulsa City and Tulsa County agreed to merge their respective planning commissions and staff into a single regional planning body called the Tulsa Metropolitan Area Planning Commission (TMAPC).[2]

These organizing efforts were followed in 1956 by a consultant report that advocated more "balanced" growth for Tulsa, with development progressing outward in a pattern of concentric circles (Wise, 1956). Following the thrust of these recommendations, Tulsa's City Commission adopted its first Comprehensive Plan in 1960.

However, development continued to proceed in directions and at rates that were likely to create major problems for future government provision of urban services and physical infrastructures (TMAPC,1965). In response, TMAPC planners began suggesting the need for new tools to more effectively implement general planning concepts (TMAPC, 1967). Concern also arose among civic leaders that Tulsa could face problems of unbalanced growth—urban sprawl to the south and southeast and deterioration of the central business district and older residential areas.

THE PLANNING COALITION

In 1970, Robert J. LaFortune was elected Mayor of Tulsa. LaFortune was among the local economic elite, the son of a wealthy family connected to the oil industry, and an important figure in the Republican party. He drew broad public support from across the community, including a large number of Democratic voters. One Tulsa politician expressed the general consensus that LaFortune "probably had the broadest base of popular political support of any political figure in the area over recent years."

Mayor LaFortune lent his influence to a major planning effort to address the region's growth issues and to update the 1960 Comprehensive Plan. Consistent with the tradition of grass-roots democratic structures, extensive citizen participation mechanisms were established, such as the Greater Tulsa Council (GTC), a 25-member elected citizen advisory committee. After establishing such mechanisms, the city hired outside planning consultants to formulate alternative patterns for future growth. The consultant report suggested three alternative urbanization patterns, and called them trendline, balanced growth, and satellite (Turner & Associates, 1972).

The "trendline" pattern projected continuation of growth trends set during the 1960s and 1970s, toward the south and southeast. These trends were viewed by the TMAPC as detrimental to the Central Business District (CBD) of Tulsa, located roughly in the northwest part of the city. The planners also feared that continuation of current trends would accentuate racial and economic segregation, and the decline of North Tulsa. The "satellite" pattern projected a shift in growth to the small towns around Tulsa. The "balanced growth" pattern projected more uniform growth over the region in an effort to slow down sprawl, benefit by in-fill, support CBD revitalization, and dampen racial and economic segregation. Of the three patterns, there appeared to be a growing consensus in favor of balanced growth. The consensus was more apparent than real, however, and two political factions developed over growth management policy along a split that had originated during debates over the issue of district elections of commissioners.

One faction, led by Mayor LaFortune, was supported by Chamber of Commerce leadership and several city commissioners, and favored incentives for development in North and West Tulsa and for redevelopment of the downtown area. The other faction was, according to an observer, "organized around a man named W.K. Warren, who merged into Gulf Oil and is one of the biggest and wealthiest men in town," and was supported by most of the development community. This group supported a more laissez-faire approach. According to one observer:

> The Warren faction and the development community has . . . basically favored a policy of unfettered growth—no interference in growth—and therefore, tended to be suspicious of growth guidance. But LaFortune was powerful enough that they were reluctant to oppose him.

Thus, despite a division among the Tulsa economic elite, LaFortune was able to engineer a coalition in support of planning and implementation of a balanced growth policy in an anti-planning political environment. A balanced growth policy was formally adopted in 1973.

THE EMERGING NEED FOR CONTROLS

The mere adoption of a balanced growth policy without detailed controls had little impact on development patterns. However, major floods in 1974 and 1976 rekindled concerns over the adequacy of urban infrastructures and the wisdom of permitting growth in flood plains, which included many of the growing areas in the south and southeastern parts of the city. These concerns in turn rekindled the division between those in favor of laissez-faire development and those in favor of planned growth.

From 1974 through 1977, the major TMAPC activity involved the creation of district land-use plans for Tulsa. During this time, TMAPC officials were investigating new approaches for addressing Tulsa's growth issues. A legal expert on urban land-use planning, Professor Robert H. Freilich, was invited to Tulsa for a luncheon meeting with Don Osgood, Director of TMAPC, Stan Williams, a member of TMAPC working on flood plain regulations, and a city commissioner. Freilich had been developing a national reputation for his expertise in establishing legal mechanisms to effectively implement land-use plans.[3]

Concurrently, the City of Tulsa began efforts to promote more balanced growth through downtown revitalization. In 1976, the City's Community Development Department was given responsibility for re-examining urban renewal and revitalization practices as part of its Community Development Block Grant Program. Accordingly, the city initiated several projects aimed at collecting data for land-use planning and decision making. The city also tried to build a policy analysis capability using quantitative, computer-based methods. These efforts of the city were joined by similar efforts to improve analytical capabilities with TMAPC.[4]

While these efforts were underway among planning agencies, more direct efforts were being made to redirect growth in the Tulsa area. The Chamber of Commerce initiated the Cherokee Industrial District aimed at encouraging movement of jobs to the north, and the Williams Company decided to build its Williams Center downtown. The Center was a $200 million private venture that covered a nine-square-block area centered around the 52-story Bank of Oklahoma, The Williams Plaza (a luxury hotel), and the civic auditorium. To complement the Williams Center, the city began development of a downtown pedestrian circulation system. Also, the Tulsa public school system began to create and maintain magnet schools in North Tulsa. Finally, Tulsa developed plans to annex a portion of Osage County to facilitate growth in the northwest. Despite these efforts, the dominant trend was still movement of new housing to the south and southeast.

GROWTH GUIDANCE

Supporters of the planning coalition were searching for mechanisms to effectively implement more balanced growth when in February of 1977 the League of Women Voters, the Junior League of Tulsa, and the American Association of University Women hosted a seminar entitled "Growth with Planning." Robert Freilich was invited back to the city, now as a major speaker at what became a large conference including participants from most sectors of the community. He focused on the legal aspects of growth management—the creation of mechanisms to achieve planning goals.

Professor Freilich was invited back once again to meet with Mayor LaFortune along with two commissioners supportive of more balanced growth. LaFortune felt that Tulsa had developed a habit of letting development lead public improvements. He wanted to turn that sequence around and guide growth in patterns more desirable to the city. He believed that Freilich could advise the city on how to do it, and decided to negotiate a consulting contract with him to develop a "Growth Guidance System" (GGS).

Freilich was engaged as the principal consultant to help TMAPC develop the GGS. The GGS was a process for arriving at a land-use plan for Tulsa that could be effectively implemented given state and local laws applicable to the public regulation of land use. At the heart of the system were the development and evaluation of several alternative land-use plans, or growth strategies. Fiscal impact analyses, along with other analyses, were necessary to support the evaluation of these alternative growth strategies; and, according to LaFortune to justify growth guidance, "the fiscal impact of that decision had to be done in some fashion." Freilich and his associates were to conduct the legal analyses as well as guide the development of the overall work plan. Planners were to handle such tasks as organizing land-use data, conducting various population and economic forecasts, and developing alternative growth strategies in consultation with various officials and citizen advisory groups.

As an outsider and principal consultant for the GGS, Freilich became a virtual lightning-rod for the controversy over growth guidance that pitted the planning coalition against those in favor of more laissez-faire growth policies. On April 14, even before Freilich's consulting was officially commissioned, a *Tulsa World* editorial implied that he had a "no growth" reputation and urged that the Mayor and City Commission "unanimously put Freilich on notice that his employment is not a mandate for a 'no growth' policy . . . ." Acording to local political observers, the *Tulsa World's* editorial position was normally with the Warren faction and the development community and, therefore, critical of growth guidance.[5]

Mayor LaFortune wanted the GGS to be conducted by TMAPC, but Don Osgood, the director of TMAPC at that time, resisted the 12-member commission's involvement given the political controversy surrounding the GGS. Ultimately, LaFortune got the support of TMAPC when it changed to a new director. He also obtained the tacit support of the Chamber of Commerce, although factions within the Chamber were opposed. Formally, the Chamber of Commerce endorsed the GGS in several resolutions and formed a committee to monitor the system.

Still, controversy over the development of a growth guidance system created difficulties early-on for the city's contract with Freilich. Initially conceived as a TMAPC staff support function, it became an important, complex, and controversial contract. In fact, growth guidance issues resulted in the establishment, on April 20, of the Freilich Contract Coordinating Committee to oversee the contracting of growth guidance activities. Even the choice of the committee chair was a politically difficult feat for the Mayor, with his initial choice for the chair being rejected by the Commission.

Despite such difficulties, by April 26, the City Commission awarded a contract to Professor Freilich for legal services to develop a growth guidance system. The various data collection and planning tasks needed to support the development of the GGS were assigned to city and TMAPC staff. In response, the *Tulsa World* continued to push the concept that the growth guidance system would be a tool of "no growth" advocates.

Soon after work began, TMAPC recognized that its land-use base, in need of revision the prior year, was inadequate to support the GGS planning analyses. Also, it became apparent to the city and GGS consultants that TMAPC needed additional professional planning assistance to complete the project on schedule. Therefore, following the initial contract, four growth guidance planning tasks originally assigned to city and TMAPC staff were contracted by the city to the Oblinger-Smith Corporation, a planning firm in Kansas City that had assisted Freilich during the early stages of the project. Additional GGS planning activities were contracted out to Frank Osgood and Associates, a local planning firm that would also assist Oblinger-Smith staff.[6] Still, the city retained responsiblity for providing the land-use data necessary to support the planning analyses to be conducted by the consultants. Figure 4.1 presents a simple schematic of the organization of the units engaged in developing a growth guidance system.

These organizational adjustments and data problems ignited a number of interagency and interpersonal conflicts between the City's Director of the Community Development Department and TMAPC's Don Osgood over the handling of the growth guidance system. Some participants believe that the Director of Community Development might have personally disliked Osgood, wished to take over TMAPC activities, wanted to become TMAPC director, wanted to take over the GGS project, or all of the above (*Tulsa Tribune*, June 15, 1977). These interagency rivalries together with the political controversy over growth guidance caused the project to be

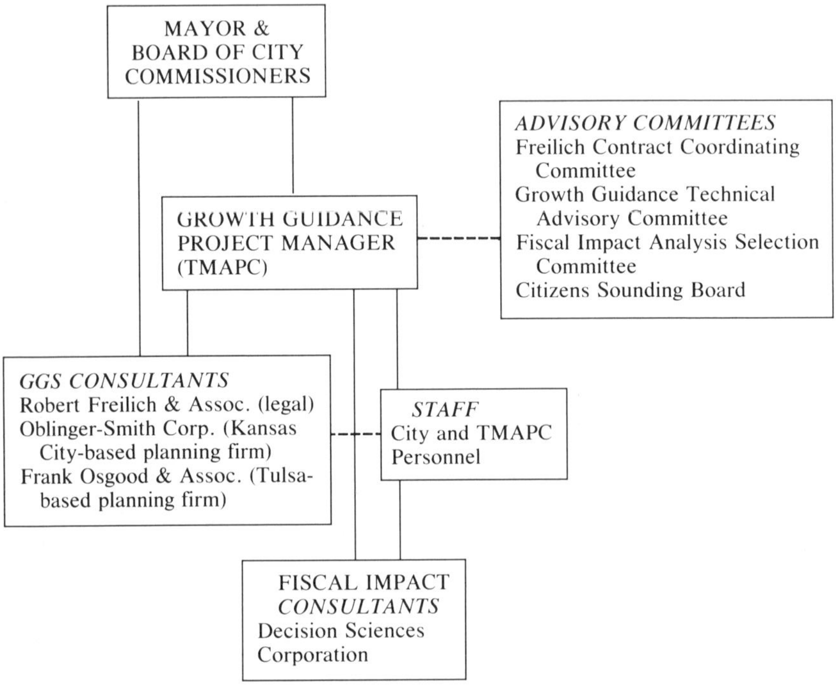

FIGURE 4.1. Simplified Organization of Growth Guidance System[a]

[a]This is not an official organization chart. It is a simplified representation of the organization as reported by participants and documents.

monitored closely and to meet with mixed reviews from the start. Early work in developing flood plain ordinances was well received, while mechanisms for establishing interim growth controls were not accepted.[7]

The Adoption of FIAS

From early discussions of growth guidance, LaFortune believed that a fiscal impact analysis was important to establishing the need for growth guidance policies. Freilich had used fiscal impact analyses in a similar consulting effort in San Diego, California. After briefings from prospective fiscal impact modeling consultants, including Decision Sciences Corporation, reviews of the city's planning documents and data, and interviews with city department heads, Freilich and his associates prepared a GGS work plan that called for a fiscal impact analysis of alternative growth strategies. On September 13, the City Commission approved an expansion of growth guidance activities, including the provision of performance specifications for a fiscal impact model.

Later that month the growth guidance project began officially. True to Tulsa's democratic tradition, an early matter of business was citizen participation. In October, the project manager, Stan Williams, recommended against an advisory committee for the Growth Guidance System. However, the City Commission disagreed and recommended establishment of a 28-member "sounding board." On November 5, Stan Williams was prodded by the City Commission to establish a broad-based citizen's advisory committee as the citizen participation arm of the Growth Guidance System. Its function was to react to reports and plans, rather than to vote or make recommendations.[8]

The Commission discharged the Freilich Contract Coordinating Committee and appointed a new Growth Guidance Technical Advisory Committee. According to the minutes of this committee, the selection of a fiscal impact analysis system was one of the first orders of business, a task they began in early November (TAC minutes, November 22, 1977).

Tulsa sought a methodology or model to help forecast alternative growth strategies as well as to evaluate their fiscal impacts (Williams, 1978). A community development forecasting methodology was needed for quantitative forecasts of Tulsa's growth over the coming years under such alternative strategies as the continuation of current trends versus more balanced growth. A fiscal impact analysis methodology was needed to calculate the public costs and revenues that would be generated by each strategy. The Technical Advisory Committee's RFP for a fiscal impact analysis system sought both kinds of methodologies within a single analytical system (Williams, 1978).

On December 27, at the City Commission meeting, Ron Mize of the City Budget Department indicated that the Fiscal Impact Analysis System Task Force was proceeding well (Mize was the principal drafter of the RFP, assisted by a list of specifications prepared by Oblinger-Smith Corporation). Shortly after this meeting, on January 6, 1978, Stan Williams mailed the RFP for development of a fiscal impact model to a list of people suggested by the American Institute of Planners and Tulsa's growth guidance consultants. Implementation of a fiscal impact model was planned to occur during the first phase of the Growth Guidance System, from September 1977 to April 1978. Alternative development patterns would be simulated, and fiscal analysis of these patterns would follow, scheduled for May–July of 1978. The RFP schedule was highly optimistic (Williams,1978). While most fiscal impact analyses calculate the *direct public* costs and revenues of development, the Tulsa RFP sought a model that would calculate both direct and indirect public and private costs and revenues. Some planning staff later referred to the RFP specification as calling for a "God Model."

Technically, the purpose of a fiscal impact model is to forecast the direct public costs and revenues of urban development patterns, or the relative costs and revenues of alternative patterns. In Tulsa's case, the conventional wisdom of members of the planning coalition was that balanced growth would be more fiscally profitable for the city than the continuation of current trends, because already existing public infrastructures such as schools, sewers, and streets would be more efficiently utilized and fewer new facilities would be needed. However, such conventional wisdom was insufficient by itself; growth guidance proponents needed to show how zoning and other land-use policies designed to guide growth would be in the public interest. Because of the major analytical and computational difficulties in forecasting these fiscal impacts, Tulsa sought a computerized model.

The city received about a dozen proposals for such a model. One early response was received from Decision Sciences Corporation (DSC) under the direction of its president, Donald Blumberg. The DSC proposal differed most from nearly all other proposals in offering to enhance an early existing model. Other respondents to the RFP indicated experience in conducting fiscal analyses, some proposed to develop a model, but very few established the current availability of a model that could meet Tulsa's needs with only some additional development. Moreover, there was a close match between the specifications outlined in the RFP for a fiscal impact analysis system and the proposed design of the Fiscal Impact Analysis System (FIAS) marketed by Decision Sciences Corporation. For example, FIAS is composed of two subsystems: (a) the "community model subsystem" (CMS) for predicting the effects of policy changes on population, employment, income, and other community development factors; and (b) "fiscal analysis subsystem" (FAS) for calculating the fiscal impacts of these predicted changes in community development factors.

Members of the screening committee believed DSC could provide the most "sophisticated" model. They were impressed that DSC had a model in hand, that it was computerized (one consultant who was highly regarded proposed a manual procedure), and that it combined a community forecast model with a fiscal impact model. The city could use the community model (CMS) to forecast the land-use consequences of alternative development or growth guidance policies. Land-use projections could then be fed into the fiscal model (FAS) to calculate the fiscal impacts of alternative land-use projections. As one influential participant in the selection process argued:

> the key thing we liked was that the financial side of the model fed off the community side; that we could play around with alternative futures and process large amounts of information and assess the impacts rather quickly; which, if you had tried to do that through the traditional planning process, it would probably take you two years per scenario to evaluate.

Finally, DSC was considered to have a better understanding of Tulsa's needs—a reflection of their extensive marketing efforts, which had included briefings and presentations to Tulsa public officials as early as the fall of 1977, prior to the development of an RFP.[9]

In March, the Screening Committee recommended that the city enter negotiations with DSC for the preparation of a contract. The City Commission was presented the committee's recommendations, which they reviewed and approved. Also, LaFortune personally reviewed the scope of work outlined in DSC's proposal. His impression was that DSC consultants knew what had to be done and what they were going to do, but that they were plowing new ground. Generally, he was convinced of the model's utility. With LaFortune's and the commission's support, the city contracted with Decision Sciences Corporation to implement FIAS in April, just as a new political coalition that openly opposed the growth guidance system was moving into city hall.

Growth Guidance Data Problems

Efforts to develop the city's Growth Guidance System were continuing during the model procurement process. But some aspects of the GGS were not proceeding on schedule. The GGS consultants met with the city's project manager to discuss the project's delays, which soon became a public issue. The *Tulsa World* (January, 15, 1978) reported that GGS project delays were due to conflicts with the local project manager's time (which was focused on flood plain ordinances), TMAPC personnel problems, and citizen participation requirements. In fact, though, the greatest delay involved completion of the land-use inventory, a TMAPC task whose difficulty was greatly underestimated.

Clearly, the land-use data were critical to the completion of many of the planning and fiscal analyses central to the Growth Guidance System. The inadequacy of land-use data was cited as a problem not only by the consultants, but also by some TMAPC staff, and is reflected in correspondence between city staff and the growth guidance consultants. While the inability of TMAPC staff to provide adequate land-use data seems to have been the cause of delays, responsibility was blurred by the controversial politics surrounding growth guidance in an election year. In fact, the GGS was being publicly criticized as the 1978 primary elections approached.

THE DEVELOPMENT COALITION

Mayor LaFortune had decided to retire as the 1978 primary elections drew near. Remaining supporters of the GGS were primarily Commissioners Franden (a Democratic mayoral candidate), Eagleton, and City Auditor Francis Campbell. Opponents were plentiful, and developers worked hard and successfully to get their candidates chosen in the primaries. According to one local observer:

> When LaFortune decided not to run for re-election in 1978 there was a Democrat on the City Commission—a street commissioner named Robert Franden. Franden sort of assumed the mantle of the LaFortune group. And some of us think that LaFortune, even though he was a Republican, might have endorsed Franden in the election because they agreed on the general thrust of growth guidance and that sort of thing. The developers strongly supported a man named Roger Randle, a state senator, against Franden in the Democratic primary and strongly supported Jim Inhofe in the Republican primary. Randle defeated Franden in the primary. So the general election was a choice between two candidates both of whom had the endorsement and support of the developers.

Inhofe, whose family is prominent in Tulsa business and society, was elected Mayor of Tulsa in April, 1978, another in the line of businessmen mayors. But Inhofe's mayoral style differed from LaFortune's. LaFortune gained a tremendous reputation for his excellent memory, his "engineering mentality," and his concern for operational details. He has been described as having the managerial style of an executive vice-president who attended to many day-to-day operations. In contrast, Inhofe developed a reputation as the political entrepreneur who delegated most day-to-day management decisions to his chief appointed officials, one of whom was John Piercey.

John Piercey, formerly with the Chamber of Commerce, took over as Director of City Development under Inhofe and became Inhofe's chief administrative officer. Trained as an economist, Piercey had been on the GGS Technical Advisory Committee from its inception as Manager of Research and Planning for the Metropolitan Tulsa Chamber of Commerce and also as Associate Director of the Economic Development Planning Group of the TMAPC. Later, he had served on the fiscal impact model selection committee. Piercey supported the city's modeling effort, favored the chosen model, and saw the model as a resource for the city in studying redevelopment proposals and generating revenue forecasts. Yet he remained cautious of the modeling effort because he saw models as limited, based on weak data, and frequently accepted too readily by uninformed users. As Director of City Development, Piercey was kept informed of the modeling process by Austin Neal of TMAPC and Ron Mize of the city.

Piercey's growth management policy preference was to increase the city's share of new growth by providing incentives for growth in desired directions without trying to prevent, limit, or otherwise "manage" growth in other directions. From Piercey's perspective, growth management might raise the costs to developers of building within the city and thereby drive new development to surrounding jurisdictions. He believed this thesis was reinforced by a slow but noticeable decline in the City of Tulsa's share of new growth in the broader metropolitan area.

Regardless of rationales, Inhofe's administration was opposed to the GGS. This opposition was reflected by the new mayor's appointments to the Planning Commission. According to one observer:

> Those who have supported Freilich and the growth guidance things have generally not been reappointed and others have replaced them and, in fact, the two most prominent supporters of that [growth guidance] were not reappointed this year.

Another participant in Tulsa politics noted that Inhofe's administration shut off the Growth Guidance System and the modeling effort. The new Board of Commissioners and the Mayor first took a "wait and see" attitude, but later this turned into an attitude of "let the thing die." These perceptions of the development coalition's move against the GGS is reinforced by a former GGS consultant who emphasized that the 1978 "election was the death-knell for growth guidance, and in many ways, for planning of any kind in Tulsa."

Thus with Inhofe's election, a new growth-oriented, development coalition emerged within Tulsa's city government. Still, on the surface, the Tulsa bureaucracy seemed to move along the previously established path with several technical documents continuing to flow from the GGS project. Continued project delays led to a June meeting to discuss the land-use data problems that forever plagued the GGS. At this meeting, August 15, 1978 was set as the date at which all work on not yet completed tasks was to be submitted irrespective of its status. When the date arrived, several reports were indeed completed. But the city argued that the reports did not provide sufficient information for conducting a fiscal impact analysis. The consultants responded that the reports were based on the level of detail and availability of data provided by the city and TMAPC and offered to work with the city to iron out the problems.

In October, the GGS consultants and Inhofe's representatives met and mutually agreed to terminate the growth guidance contracts. Will Neal replaced Stan Williams as Project Director for the Growth Guidance System in that month. Some accused Williams of mismanaging the project, but others saw Williams' replacement as one more step in dismantling the GGS. The new project manager immediately corresponded with the consultants and acknowledged the city's data problems, particularly with land-use information. He also requested all documentation—work notes, working papers, files, and data—utilized by the consultants. What followed was a series of letters, memos, meetings, and phone calls focused on establishing the final payments to the consultants.[10]

The election of Inhofe had indeed ended political support for the GGS. While the decision to end GGS was rationalized on technical grounds—the poor quality of land-use data, the delayed completion of tasks, the performance and organization of the project, and even the personality of individuals associated with the GGS—these were secondary considerations. The loss of political support was the key. The technical problems merely rationalized an earlier political decision to end the GGS. By the end of February 1979, contracts with all the GGS consultants had been mutually terminated, with the consultants fully compensated for the tasks they had performed. However, the growth guidance program was not totally eliminated; it was scaled down to a TMAPC activity that was given the label of "growth planning" rather than "growth guidance." Planners still expected to evaluate alternative growth strategies using the FIAS model.

MODEL ADAPTATION

The adaptation of the FIAS model to Tulsa's specific needs had been proceeding since the city contracted with Decision Sciences Corporation in April 1978. Broadly, the adaptation process moved through five steps following its adoption—redevelopment, transfer, reinvention,[11] utilization, and rejection (Table 4.1). By the time utilization ocurred, political support for regional planning had eroded so seriously that both the modeling effort and TMAPC were terminated.

Redevelopment

Shortly after DSC contracted with Tulsa, DSC staff began to focus their time on the further development and enhancement of FIAS, mainly on

TABLE 4.1. Phases in Tulsa's Modeling Effort

Phase/Step	Approximate Dates	Events
Adoption Phase		
Adoption	September 1977 April 1978	Approval of fiscal analysis tasks. Development of RFP and search process. Proposal evaluation. Approval of contract for FIAS.
Adaptation Phase		
Development	May 1978–December 1978	Development, customization, and enhancement of FIAS by consultants to meet user specifications.
Transfer	December 1978–September 1979	Data collection. Transfer of programs and data set. Adapting model to operate on Tulsa's computer system. Training analysts to use the model.
Reinvention	July 1979–May 1980	Local development of fiscal impact models.
Utilization	May–July 1980	
Rejection	August 1980–September 1980	Analysis of growth strategies. All modeling efforts are shelved.

redesigning and customizing the community analysis (CAS) portion, to meet Tulsa's needs.[12] Their work was monitored and coordinated in Tulsa by the Assistant Director for TMAPC (Stan Williams) and on a day-to-day basis by Austin Neal, at that time a planner with TMAPC.

Neal was politically astute, and personally conducted an extensive marketing effort in an attempt to allay some fears of various local government officials involved with the implementation process. Neal dealt directly with the President and staff of Decision Sciences Corporation. To DSC staff, Neal was a valued problem solver and facilitator. DSC would submit monthly progress reports to Neal that would be signed off by Stan Williams and Ron Mize of the Budget Department.

Beyond the monthly progress reports there was frequent contact with DSC. For example, Neal was on the phone with DSC, over a period of eight to nine months, sometimes as often as twice a day. In addition, DSC sent a staff member to Tulsa when Neal needed help, and generally did a great deal to complete the transfer of FIAS. In addition, a "Citizen's Sounding Board" was incorporated within this process to obtain the input and support of a board array of interest groups.

Transfer

The transfer phase started by December 1978, when DSC began to send data collection forms to Neal. The completed data forms filled as many as six three-ring notebooks when they were returned to DSC. With this data base, Tulsa's enhanced version of FIAS was then finalized and tested on DSC's prime computer system. These tests provided an initial analysis of alternative growth scenarios which identified no single growth strategy to have been more fiscally profitable than any other. However, the test runs did suggest that some growth scenarios were unrealistic (i.e., assuming more growth in an area than could be supported by available land area).

By June 1979, Decision Sciences Corporation began the physical transfer of the FIAS programs and data sets for use on Tulsa's Honeywell computer system. In the midst of this transfer process, Austin Neal resigned to accept a position with the Chamber of Commerce. Jim Johanning, trained in transportation planning and modeling, took Neal's place as Program Manager for Economic and Fiscal Planning in May, and was joined by planner Jim Robertson in July. They were supported technically by a programmer/analyst familiar with FORTRAN (the language in which FIAS was programmed) and Tulsa's Honeywell system.[13] They were briefed by Neal as well as by a DSC staffer who visited Tulsa for a week in July.

During that week, the fiscal analysis (FAS) portion of FIAS was run satisfactorily with two minor problems, but the community model (CMS) portion presented more difficult conversion problems, requiring DSC and Tulsa staff to communicate through August and September to solve them and make the necessary coding changes. During the last week of September 1979, DSC staff spent one more week in Tulsa and managed to successfully install the entire model, including the CMS component. A few months later, city officials signed-off on the transfer of FIAS and all payments were made in full for its delivery. However, the new planners were not content with FIAS and launched a local redesign effort.

Reinvention

Soon after the new TMAPC planners—Johanning and Robertson—were in place, they began to raise concerns about the fiscal impact modeling effort. Primarily, they doubted the accuracy of the data that TMAPC had provided Decision Sciences Corporation. The major difficulties stemmed from such problems as changes over time in the names of departments, funds, and programs, that confused attempts to consistently estimate historical revenues and expenditures by categories that reflected the current structure of the city's budget. Also, there was uncertainty over the proper schemes for allocating different revenue funds back to department budgets. As a result, there were four to five major revisions of the financial data base such that in the end, city budgeting staff applauded the financial data base as one of the most valuable products of the modeling effort.

In addition to these difficulties, the new planners perceived the modeling approaches of FIAS as inadequate. FIAS conformed to specifications worked out with former TMAPC staff, but the new planners had different views on the design of a fiscal impact model. For example, FIAS was a large program that consumed considerable computing resources in terms of internal computer memory and run time. Its size was a function of such feaures as detailed documentation, the option of operating CMS in a conversational mode, a large variety of options in computing the various forecasts, and nicely formatted reports. To many users of a fiscal impact model, the benefits of such features would be worth the use of additional computing resources, but the new TMAPC staff came to prefer economy. First, they became frustrated in their early efforts to get FIAS to run properly. Their in-house programmer worked with DSC staff for several months to make the appropriate changes in the job control language and the source program to successfully run FIAS on the city's Honeywell computer. Second, they were frustrated that the run time and core storage requirements of FIAS necessitated running the program on the night shift and even then with such low priority that three-day turnarounds occasionally occurred. In short, the new staff preferred a streamlined model without all of the "bells and whistles" incorporated in the FIAS model.

The new planners became concerned with the model's comprehensibility as well as its economy. Initially, they did not understand all of the model's operations in sufficient detail to confidently defend the model results. Taken together, the uncertainties that the analysts had over the data base and the model's operation were substantial indeed. As one TMAPC planner noted:

> our concern was that nobody really knew just how they (the departments) came up with the raw figures . . . [and] Well, they [analysts] couldn't tell just how in the world the model took all of this raw information and came out with the answers.

Given these data and model concerns, the new TMAPC planners began to develop their own fiscal impact models. They began this reinvention process by developing the Tulsa Area Growth Allocation Model (TAGAM) that overlapped parts of the FIAS community model. By November 1979, when the FIAS model had been installed completely on the city's Honeywell system, the in-house computer model TAGAM also was installed and operational. In early 1980, the planners began testing the FIAS and TAGAM models and then moved on to develop additional models, including a revenue-forecasting and an expenditure-forecasting model. By the summer of 1980, the local development efforts were completed. FIAS was still available, but the local planners believed their own models better met their analytical needs.[14]

MODELING AGENDAS

The planner's work on the fiscal impact models occurred outside the limelight of growth politics. At the same time, several groups and agencies were planning for the use of a fiscal impact model, largely unaware that the new in-house models would replace FIAS as the preferred tool for fiscal impact analysis. Various planning groups within TMAPC, the city's Budget Department, and the Chamber of Commerce each had different and sometimes competing agendas.

TMAPC staff planned to use a model to evaluate the fiscal impacts of alternative growth strategies as part of the "evaluation phase" of the growth planning project. The evaluation phase was not expected until after the April 1980 elections, but three growth scenarios were being prepared for evaluation:

1. *Sounding Board Alternative:* assumed that growth would be more rapid than historical trends and that all sectors of the city could have equal (balanced) rates of growth.
2. *Central City Enhancement:* assumed more growth would occur in and around the CBD by the year 2000.
3. *Staff Forecast:* assumed more growth near employment centers, more movement back to the CBD, and higher-density housing development.[15]

The major TMAPC staff activity during April and May centered on finalizing these growth scenarios with involvement of the Planning Commission Staff, the Growth Plan Technical Advisory Committee, the Citizens Sounding Board, and City Commissioners. In addition, the planners in charge of the modeling effort sought to inform these potential users about the role of models and fiscal analyses in plan evaluation.

Some TMAPC planners tried to establish less grandiose roles for the modeling effort. They felt that FIAS and the locally developed models might be more useful tools for capital improvements programming in the short-term than for assessing the fiscal impacts of long-range plans. At the heart of the short-term issues was the cost-revenue analysis of specific capital improvements.

The planners also viewed FIAS as a tool for an active approach to revenue-generation.[16] FIAS could help generate revenues in two ways. First, it could be used as leverage in negotiating with developers over specific development projects by helping to quantify the costs of specific developments. Second, FIAS could be used as a lever in developing public support for efforts to raise additional public revenues by demonstrating the need for new revenue for capital improvement projects.

Whereas various planners viewed the modeling effort as a tool for plan evaluation, capital projects programming, and revenue-generation, budget analysts in the city viewed it as a tool for enhancing administrative control through the budget. Historically, efforts to centralize administrative control through the budget were hindered because information about operating departments was fragmented. Budget Department managers saw the integrated city-wide data base created by the modeling effort as a major information resource. But the new financial data base was less popular with department managers. Their concern centered on the loss of department control over financial data—both historical and projected. According to a former planner:

> The department heads are very territorial. They've got their turf and, by God, they don't want anybody treading around on it. . . . we know that some of them were going to get clubbed over the head with what we were going to be coming out with. The fiscal impact system, put in the hands of the politicians, means to really evaluate what in the past, . . . you really just had to take the old department head's word for.

The Tulsa Chamber of Commerce had still another agenda for the modeling effort. The Chamber was embarking on the "Tulsa's Futures Project" and expected FIAS to be used to assess the Chamber's recommendations for capital improvements and alternative development plans. A Tulsa politician noted that the Chamber's study sought to resurrect some of the goals formerly sought by the Growth Guidance System. Presumably, the reputation of the Chamber combined with the mystique surrounding the model would lend more credibility to growth guidance.

Finally, the modeling effort was seen as a possible means of re-establishing the viability of TMAPC—an organization beset with political problems. First, since growth guidance has been coordinated through TMAPC, the collapse of political support for growth guidance weakened political support for TMAPC. Second, some TMAPC functions overlapped functions of the Indian Nations Council of Governments as well as the city's Department of City Development, thereby weakening the perceived need for TMAPC. Third, there were rumors of impending federal budget cuts that would deplete TMAPC's financial resources, since the agency depended in large part upon federal funding. Faced with these political problems, some TMAPC members hoped that FIAS might offer an opportunity to shore-up the agency's image, provide a valuable service to its member jurisdictions, and generate political support. By providing fiscal impact analyses to various groups, organizations, and jurisdictions TMAPC could increase its services, revenue, and credibility.

TULSA'S ANALYSIS OF GROWTH STRATEGIES

Model Utilization

In the city elections of April 1, 1980, Mayor Inhofe was re-elected. The pro-growth, anti-planning Commission remained intact. Issues in the election were pot-holes, street improvements, water pressure, and increasing sales taxes. (The data collected in implementing the fiscal impact models were successfully used in the summer to support a one percent sales tax increase for Tulsa's capital improvements program.) Growth was not an explicit issue, although closely related to all these capital improvement and revenue issues.

Also following the election, TMAPC staff proceeded through the evaluation of the three long-range growth strategies using the models developed in-house. The staff's analytical assumptions and preliminary results were reviewed by the Technical Advisory Committee and the Citizen's Sounding Board. In July, these preliminary results were presented to the City Commission in a slide show format. As one participant noted, most commissioners did not want to know the "what ifs." Only one or two elected commissioners attended parts of the presentation, which focused on the technical details of the analysis and provided no clear substantive findings.

To the relief of city commissioners who did attend, TMAPC's fiscal impact analysis of alternative growth strategies suggested only minor differences among the growth strategies. One analyst said that "no one option stood out." Overall, the fiscal impact of the Staff Forecast (basically current trends) and Central City Enhancement were somewhat more fiscally profitable than the Sounding Board option. However, each strategy was better on some counts and not on others. Another analyst said the findings suggested that the best strategy is "to do what Tulsa has been doing over the last 20 years." In short, the analysis not only failed to support the planning coalition's growth guidance policy, it reinforced the development coalition's laissez-faire development policy.

Rejection

In response to the presentation, the City Commission requested that no recommendation be made on behalf of any growth planning strategy. Soon after the meeting, all TMAPC's fiscal impact models—FIAS, TAGAM, TAGRevenue Model, and TAGExpenditure Model—were shelved. TMAPC was dissolved on October 1, 1980 with its staff divided among the Department of City Development and the Indian Nations Council of Governments. The Director of the TMAPC had resigned to accept a position with Williams Realty Corporation. Robertson accepted a position with the Tulsa Urban League. Johanning accepted a position as a chief of the research division with the Indian Nations Council of Governments. By October, all fiscal impact modeling efforts were scrapped. A series of technological innovations had been rejected.

NOTES

1. This case study is based upon field interviews and public documents. The interviews, numbering over twenty, were the most important source of information, given many undocumented events and controversy over the meanings of records, reports, and other documentation that were available. All interviews were unstructured and nearly all questions open-ended. Each respondent was encouraged to describe the FIAS implementation process and his or her role in that process from a personal point of view. Respondents were encouraged to discuss whatever they perceived as relevant to the process. The interviewer sought clarifications and expansions of points. In addition, when inconsistent accounts were provided, the interviewer identified conflicting information and requested additional clarifications.

   Most of the personal interviews were conducted in Tulsa during late March 1980. Interviews were tape-recorded in most cases with assurances that the identity of respondents would be kept confidential. Typed transcripts of the interviews were analyzed in conjunction with the other documentation gathered while in Tulsa. A variety of telephone interviews preceded and followed the site visit. Finally, an early draft of this chapter was sent to several respondents as well as important participants in the events described who were not personally interviewed. Additional telephone and personal interviews were conducted to resolve issues of fact and interpretation raised by the early drafts. Regardless of these efforts, there remain ambiguities and inconsistencies. Every participant in this case had a unique perspective and, therefore, holds unique perceptions of events and motivations. Furthermore, the events discussed in this case are controversial, raising opposing views based on many strong feelings and opinions. These ambiguities and inconsistencies are identified where appropriate.
2. TMAPC had a nine-member board of commissioners: four representing the City, four representing the County, and one member from the community

who was chosen by the others. All but the community member were elected officials.

3. Robert H. Freilich is Hulen Professor of Law, School of Law, University of Missouri-Kansas City, and author of numerous articles on land-use zoning law, including Freilich and Stuhler (1981), Freilich and Ragsdale (1974), and Freilich (1974).
4. In 1976, the Economic Development Administration of the U.S. Department of Commerce awarded an Economic Development Planning Assistance Grant to the City of Tulsa. This grant was used to develop the Economic Development Planning Group of TMAPC, whose purpose was to plan, coordinate, and implement economic development projects. This planning group was charged with providing economic research and analysis, information, and economic impact studies to both the public and private sectors.
5. The "no growth" label was pinned on Freilich because of his role as a legal consultant to a community in New York that chose to institute strict growth controls. The major local paper sent a reporter to investigate Freilich, gathering material for a series of editorials in the *Tulsa World*.
6. Formally, Oblinger-Smith's contract with the city was supported by an amendment to the Freilich contract. This pass-through was designed to expedite the completion of these planning activities and avoid a lengthy RFP process.
7. On June 10, the first overall work program entitled "Growth Guidance System for the City of Tulsa, Oklahoma" was submitted by Robert Freilich and his law partner, Martin L. Leitner (1977) with the assistance of the Oblinger-Smith Corporation. This would be revised on November 4 of 1977. In the plan, separate contracts were developed for each phase of the growth guidance work.

    Also on June 10, a document called "Flood Plain Regulations" was completed by Freilich and Leitner. This technical memorandum provided a set of proposed ordinances for the regulation of development on flood plains. To some Tulsa officials, this report justified the Freilich contract on its own. However, two proposals submitted in June were controversial. These were an "interim development control" and a division of "the metro into 'tiers' or sectors where different growth controls would be imposed." Both proposals fed the concerns of those in favor of growth and, therefore, were modified.
8. During the height of the controversy over growth guidance the board was fairly active. Later, after the growth guidance contract was terminated, the controversy and interest of board members also died down. By 1980, it would be difficult to get members to attend meetings. But interest was expected to re-ignite once the fiscal impacts of alternative growth scenarios had been assessed.
9. In the fall of 1977, Don Blumberg of Decision Sciences Corporation was invited by TMAPC to brief Tulsa officials on fiscal impact analysis systems (Blumberg, August 21, 1981, personal correspondence).
10. On December 12, 1978, a determination was made that all documentation, files, and materials had been received. The resolution of final payments to the consultants continued into January and February 1979.

11. Re-invention is a concept developed by Rice and Rogers (1980).

12. Jim Kerrigan was the major staff analyst involved in this development work. He was supervised by the project manager, Warren Suss.

13. Tulsa uses a Honeywell 6400 system with batch and on-line processing through a TSS (time-sharing system) similar to IBM's TSO.

14. An objective assessment of the relative quality of FIAS versus the local models is beyond the scope of this paper. Moreover, any expert judgment of quality is irrelevant to this case. The subjective opinions of the local analysts were the determining factor in Tulsa.

15. Two additional scenarios were sometimes discussed, called "Historic Trend," and "Adopted Control Total Base Case." Both were disregarded later because they were very similar to the "staff forecast."

16. This "revenue-generation" concept is developed in Kirlin and Chapman (1980).

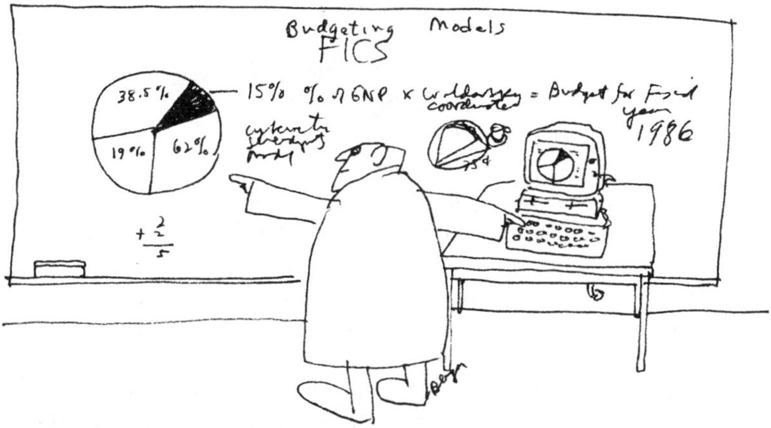

5.
Modeling for Mutual Gain

This final case study focuses on the repeated use of fiscal impact modeling by a city government and the emergence of counter-modeling by development interests. Despite considerable controversy surrounding its use, modeling was eventually incorporated into the on-going planning processes of the government. This is because it helped to forge a new political compromise on development as it simultaneously destroyed the old political compromise. The old compromise was in jeopardy before the model came along—a result of rising taxes, inflation, environmental protection and quality-of-life concerns that had been building in the city for years. The model helped to seal that compromise's fate by making explicit for the first time the public costs of development. At the same time, the model created the basis for a new compromise by giving attention to citizen concerns about fiscal impact and by indicating the prerequisites for development. When the developers accepted these requirements as the price for continued development, a new compromise had been struck.

DEVELOPMENT LAND

For nearly three decades, the city of Anaheim has been quietly building an image as the growth machine of Orange County, California. Before it entered into its period of expansion, Anaheim, the oldest city in the county, was a sleepy little community of 14,000 residents and 4½ square miles. As people and commerce began pouring into Southern California in the 1950s, Anaheim's city fathers led the locality down the classic pathway to economic health by annexing increments of developable land at the city's borders, in hopes of capturing the tax benefits of growth. The 1950s were a city-building era: the same decade in which Walt Disney opened his park in the city also saw Anaheim grow to 25 square miles and 104,000 people. The city maintained its expansionist activity in the 1960s, although at a relatively slower pace of growth. Two major public development projects—Anaheim Stadium and the Convention Center—were christened, helping to stimulate the healthy tourist trade that Disneyland attracted to the area.

In 1970, the city's population of 167,000 was spread out over 33 square miles, with opportunities for still more growth primarily to the east of the city in the largely undeveloped Santa Ana Canyon area. By this time, the rate of land acquisition and development was slowing, mostly as a result of changing circumstances in the canyon area. Residents who had moved to this newly created neighborhood for the low densities and open spaces it offered began to complain at the prospect of more people moving in. They associated further annexations and new housing tracts on nearby hills with increased congestion and pollution, bulldozed hillsides, and a harsh property tax burden. By the early seventies, Canyon residents began to organize homeowners' associations to protect their interests in the face of the "bigger-is-better" attitude of the city council and management. The battle over the future of the Santa Ana Canyon had been joined.

The land in question was a beautiful expanse of golden hillsides and canyons, a piece of prime real estate covering over 20 square miles, held by a few large landowners, and constituting one of the largest tracts of undeveloped territory in the northern portion of an increasingly urbanized Orange County. The battle over this land centered on issues of economics and control: Which jurisdiction would regulate and benefit from the development of the then-unincorporated land? The interested parties were many, including the cities of Anaheim, Orange, and Yorba Linda, the County of Orange, and perhaps some yet-to-be-incorporated municipality. Which group would profit from the use of the Canyon area: The local residents, favoring slow growth and expecting their land to gain higher property values while wishing to preserve access to open space? The building and real estate industries, eager to profit from residential construction in the Canyon? Or the City of Anaheim, torn between its long-term interest in annexing and developing land to broaden its tax base, and its short-term need to respond to public demands for property tax relief by foregoing new bond measures for capital improvements to service future development?

This battle has now gone on for nearly a decade, with shifting actors and alliances, strategies and weapons, winners and losers. But while the decision-making environment has changed, the formal battlefield has remained constant: Anaheim City Hall, where council members, planners, and interest groups have worked their way through a number of land-use decisions that have shaped the destiny of the Canyon area. Over the years, the partisans have drawn their arguments from the kinds of documents that are common in land-use debates: population projections, general plans, market analyses, budget statements, and environmental impact reports. In this case, though, a new technical tool has entered into the analytic—and political—fray: the fiscal impact analysis.

THE BATTLE FOR SANTA ANA CANYON

At the start of the seventies, little conflict existed among the Anaheim leaders about the city's policy toward growth. Development offered the winning formula for fiscal health. The Anaheim City Council regularly supported the recommendations of Manager Keith Murdoch for zone changes, annexations, capital improvements, and plans for the nearby Anaheim Hills, at the western entrance to the Santa Ana Canyon.

Murdock, who had been the city's administrative officer since 1950, played a central role in guiding the development process in Anaheim. An intelligent, articulate, and amiable man, Murdoch was a leader as much as a manager. He was a man of vision and action, the one whom many credit with bringing Disneyland, the Stadium, the Convention Center, and prosperity to the city. Years before, Murdoch had had the wisdom to learn from other California cities, such as Bakersfield and Fresno, that had failed to annex the urbanizing lands at their borders and later found themselves strapped with a tax base inadequate to support the increasing costs of municipal services. Murdoch read the message and convinced his colleagues to take heed: growth was occurring around the city and the local government would do well to put itself in a position of control over it, to annex new land, to encourage high-quality development, and to capture the tax benefits for its treasury. As in most localities in Southern California at the time, few people talked of the service-cost side of new development. Cities were competing to attract commerce and people; many were offering tax incentives to get them there. Under Murdoch's guidance, Anaheim adopted this goal early on and prospered under the pro-growth philosophy of the time.

Pressures for Development

In 1970, Anaheim Hills, Inc., a local development company, opened up a large residential project south of Route 91 at the western edge of the Santa Ana Canyon Area. This low-density subdivision was one of the initial phases of the company's long-range plans for developing miles of

Santa Ana Canyon land. Despite the prospect of high property taxes in this neighborhood, the location offered many attractions: a prestigious address in a high-priced, planned community; proximity to numerous freeway interchanges for convenient commuting; good schools and affluent neighbors; miles of tree-lined streets and riding trails; and thousands of acres of golden hillsides and rugged canyons. Hundreds of families purchased homes in the Anaheim Hills, so that by 1970 the population in the Canyon area was nearly 5,000.

Shortly after moving to Anaheim Hills, many new residents began to turn their backs on the organizations that had made their homes possible: the Anaheim City Council and Anaheim Hills, Inc. Residents had heard of the plans for the next phases of development in the Canyon—plans that included high-density residential and commercial projects near the freeway and new housing on nearby hills. To many newcomers, such plans meant only the prospect of paying higher property taxes in order to share diminished environmental resources and service levels with thousands of other people. Some of the more politically active residents believed that if they wanted to hold on to what they had purchased, they would have to act quickly to try to influence some of the impending land-use decisions for the Canyon area. Many homeowners formed associations within their local subdivisions. Nearly a thousand households joined the Santa Ana Canyon Improvement Association, an organization established to defend Canyon residents' interests before the Anaheim City Council and the Orange County Board of Supervisors.

By the summer of 1972, Canyon residents had become actively involved in the land-use planning and development process, airing their views at public hearings and in petitions to local governments. This coincided with efforts undertaken by local agencies to prepare state-mandated open-space and conservation plans for the Santa Ana Canyon area. At the request of several citizen groups, the Orange County Board of Supervisors established the Santa Ana Canyon Study Committee, originally comprised of the County's Chief Administrative Officer, Planning Director, and Greenbelt Coordinator, and the Chief Engineer of the Flood Control District. The Board charged the Committee with exploring options for the development of the unincorporated land in the Canyon. Residents within the boundaries of Anaheim and those in nearby cities of Orange and Yorba Linda asked their governments to cooperate with county planners in the Santa Ana Canyon Study, as the land in question was within these cities' spheres of influence as officially designated by the Local Agency Formation Commission. By the fall of 1972, all of these localities had passed resolutions to jointly study development issues of mutual concern.

Joint Cost/Benefit Study

County Greenbelt Coordinator Rod Sackett played an instrumental role in organizing the study. Sackett proposed that the localities utilize an "environmental cost/benefit analysis" to explore development options. Sackett, a planner by training, was familiar with innovative methodologies being used in other cities experiencing growth pressures. One study that had received some attention in the planning literature was the Palo Alto report, prepared by Livingston and Blayney (1971). These consultants had developed a crude technique for forecasting the future costs and revenues to a city of alternative land-use plans. Sackett proposed that the Santa Ana Canyon Study Committee utilize a similar methodology to analyze future development in their region. In October of 1973, the Board of Supervisors authorized the development of a non-computerized economic model for determining public costs and revenues of alternative land-use configurations in the Canyons.

In Anaheim, the city manager and planning department supported this idea as well. As far as Murdoch was concerned, here was a legitimate and inventive way to cope with a touchy political issue. Murdoch had had a long standing personal fascination with technological innovations, an interest he had demonstrated inside City Hall on numerous occasions.[1] Moreover, Murdoch was attracted to the forecasting methodology itself—an interest shared by many members of the planning staff. The technique promised to provide planners with a new capability to generate information useful for analyzing the probable impacts of development options. Citizen activists were demanding just such analyses, and the economic model that Sackett proposed seemed to the planners a way to meet that informational challenge. To Murdoch, the economic model could serve perhaps another need as well. As one of the manager's former colleagues recalled:

> Murdoch had a political problem. This study helped him solve it. It gave him a way to diffuse public resistance to development itself: Let the Canyon residents see the city doing the study; let them participate in developing the techniques; let it win them over to development. Of course, all the while he expected it to support his own—and not their—position on new development. He expected it to prove without a doubt that development was financially beneficial to the city, so that the results would quiet the fears of the people and justify the city's annexation and development policy. Given that expectation, he put everything behind it.

If Murdoch had not supported the project, Anaheim might never have become involved in developing a fiscal impact model, as there was little interest in such a methodology among the politicians or the council. To them, it was a non-issue—a no-cost proposition which they supported at Murdoch's recommendation.

At the end of 1972, the city council agreed with neighboring localities to conduct a "Joint Environmental Cost/Benefit Study." The study's purpose was "to derive quantitative measures of the desirability of various political uses of project area lands, taking into account economic, public service and safety, environmental and social factors . . . to provide a basis for efficient County and City land-use decisions."[2] The study area—the Santa Ana River/Santiago Creek area—included land within the jurisdiction of all the participating local governments: the County of Orange; the Cities of Anaheim, Orange, and Yorba Linda; the Orange County Flood Control and Sanitation Districts; and the Orange County and Placentia School Districts.

Planners from the participating governments met several times over the following months, with Rod Sackett serving as the study coordinator. In September of 1973, they applied to the U.S. Department of Housing and Urban Development for a Comprehensive Planning Assistance Grant to construct the land-use model.[3] The application outlined three components: Phase I, collection of cost and revenue data and development of a manual model to forecast fiscal impacts for a variety of land-use configurations; Phase II, identification, forecasting and weighting of nonmonetary factors, such as public safety, environmental and social impacts; and Phase III, design of a computer program to transform the manual systems to a computer model. The application asked for $35,000 in federal 701 funds, to be matched by local contributions. Most of the $70,000 would pay for writing the computer model, with the localities donating in-kind services to perform Phases I and II. Work on all three components was expected to take two years.

Even though this grant application was denied, the localities continued with their work on Phases I and II: data collection and development of the manual system. Contributions of planning staff resources varied across the localities, with Orange County and the City of Anaheim exhibiting the greatest commitment over the year. In 1973, Anaheim hired an economist/planner, Bill West, to serve as project director. But without special funding, work on the model was often interrupted by other projects and the projected completion date for Phase I slipped from October 1973 to July 1974.

Canyon Politics and the City Council

As work on the Joint Cost/Benefit Study quietly progressed at the staff level, local citizen groups shifted the focus of their fight against Canyon development. Leaders of the homeowners associations tried a more direct route to ensure a significant change in the city's growth policy: a shake-up of the membership of the city council to create a majority favoring slow growth. The Santa Ana Canyon Improvement Association, led by activist Mary Dinndorf, focused attention on the 1974 race for mayor, favoring candidate Bill Thom.[4] Thom had been elected to the council in 1970 and had gained a reputation as an outspoken, independent populist. He appealed to Canyon activists because he opposed the city's traditional growth policy. On numerous occasions, Thom had expressed concern that the city was approving annexations and development in the Santa Ana Canyon area so fast that it could not maintain adequate levels of service to other neighborhoods in the city. Thom's preference for slow, sequential growth isolated him from the rest of the pro-development council. To Canyon residents, Thom represented the person to champion their cause. Thom put his name behind two new council candidates, John Seymour and Miriam Kaywood, both of whom were former planning commissioners. All three campaigned on a platform that included "quality growth," low-density development, open spaces, and no new capital obligations or tax increases without voter approval. When Thom, Seymour and Kaywood won, they constituted a new majority on the five-member council.

Shortly after taking office, the new council held an informal working session with members of the planning commission, City Manager Murdoch, department heads, and planning staff. The purpose of the meeting was to review the status of ongoing projects and to set priorities for future staff work. The council designated two long-range issues as priority items: revision of the Santa Ana Canyon General Plan, an outdated document which conflicted with regional and county growth policies as well as with the attitudes of the new council; and completion of the Joint Cost/Benefit Study.[5]

In the status report they submitted on the Cost/Benefit Study, the planners indicated that in-house work had so far concentrated on the first phase of the project, determination of the fiscal impact factors.[6] The staff was receiving assistance from outside groups for the other components of the project: Faculty and students at the University of California at Irvine were helping to identify and collect data on non-monetary impacts; and John Rau, an economic analyst at the Irvine-based consulting firm of Ultrasystems, Inc., had begun a review of the state-of-the-art of computer forecasting models. These individuals were donating their services to the effort. Rau lived in the Canyon area and had heard of the project through his involvement with Mayor Thom and the campaign for slow growth. Rau believed that his unpaid contributions to the study would benefit not only the timely development of the technique itself, but also his own firm's interests in economic analysis as well. As Rau later explained, "We decided it was really good for us to get into the area of fiscal impact modeling. . . . So we obviously had some kind of ulterior motive. We expected that there would be some kind of money somewhere down the line. We had no idea how much, so we took a gamble by donating our services up front (Rau, June 27, 1980, interview). During this period Rau was spending a fifth of his time working with the local planners on the Cost/Benefit Study.

Toward the end of the summer, the council had devised a strategy to deal with the Canyon growth issue: At the July 29 meeting, Council member Seymour proposed the establishment of a task force devoted to the revision of the Canyon Area General Plan.[7] Seymour identified several advantages that a special panel could offer over keeping the project under the council or planning commission. It would focus public attention on the Canyon District; its members could specialize in the development concerns specific to that area, making use of the technical expertise of the planning staff and the information from analytic techniques such as the Cost/Benefit Study; and it would ensure participation by representatives of all interested parties in generating and considering general plan alternatives. The panel would have a mixed membership: council members, planning commissioners, representatives from homeowners associations and developers, and planning staffers. After Seymour's proposal received the backing of Mayor Thom and most of the commission members and interest groups in attendance at the meeting, the council approved the approach. And from this point on, the fate of the Cost/Benefit Study was formally merged with that of the General Plan process for the Hill and Canyon Area.

Support for Model Development

It took several months to organize and appoint the Santa Ana Canyon General Plan Task Force. Meanwhile, Anaheim planners interpreted the comments from city administrators and council members as a renewed commitment to the Joint Environmental Cost/Benefit Study. Anaheim planner Bill West worked with Rod Sackett from the county staff to draft a new application for funding for the project. This time they located an agency that found their project interesting; they requested another HUD 701 grant through the state's Office of Planning and Research (OPR).

OPR was preparing an "Urban Strategy for California," a policy that encouraged urban growth on lands adjacent to developed areas and supported local governments' adherence to a managed-growth approach (State of California, 1974). West and Sackett reasoned that their analytic technique fit well into this strategy, designed as it was to enable local governments to better analyze the likely public costs and revenues associated with new development. To sell their idea to OPR, they characterized their model as having general applicability for all cities facing development pressure. The grant proposal they drafted in January 1975 described their completed work on Phases I and II of the project, using data and parameters specific to the Orange County area. The request to OPR outlined a $45,000 project—$30,000 in federal money, combined with $15,000 in in-kind local contributions—to fund Phase III. Specifically, this would cover computerization of the manual model that had already been designed to analyze the economic, public safety, environmental, and social impacts of land-use developments. Also, the new model would be tested on five strictly hypothetical land-use alternatives for a major tract of undeveloped land in Orange County. The language of the proposal included a promise that the study would be understandable to lay citizens, applicable to various sorts of development projects, and comprehensive in its treatment of impact factors.[8]

When OPR and HUD finally decided to approve the project that spring, the state stipulated that the end product be a generally applicable methodology. The state was willing to authorize and use public money to pay for the development of a technique that many cities could use. This meant a flexible system, one whose users would have multiple options of measuring and calculating cost and revenue and non-monetary impacts. Additionally, it meant a non-proprietary computer program so that localities would have access to the code and could learn to operate the system in-house. The Orange County consortium, by now limited to Orange County and the cities of Orange, Anaheim, and Yorba Linda, accepted these conditions when they signed the contract with the state in July.

Development of the Model

Ultrasystems submitted the winning bid for the programming work. Over the next months, John Rau and mathematician Russ Egbert of Ultrasystems worked with staffers of the Project Working Committee to review the manual system and to design the computer model. Rau and Egbert worked with planners Bill West of Anaheim, Phil Paxton of Yorba Linda, and Rod Sackett, who, though by this time he worked for the City of Orange, continued to serve as Project Coordinator. A Steering Committee of the chief administrative officers of the participating jurisdictions directed the overall work plan.

Rau has subsequently described the initial stages of the funded project as "creative plagiarism" (Rau, June 27, 1980, interview)—a process which started with a complete search of the literature on the few computerized models then available, in order to identify and borrow from the best components of different systems. The planners carefully analyzed experiences of cities with different modeling approaches in hopes of devising a flexible, workable system for Orange County. They spent hours talking to the Working Committee in order to derive equations and assumptions that represented "real world" urbanization and development processes. The Working Committee managed to agree on criteria for selecting impact factors, stipulating that they be "important and relevant in land-use decisions," "comprehensive," and susceptible to quantification in terms of variables that could be easily understood, estimable, and for which quality data existed. But as Bill West explained, the Committee had more trouble in specifying the actual measures and assumptions to include:

> It was very difficult to get agreement. Every person wanted his own equations or parameters built into the model. That meant that there had to be at least four ways to compute everything, one for each jurisdiction. For months, no one could agree on the locality to use as the basis for the numbers we would use. . . . Actually, I think this conflict was good for the model. The equations and assumptions we eventually used came out of a long discussion process. Some parameters were eliminated as unworkable or too [controversial]. The ones we could agree on eventually got back into the model. (West, August 19, 1980, interview)

The approach the committee finally settled on was a method for quantitatively comparing developments that differed from one another in terms of land-use type, density, rate of development, market value, and so forth (Figure 5.1). The first component—a semi-independent fiscal impact routine—analyzed the set of alternative development configurations by computing scores on an array of fiscal impact measures: public capital and operating costs (e.g., for sewer lines, street lighting, school construction and operation); and public revenues (e.g., property taxes, development fees, revenue sharing). A second component generated data on three categories of non-fiscal impacts: public safety (e.g., fire and police protection); environmental (e.g., air and noise pollution); and socioeconomic (e.g., employment and energy consumption).

For its end result, the model computed a composite "desirability score" for each development alternative. This score had no intrinsic meaning, but enabled comparison of one particular development proposal to other specific alternatives, given the assumptions and data provided to the model by the user.[9] This condition was what allowed the system to satisfy the needs of the state for a flexible, broadly applicable model. For the program to generate the desirability score, the analyst had to: agree to the general assumptions underlying the model; select one of various options for computing costs and revenue factors; supply specific data on the relevant characteristics of alternative projects; and supply values for the relative importance of different impact factors, as derived from the Delphi technique or some other method for weighting the factors.

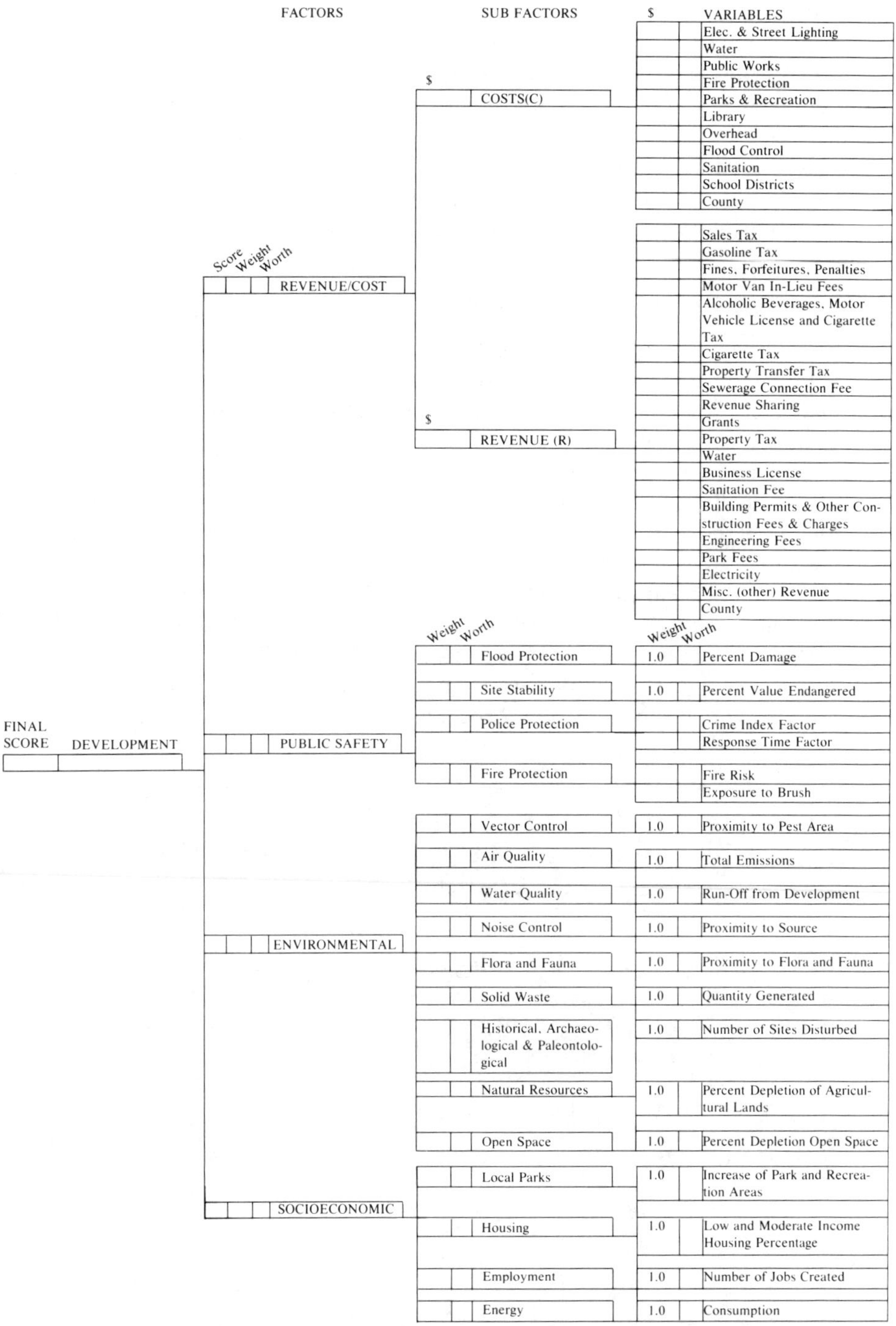

FIGURE 5.1. Land Use Decision Model: Measurement Factors and Variables[a]

[a]*Source:* County of Orange, et al. (1976).

It took the Working Committee and the Ultrasystems consultant the better part of a year to specify these options and to write the computer program for the "land-use decision model." By the time they were ready to test the full model with real data in the spring, the Santa Ana Canyon General Plan Task Force was prepared to supply them with a set of alternative general plan proposals it wanted analyzed.

Santa Ana Canyon General Plan Task Force

The Task Force had been meeting steadily since the start of 1975. The council had appointed to it a group of twenty individuals: two councilmembers (Seymour and Kaywood), three planning commission members, eight homeowner representatives, and seven development representatives.

The Task Force members argued as much over process issues as growth policies during the earliest work sessions, as they attempted to plan how they would complete the task of revising the Santa Ana Canyon General Plan. Members had to agree on the scope and the goals of their mission; they had to obtain formal recognition to gain the cooperation of the county; and they had to be informed of the technical issues associated with general planning in the Canyon area. After meeting regularly for several months, the Task Force backed an action of the council formally requesting that Orange County recognize Anaheim's attempts to plan for

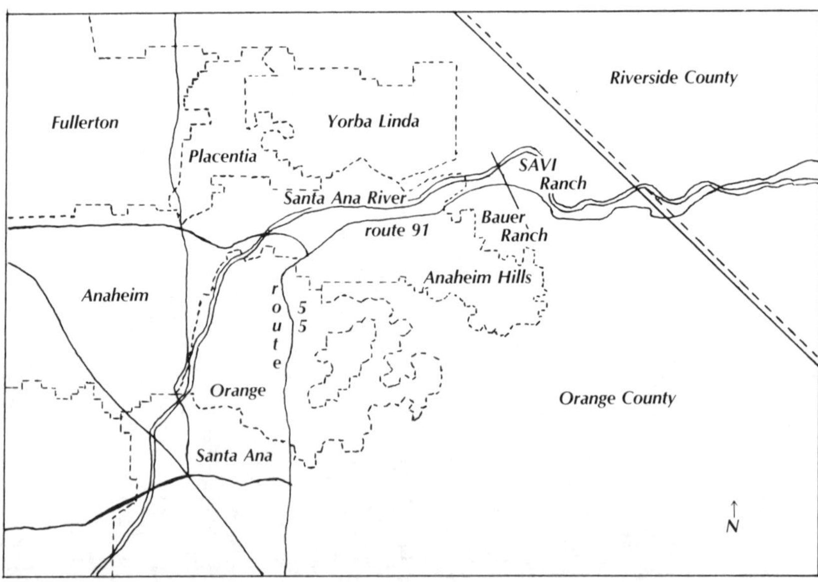

FIGURE 5.2 Map of Anaheim and the Santa Ana Canyon Area

TABLE 5.1. Comparison of Development Options[a]

		Extent of Urbanization	Ultimate Population	Ultimate # Dwelling Units	Acres of Open Space and Parks
#1	Restricted growth	No development beyond 1970 city boundaries	43,000	13,000	8,770
#2	Modified growth/Low density	Low density beyond 1970 city boundaries	54,000	16,700	6,715
#2A	Modified growth/Low density	Low density beyond 1970 city boundaries	59,000	18,000	5,415
#3	Modifed growth/ Clustering	Only clustered development beyond 1970 city boundaries	58,000	19,400	7,315
#3A	Modified growth/High density clustering	Only clustered development beyond 1970 city boundaries	65,000	23,200	8,320
#4	Full growth with shopping center	Mixed density development throughout Canyon area	73,000	22,100	4,065
Preferred Option:					
#2B	Modified growth/low density and clustered	Low density beyond 1970 city boundaries with clustered settlements	65,000	20,200	5,425

[a]*Source:* City of Anaheim, Planning Division, "Canyon Area General Plan—Land Use Decision Model Findings," December 7, 1978, pp. 3–8.

the future development of the unincorporated Canyon territory. The city asked the county to change Canyon land then-designated as open space "preserve" to "planning reserve" status and to place all land under Anaheim's sphere of influence (8,000 acres) into the "planning reserve" (Figure 5.2). The entire study area covered 14,400 acres, a fifth of which was developed. Population in the Canyon area had already passed 15,000.

Following their endorsement of this move, the Task Force began identifying and analyzing alternative land-use configurations for the area. According to member Mary Dinndorf, everyone on the committee assumed that *some* new development in the Canyon would occur, but considerable conflict existed over the timing and extent of allowable growth. Task Force members took extreme positions on these issues, with public officials tending to play a mediating role between the opposing interests. Consequently, the planning staff prepared four land-use alternatives for Task Force consideration; soon after, the Task Force added two more mid-range variations to this list. These proposals differed in Table 5.1.

After carefully reviewing staff reports on these six alternatives, the Task Force settled on a variation of Option #2A as the preferred compromise alternative. This modification, termed #2B, differed from #2A in that it allowed for higher-density development to cluster near the freeways at major crossroads. This would ultimately result in a higher number of residents but the same amount of open space (see Table 5.1).

This set of seven alternatives is the one the Task Force gave to the planning staff for analysis by the new Land Use Decision Model. Consensus on these options was reached just as the city received word that HUD would fund a second-year 701 grant for the refinement of the cost/benefit model. The new $30,000 grant would fund Phase IV, essentially a practical application of the computer methodology using actual data and growth alternatives for the Santa Ana Canyon area. It would also support the preparation of documentation materials and a workshop on use of the model. For this grant, the City of Anaheim would serve as the lead agency, with Ultrasystems again receiving the consulting contract. The 701 funds arrived in July 1976—a time that coincided precisely with the Task Force's preparation of the seven alternatives for the Santa Ana Canyon General Plan.

Model Use for the Canyon General Plan

Later in the summer of 1976, Bill West and John Rau recognized a need for collecting data on growth-related attitudes of community members in order to derive "weights" for the model's various impact factors. They used a Delphi technique to poll the members of the Task Force, asking them to rate the relative importance to them of fiscal, environmental, social, and public safety factors. Rau and West explained the procedure to the participants, as well as how the information would be used in the model to compute the "composite development score." The numbers that emerged after several rounds showed that there was little variance among members' preference for the four primary impact factors and the many secondary factors. Therefore, the staffers used these ratings (shown in Table 5.2) in the model to weight the importance of the various impacts of development. Final computer runs were conducted by the consultants.

When the planners came back to the Task Force with the results of their analyses in December, the study caused quite a stir: Alternative #1, the restricted growth option, came out ahead of all of the others in its overall development score (Table 5.3).[10] These results meant that even

TABLE 5.2. Weightings Used For Impact Factors in the Model[a]

	Weighting	
	Secondary Impact Factors	Primary Impact Factors
Revenue/Cost		
Costs	a[b]	
Revenues	a	
	100	27
Public Safety		
Flood protection	20	
Site stability	23	
Police protection	29	
Fire protection	28	
	100	26
Environmental		
Air quality	16	
Water quality	15	
Noise quality	12	
Flora and fauna	13	
Solid waste	11	
Historical, archaeological and paleontological	9	
Natural Resources	10	
Open space	14	
	100	25
Socioeconomic		
Local parks	26	
Housing	18	
Employment	24	
Energy	32	
	100	22

[a]*Source:* City of Anaheim, Planning Division, "Canyon Area General Plan—Land Use Decision Model Findings," December 7, 1976.

[b]a = (dollar value of specific subfactor) ÷ (total dollar values for all subfactors)

though the model had used the stated preference weights generated through the Delphi polling of Task Force members, the model projected that the restricted growth scenario would minimize the combined negative impacts on the Canyon and the community. This struck many participants as ironic, since even though the Task Force was numerically dominated by home-owner interests, the members had informally managed to come up with

TABLE 5.3. Composite[a] Cost/Benefit Analysis Results[b]

	Alternative	Composite Development Score	Ranking
#1	Restricted growth	62	1
#2	Modified growth/Low density	40	2
#2A	Modified growth/Low density expanded	35	3
#2B	Modified growth/Low density and clustered	35	3
#4	Full growth with shopping center	16	4

[a]Combined economic/environment/social/safety impacts
[b]*Source:* City of Anaheim, Planning Division, "Canyon Area General Plan—Land Use Decision Model Findings," December 7, 1976.

a compromise alternative that was more favorable to developers' positions than were the model's findings. The members had assumed that the model would make similar trade-offs in its calculations; its strong conservationist result therefore surprised many members. No one on the panel understood how the model really worked, and its unexpected results caused some people to question whether it was inherently biased against development.

This attitude was reinforced by the results of the fiscal impact portion of the model. It projected that given the then-current tax structure of the city, *every* alternative would be a fiscal liability to the city over the next 25 years (Table 5.4). The staff attributed these negative impacts to the large capital outlays (for roads, sewer and water lines, and other infrastructure development) needed to service the increased population as well as to the costs of extending those services to the distant portions of the Canyon. Additionally, they reasoned that any residential neighborhoods lacking industrial or major commercial activities would generate fewer tax revenues than service costs. Finally, the staff identified several policies which could mitigate the negative impacts of any alternative: (a) directing new residential development onto or next to areas where city facilities or services already existed; (b) requiring developers to provide all facilities in unserviced or non-contiguous areas; (c) foregoing future annexations to the city in the Canyon; (d) shifting the city's tax policy to lessen reliance on bonds and to set up special assessment districts, higher property taxes, or development fees; or (e) looking for ways that other activities in the city could pay for the service needs of the residential Canyon area (City of Anaheim, 1976).

The fiscal impact projections provoked another round of discussion

TABLE 5.4. Fiscal Impact Model Results[a]

	Alternative	Total 25-Year Revenue-Cost	Total 25-Year Revenue-to-Cost Ratio	Average Annual Deficit or Surplus	Ranking
#1	Restricted growth	$14.3 m.	.93	$ 731,200	1
#2	Modified/ Low density	$50.1 m.	.869	$2,018,800	2
#2A	Modified/ Low density expanded	$57.1 m.	.85	$2,283,600	3
#2B	Modified growth/Low density and clustered	$57.4 m.	.857	$2,297,200	3
#4	Full growth	$82.3 m.	.819	$3,290,800	4

[a]*Source:* City of Anaheim, Planning Division, "Canyon Area General Plan—Land Use Decision Model Findings," December 7, 1976.

at the Task Force, but the compromise alternative #2B remained its preferred option. Everyone recognized that the restricted growth option—the one the model designated at least costly across all impact measures, but especially in terms of fiscal impacts—was a political lemon. Even the most ardent opponents to growth realized the Task Force would lose all credibility with city officials if they held out for such a politically infeasible scenario. And the developers on the Task Force refrained from pushing for the full growth option; many had already decided that the market would not support those projects anyway, after a re-analysis of the costs of building in the steep sections of the Canyon using the city's strict new grading and construction codes. The Task Force remained in favor of alternative #2B primarily because, assuming a margin for error in the model, the members believed that the absolute differences among the mid-range alternatives were small and because option #2B allowed for considerably more people to move into sites appropriate for development.

Additionally, the Task Force took advantage of staff suggestions for reducing negative impacts when it drafted and passed its recommendations for Canyon General Plan revisions. The Task Force then sent its recommendations and the results of the technical studies to the planning commission and city council for review. On February 14, the commission approved General Plan Amendment (GPA) #142—the Task Force's option #2B—which called for lowering population densities and the amount of developable land from what was allowed under the existing plan.[11]

Debate on Canyon Policy

The city council held a public hearing on the proposed plan revision three weeks later. Many public officials and citizens presented testimony covering a broad range of issues touched by the Plan—densities, recreational opportunities, annexation policy, environmental capacity, resource supply, housing needs, and fiscal impacts.[12] Most of the speakers praised the recommendations of the Task Force and planning commission and emphasized the long hours of detailed study, heated discussion, and careful compromise leading to the GPA proposal before the council. Council member Don Roth, however, questioned the prudence of annexing and developing more Canyon land when the fiscal model had indicated that all of the alternatives would be costly to the city.

Roth's concerns led to a lengthy public discussion of fiscal impacts and the nature of the information provided by the city's computerized cost/benefit model. Many of the people in council chambers were aware of the results of a critique, prepared by the Orange County Environmental Management Agency, of the Joint Environmental Cost/Benefit Model. This report, issued at the end of 1976, raised a number of technical issues about the fiscal impact methodology—issues affecting the potential validity of the Fiscal Impact Model (FIM). For example, it identified cost or revenue variables likely to be over or under-estimated, given the use of other assumptions that were as plausible as the ones used in the model. Also, it questioned the completeness of the revenue variable list, "given the failure to include 'spin-off' or secondary effects of new development on existing property values" (Malone, 1976, Appendix). One section of particular interest to partisans in the Santa Ana Canyon growth debate stated:

> What is perhaps most significant about current or future applications of the model is the potential for inordinate reliance on the results or scores that are to indicate if one alternative is more desirable than others. . . . There are "great demands on elected and appointed officials to justify quantitatively the economic impacts of their decisions on taxpayers." While the model can be considered as enhancing the "state of the art" of computerized simulation, and therefore may be a helpful tool to assist decision makers, caution should be given to the use of this or other similar model application results as the only information for making a decision. . . . As this for other models are considered to be increasingly sophisticated or able to simulate potential "real world" situations, the importance of or dependency on such a model may also increase. However, to achieve further sophistication. . . . will probably require extensive resources including technical knowledge that may not yet be available. (Malone, 1976 pp. 3, 6)

Several individuals presented testimony reflecting similar concerns.In defense of the Task Force recommendations, member Mitzi Ozaki tried to put the numbers into context by explaining that the model could not attribute possible revenues from city-area industrial development which might be related only indirectly to an increase in Canyon housing. Another Task Force member, Phil Bettencourt of Anaheim Hills, Inc., remarked that because economic forecasts were a "newly emerging art," they should only be used for understanding expected impacts in a general way and not become a basis for actual decision by politicians. Gil Ferguson, also representing development interests, contended that the model underestimated jobs and investment money brought to Anaheim with the construction in the Canyon. By the end of the testimony, Council member Roth claimed that the preceding arguments had convinced him to support the compromise GPA. Before a vote was taken, Mayor Thom indicated his own reservations about approving the GPA, given that public service levels in some areas of the city were already inadequate and that new Canyon development could further tip the imbalance. Nonetheless, when he put GPA #142 to a vote, the council approved it unanimously.

This vote marked a temporary end to the debate over the Canyon's future. It capped a two-year period of intensive study and negotiation by the Task Force, a process that had moved the city's politics from a seemingly unresolvable confrontation between homeowner groups and developers to a welcome compromise among affected parties. City politicians were happy that the interest groups had settled their differences on their own; this made it easier for them to accept the plan the Task Force had recommended. Even those officials who has supported the Task Force's creation as a way to deflect political conflict were relieved when the process actually seemed to reduce it.

The council vote came as a relief to Canyon residents, too, since they assumed it meant their interests would be protected by official city policy. After years of campaigning for their position, they felt they could relax a bit without jeopardizing their interests. This expectation was reinforced by the city's decision to create the Hill and Canyon Municipal Advisory Committee. HACMAC, with members representing both homeowners and developers, would review specific development projects, general plan amendments, and annexation proposals for the Canyon area. It would send its studies comments, and recommendations to the planning commission, which in turn would make recommendations to the city council. Among the members appointed to HACMAC were former Task Force activist Mary Dinndorf and model consultant John Rau (also a Canyon resident). These appointments satisfied many Canyon residents that they no longer needed to monitor closely what was happening in City Hall concerning Canyon development decisions.

Reactions to the Modeling Experience

Many of those who had participated in the Canyon Plan revision felt the cost/benefit model had been a useful part of the process. At the planning department, the experience of using the FIM to analyze a set of actual development options was important for securing a place for the technique in the planners' kit of tools. The Canyon Plan analyses provided the vehicle for operating and debugging the computer program, using real data, project proposals and doing so within specified time constraints. Up until then, all the runs had been performed at Ultrasystems. After seeing the usefulness of the model for analyzing development options, the city made a strong push to bring the model in-house.

The city had recently hired a new manager, Bill Talley, to replace Keith Murdoch, who had been gradually pressured to resign as a result of disagreements with Mayor Thom and the city council. Talley was a more typical professional manager than his predecessor, and he quickly lent his support to utilizing and showcasing the planning department's FIM. The city hired a new staffer, Pam Lucado, as the Department's resident FIM specialist (Bill West had left the city). Planner Joel Fick took over responsibility for the FIM project leadership. The city underwrote several months of staff time as Fick and Lucado, the latter an urban geographer with some limited experience with computers, worked with the Ultrasystems modelers to understand the model, to learn how to operate it, to help write the FIM User's Manual, and to conduct a user's workshop—all needed to satisfy the conditions of the HUD grant.[13] By June 1977, the changeover of personnel, the writing of the manual, and the transfer of the model were complete.

For other groups in City Hall, the use of the model for the Canyon General Plan analysis had different benefits: The Fiscal Impact component had produced interesting results, opposite to what many city officials had expected when they originally supported the model's development nearly five years before. The findings were more in line with the slow-growth position of the current council majority and this outcome greatly affected the attention people gave to the model.

On one level, the use of the FIM had revealed information useful for comparing alternative development configurations. Given the assumptions of the model (which, incidentally, were poorly understood by nearly everyone except the model designers, Bill West and John Rau), it helped participants in the Canyon debate see the fiscal impacts of marginal changes in the density and location of residential development. In commenting on this process at a much later date, Bill West said:

> I think it was the closest the council ever came to grasping what they had, in terms of an analytic tool. When manager Bill Talley showed the fiscal impact results to the members, saying that all alternatives were net revenue drains on the city treasurer, it gave the council a greater impetus for a managed growth approach. The information generated by the model gave the decision makers some idea of the effects of regulating the timing nd configuration of development in the community. I'm not sure they knew whether to believe them or not, but since the numbers had hit the press headlines, they pressured the council to take a more restrained attitude toward growth.

Even developers' representatives recognized this was a useful consequence of fiscal analyses:

> We did not change any of our land-use objectives because of data we learned from the analyses. Those goals remained constant. But there were some conclusions we began to reach based on this information. For example, the testing of the five alternatives for the Canyon showed that negative fiscal impacts were lessened as densities increased. We learned that most of the ideas about low densities didn't make sense fiscally. This supported our existing conception that the market just couldn't bear all of the estate development that little cities in Orange County have been clamoring for.

Many policy makers said that FIM was useful to them in revealing the fiscal advantages of phased, incremental growth in moving the already serviced western portion of the city eastward toward the undeveloped parts of the Canyon. Former Manager Murdoch explained another impact of FIM:

> It pointed out that there could be a better or different method for providing services or infrastructure for new development, off of the public tax structure. Previously, we had always issued bonds for capital expenditures. From the 1950s on, we also used connection charges to make each development pay a goodly portion of its own service costs. But large, up-front expenditures came from bonds. . . . After the FIM and the Canyon General Plan, the council began to believe that each development would have to pay its full tax burden, to keep from expanding the general tax base of the city. Now the council's taking a more careful look at new ways to pay up-front costs.

On another level, the FIM played a role in the political debate by providing ammunition for those whose interests the numbers supported, and providing a target for those they opposed. Mayor Thom explained the political utility of information generated by FIM:

> Once it came out with information contrary to developing the Canyon, I could use it to beat the developers over the head. For me, then, it became very important. It allowed me to drag up problems with their projects, and maintain a little power over the kind of projects the developers could get away with. They would have to cough up more services as concessions for passage. . . . For political and economic reasons, I knew it would be impossible to stop these developers from moving ahead completely. But I could control them a little better once that information came out in support of what I wanted. I used it to the hilt. . . . To me, the FIM provided just one more argument I could use, among a whole repertoire. The important thing was that it reinforced what I wanted to do anyway, so then I could exploit it.

Other slow-growth proponents took advantage of the numerical "evidence" on the FIM print-outs. One planner explained how the very fact that the numbers were generated by a computer instead of manual calculations enhanced their status in the political debate:

> This was the first use of a computerized model in our area. . . . The computer has several attributes that are special: To begin, the analysts find their work more interesting with computers; they can do calculations they couldn't do by hand. So they end up working harder to support the validity of their numbers and the technique. More importantly, I think the computer has symbolic power: It's useful to make it seem like they know more about what they're doing.

In the Canyon Plan debate, it didn't take long for the pro-growth strategists to understand the new kind of power the model's results represented. One developer explained:

> Public officials are a cautious lot these days; they feel they need evidence to justify what they do. They need documentation to enable them to act. Isn't it the case for environmental impact reviews, and now for fiscal impact analyses? No one makes up their minds on the basis of those numbers; they're just used by partisans to argue for or justify their case. The new technique is an attractive technology. The information is politically useful; it can be used selectively by whoever controls it. And the technique has a life of its own. Once someone has one, everyone else has to have one too, just to look competent or knowledgeable in the face of the other side's numbers.

Outside City Hall, then, the Anaheim FIM produced an interesting effect on developers' activities, quite apart from helping them analyze the market for different projects. The FIM forced them into the business of producing fiscal impact statements of their own. After the battle over the Canyon General Plan revisions, it took developers little time to respond with their own models. The first such response occurred only a few months after the Canyon debate, when Anaheim Hills, Inc., requested another General Plan Amendment for its Canyon land.

Anaheim Hills General Plan Amendment #144

On August 29, 1977, the Anaheim Planning Commission began the formal process of reviewing Anaheim Hills' request. The proposed General Plan Amendment (GPA) #144 included two large tracts of unincorporated land where the company sought to change the densities established in the new Canyon Area General Plan. On one 300-acre area of undeveloped land, the overall densities would be reduced, with the total units dropping from 1,230 to 730 and being resituated together in one section of the land. For the other 90-acre tract, Anaheim Hills sought to change the entire land-use scheme from the existing plan for open space and estate-density housing to a mixture of general commercial, low-density housing and medium-density residential development.

Among the documentation Anaheim Hills, Inc., presented in support of GPA #144 was a fiscal impact study prepared by Ashley Economic Services of Newport Beach. One Anaheim Hills spokesman later explained why the company wanted its own fiscal impact analysis:

> When the Ultrasystems [FIM] study came out for the general plan, the City dropped it like a bomb. It reported that Santa Ana Canyon development was going to cost the City $50 million. It was a real cheap shot; it got lots of attention. But it was so complicated that it was unintelligible to non-experts. It was like handing a copy of *Gray's Anatomy* to a housewife to deal with her kid's cold. . . . So we asked Ashley to analyze it for us. They put it into context for us. And we asked them to help us do our own analysis. We knew we were going to have a problem on our hands, with a hostile mayor using numbers to beat us. So we needed our own experts to counter theirs. We had to hire an economist just to get back on equal footing with the City.

Using a methodology different from the Anaheim FIM, Ashley forecast the city's annual tax revenues and service costs for the proposed projects. These results showed "a very positive fiscal impact," an annual surplus of $153,020 for the commercial and residential developments combined. These results differed significantly from those of the previous winter's FIM analyses, which had indicated negative impacts for residential developments in the Canyon. So the planning department set about to discover reasons for the discrepancies.

Meanwhile, HACMAC was conducting its own review of the Anaheim Hills project. When they discussed it in October, many HACMAC members expressed concern that the recommended changes in location and density of development in the Canyon were premature, given that it had taken several years to obtain the new General Plan, which was then only six months old. The Committee voted unanimously to recommend against approval of the GPA.

The planning commission took up the matter soon afterwards. Discussion at its October meeting centered on the adequacy of the environmental impact statement for GPA #144. The commissioners voted to delay a vote on the proposal pending further study of hillside gradings, traffic, and airflow impacts. By the time the commission was ready to review these studies in November, the planning department had completed its own analysis of the projects' economic impacts. The staff had run a fiscal analysis of Anaheim Hills' preferred development proposal, using the existing Plan's land-use configuration and five other options for comparison. For the first 300-acre site, the Anaheim Hills proposal projected the worst fiscal impacts for the city, with the existing plan's scheme ranking third; and the FIM showed that over time (beyond ten years after development), the Anaheim Hills project would cost more in annual services than it would produce in revenues. For the 90-acre tract, the Anaheim Hills alternative showed net positive impacts over the entire 25-year time horizon and ranked fifth ahead of the existing General Plan.

The planning commission held a lengthy hearing on the GPA on November 21. Phil Bettencourt made the case for Anaheim Hills, that its interests were not reflected in the existing Plan, given the overabundance of homeowners on the Task Force. Bettencourt argued that the General Plan was a dynamic document, to which the state allowed three amendments each year. Additionally, six months had passed since the plan's adoption—enough time for market conditions to change and for developers to rethink their specific plans. Bettencourt's comments sparked considerable debate among members of the audience: many speakers defended the integrity of the land-use scheme in the existing Plan; others cautioned about trusting the company's promises. Eventually, the commission voted unanimously to recommend approval of lowered densities for the larger tract and rejection of higher densities for the smaller site.

The ultimate responsibility for decision remained with the city council, which decided to consider the GPA before the end of 1977. Over the preceding months, several events had occurred which affected the council's handling of the Anaheim Hills proposal. Mayor Thom had announced he would retire from the council when his term ended in the spring. This put the mayorship up for grabs. Among the candidates who quickly emerged was Council member John Seymour, part of the old troika that guided the Canyon area down a slow-growth path. But in his push for support for his mayoral campaign, Seymour accepted financial assistance from the real estate and construction industries in the region—not an altogether unnatural association, given that Seymour was a prominent realtor in Anaheim. In the months prior to the announcement of his candidacy, Seymour had already begun to distance himself from Thom, while another council member, the outspoken and unpredictable Bill Kott, began to align himself with the Mayor. Kott was mayor *pro term* at the time, and he and Seymour were starting up a rivalry. Council member Miriam Kaywood also began to move away from Thom, since she believed that her interests lay in working with Seymour to build a new leadership coalition on the council. These shifts were subtle at the time, but significant for the council's decision on the Anaheim Hills project.

The council met on December 20 to consider GPA #144. A HACMAC representative spoke at length to explain the reasons behind the committee's recommendations for rejecting the proposed GPA. Bettencourt presented the developer's position, explaining the company's careful work to mitigate the problems identified in previous staff and committee analyses. Bettencourt did, however, argue for only qualified consideration of the staff's analysis:

> The staff has utilized the financial impact model and determined that the plan should have an overall positive impact on the City at least through the first ten years of development. 'Factor prediction after a ten-year time frame becomes speculative since it is based upon current conditions forecasted under assumption.' [Quoting from the staff report.]

Bettencourt urged the council to approve both portions of the GPA.

After considerable public debate, the council voted with the planning commission, and against HACMAC's advice. Seymour led a majority vote to approve a reduction in density for the larger tract (Thom and Kott voted against this change) and to deny the increased density plan for the smaller site.

Shifting Political Conditions

Despite the substance of this action, which actually reduced the total number of households that could be located in the Canyon area from what the existing plan had allowed, the act of changing the General Plan so soon after its passage had symbolic importance for the former activists from the Canyon. Many read the council action as a betrayal. They wondered aloud why they had worked so hard to carve out a compromise planning document, when the developers could now come before council and undermine the Plan's overall integrity through incremental changes. One HACMAC member expressed this frustration:

> We began to think our time had been completely wasted and our studies were as good as useless. When Anaheim Hills came in and argued that so many conditions had changed and then got away with it, we couldn't believe what was happening. By this time, people were so tired of attending meetings that we had felt we didn't *all* need to be in council chambers for *every* meeting for our presence to be felt. We figured the document had some weight of its own. . . . We were so naive. . . . We were devastated when they undercut the Canyon Plan. It made us feel like we'd invested two years in just spinning our wheels. What a waste of time.

In some ways, the vote on GPA #144 had more than symbolic importance; it marked a real transition in council policy toward supporting development interests in the Canyon. City elections formalized this shift. Seymour won the mayoral election. Another realtor, Llewellyn Overholt, won the council slot opened up by Thom's departure. With Seymour's help, Kaywood and attorney Don Roth were both re-elected to council. Together, these members saw their political interests in working as a team. In regard to Canyon growth policy, this alliance extended considerable support for developers' initiatives. Only Council member Kott maintained a degree of independence—and risked alienation—from the rest of the council.

In June, soon after the spring council elections, Anaheim residents went to the polls again to vote on Proposition 13, the statewide initiative to roll back property taxes. The Anaheim tally showed strong support for tax relief, with the measure passing by a three-to-one margin. As in most localities throughout the state, city officials in Anaheim were uncertain about how the new law would affect the city's ability to provide services to its residents in the years to come. But even in mid-1978, city managers expected it to force the city to look more closely at the economics of annexing and developing new land—at least to figure out ways to enable development to occur within the confines of Proposition 13, given that the new taxing circumstances arose at the same time as the city voters approved a council more sympathetic to growth than in the past four years. This paradox and the problems it created for the city manifested themselves quite clearly in the city's reaction to the next Canyon area development proposal.

BAUER RANCH AND OTHER SKIRMISHES

Bauer Ranch—Round One

A short-lived but angry struggle over Canyon development broke out during the summer of 1978. It began when Kaufman and Broad, a major development company from Irvine, California, announced its plans to build a large-scale planned community on the Bauer Ranch, a 375-acre tract of unincorporated land just east of the Anaheim Hills. This land fell under the City of Anaheim's official sphere of influence for planning purposes, and Kaufman and Broad initiated the steps to plan, annex, and develop the land under the city's regulatory machinery. In late spring, the company submitted to Anaheim a pre-annexation zone change request (from the existing agricultural designation to a planned community district) and a draft environmental impact review (EIR) for its proposed 1,350-unit project.

These plans seemed like the last straw to the Canyon residents who had already spent countless hours fighting to slow down the pace of development in the area. Residents in both the city and county portions of the Canyon acted immediately to organize against the Bauer Ranch project.

For the residents of the Anaheim Hills, Kaufman and Broad's proposal represented one more attack on the managed-growth policies written into the City's 1977 Canyon Area General Plan. Several HACMAC members examined the adequacy of the Bauer Ranch draft EIR and the reasonableness of the zone change request. HACMAC formally presented these analyses and recommendations to the planning commission on June 19, when it took up consideration of the matters.

Although discussion at the meeting covered a broad range of topics, the commission addressed only a few narrow issues concerning the Bauer Ranch EIR and zone change request, viz., Does the Bauer Ranch general plan for development (including the conceptual design and a land-use element identifying the specific location, number and types of housing units and land-use categories) conform to the Canyon Area General Plan's development policies for that area? Does the draft EIR adequately identify and propose ways to mitigate the adverse environmental impacts of the proposed project? Kaufman and Broad's position was articulated at the meeting by Anaheim's former city manager, Keith Murdoch, who along with former planning director Alan Osborne had been hired by the company as a consultant. Murdoch argued that the Canyon Plan was a flexible and general policy document, and that Kaufman and Broad's conceptual design conformed to—even improved upon—the Plan's guidelines for Canyon development.

Nearly everyone at the meeting, including several of the commissioners, disagreed with Murdoch. Anaheim planners explained that Kaufman and Broad's development plan for 1,350 housing units constituted a significant departure from the Plan's designation of 800 units for the area. Similarly, the proposal would nearly double the overall average density (from 3.2 to 5.8 persons per acre). Finally, the draft EIR analyzed the impacts of a project of 1,110 units, instead of the full 1,350 described in the development proposal. The city attorney cautioned the commissioners that if they approved both items, and the city were subsequently sued, the city might have a difficult time convincing a court that the zone changes and later subdivision permits were consistent with the Canyon Area General Plan (as required by state law) and that the EIR had adequately analyzed the project's impacts.

The commissioners seemed most strongly persuaded by the next line of argument. Long-time activist Mary Dinndorf, president of the Canyon Homeowners' Improvement Association, expressed her group's adamant opposition to the Bauer Ranch development and Anaheim's impending annexation of the tract. Dinndorf reminded the commission of the Plan's policy to delay annexation of land in this area until 1985, in order to reduce sprawl and to postpone congestion and loss of natural resources. She also raised the issue of equity to the rest of the city's taxpayers in underwriting the high costs of servicing a large, distant subdivision ahead of need. These sentiments were reinforced by HACMAC Vice-Chairman John Rau, the Ultrasystems consultant who had worked on the Anaheim FIM. HACMAC criticized Kaufman and Broad's plan for developing Bauer Ranch prematurely, inducing sprawl, and imposing severe negative fiscal impacts on the city in the wake of Proposition 13.

Raising this question of the project's public cost burden proved to be an effective strategy for the opponents, at least for the short term. The recent passage of Proposition 13 had made city officials uncertain about how to finance existing city services, much less new projects. This caution was reflected in the planning commission's handling of the Bauer Ranch requests. While most members were predisposed to support owners' rights to develop their property as they saw fit, the commissioners felt compelled to deny a request where the development would overburden current city taxpayers. The commissioners postponed the EIR review and zone change request until October, giving Kaufman and Broad time to produce an up-to-date fiscal impact analysis, a revised EIR and a whole new general plan amendment to bring the zone change into conformance with the Canyon Area General Plan.

Vista del Rio Annexation Attempt

Meanwhile, other groups were considering different ways to cope with the pressure for canyon development. News of Anaheim's delay of the Bauer Ranch project provided the opportunity for the handful of county residents living in the sparsely populated sections of the canyon to organize to fight against further urban encroachment eastward. The campaign backed the establishment of a new city, called Vista del Rio, to stretch from the edge of Anaheim on the west all the way to the county border on the east, with the entire 11,500 acres located south of the Riverside Freeway. This tract included the Bauer Ranch and portions of other undeveloped ranches as well. Vista del Rio supporters sought to incorporate as a way to protect the rural character of the area from developers' bulldozers. The incorporation petition, containing the names of 31 of the area's 40 registered voters, was filed with the Local Area Formation Commission (LAFCO) on July 6. This set in motion a lengthy process of public hearings, technical reviews, and approvals by LAFCO and the Orange County Board of Supervisors, even before the public election on the question could be held.

LAFCO's treatment of Vista del Rio as an independent agenda item proved significant for the fate of the proposed city, in light of other events taking place at that time. Kaufman and Broad had been paying close attention to the incorporation drive and the motivations behind it. Recognizing the importance of working through Anaheim's regulatory process instead of through Vista del Rio's, Kaufman and Broad moved up its own timetable on the Bauer Ranch annexation proceedings. Early in the summer, the owners of the ranch and other nearby property owners filed annexation papers with LAFCO for a 1,265 acre parcel just east of the city. All of this land was inside the boundaries of the proposed city of Vista del Rio, for which papers had not yet been filed. LAFCO set the hearing date for annexation on December 13. When the Vista del Rio petition came in shortly afterwards, LAFCO scheduled its consideration date for January 17, 1979, despite demands of the backers to treat it before or together with the annexation issue.

Anaheim became directly involved with these annexation proceedings because it had to review the EIR for the annexation. Despite a number of unavoidable adverse impacts associated with developing the unincorporated area and despite written opposition from the chief administrative officers of the City and County of Orange, Anaheim approved the EIR in the fall and formally recommended to LAFCO that it approve annexation of the Bauer Ranch as a means for Anaheim to retain control over development in the Canyon area. Shortly thereafter, LAFCO approved the annexation bid, followed eventually by formal annexation in March 1979. This in effect was a denial of the Vista del Rio incorporation attempt, since annexation brought all of the proposed city's backers inside the Anaheim city limits.

Bauer Ranch—Round Two

The Anaheim leadership's position on the annexation-vs.-incorporation debate was intimately related to its attitudes about Bauer Ranch development. Just as the planning commission was considering the EIR supporting annexation, it also had to review Kaufman and Broad's revised project plans, which had gone back to the drawing board after the June meeting. Over the summer, Kaufman and Broad decided it preferred to avoid the controversial and time-consuming general plan amendment, opting instead to redesign the project to bring it into conformity with the existing Canyon Plan requirements. The new development plan for the Bauer Ranch reduced the total number of housing units from 1,350 to 900, and lowered densities throughout the project area to bring them in line with the General Plan. These changes helped Kaufman and Broad argue against rewriting the original EIR, which the company believed to be more than adequate since it forecast the impacts of a 1,100-unit development.

When Kaufman and Broad delivered its project revisions in October, it also brought a draft of the fiscal impact analysis. Ashley Economic Services of Newport Beach prepared this analysis, which took into account the public-sector cost and revenue impacts of Proposition 13 as well as specific revisions made to the Bauer Ranch project. For yearly impacts, it predicted an average annual surplus of $123,022, across all residential and commercial phases of the project and over the initial ten years of the project. The analysis attributed no real costs to capital improvements, which were analyzed separately from annual operating costs, since the expenditures needed to finance those facilities needed for development of the Bauer Ranch would be advanced to the city by Kaufman and Broad. Therefore, the development would pay its own way, even bringing in more revenues than it cost.[14]

The fiscal analysts on the Anaheim planning staff were clearly surprised by these conclusions, given their experience analyzing impacts of alternative development configurations for the Canyon General Plan back in 1976. The Ashley report, showing net positive impacts, looked suspicious to planners Joel Fink and Pam Lucado: the City's fiscal impact model had consistently projected *negative* overall impacts for projects dominated by low-density residential uses. Those analyses had been run when property taxes were not frozen to fixed rates of increase, as they now were under Proposition 13. Logically, residential developments coming in under current conditions should project *worse*, not better, fiscal impacts. So the planners decided to run the Bauer Ranch specifications through the Anaheim FIM, compare these results to the Ashley statistics, and determine the sources of variation between the two estimates.

As expected, the FIM predicted the Bauer Ranch project would have significant adverse impact over the first ten years, with $9.17 million more in costs than revenues.[15] By examining both these results and the Ashley methodology, Lucado discovered why Ashley's numbers differed so significantly from FIM's. Each analysis took into account both annual costs and revenues along with initial capital expenditures, but they made a number of different assumptions in computing fiscal effects. For example, they used different methods for attributing city revenues and costs to new development. The FIM calculated only those that could be directly associated with a development's impacts on the city's regulatory process, its service provision, its property tax base and its population size. The Ashley model brought in another set of indirect impacts, assigning a portion of general revenues (e.g., revenue sharing) and costs (e.g., administration) on a per capita basis for different categories of land-use. These differences accounted for FIM's predicting average annual deficits while the Ashley model forecast surpluses.

In addition, the models treated financing of capital improvements differently. FIM utilized existing city policy, with the city providing large regional facilities necessitated by a new project and charging that project the portion of the costs associated with its residents' use of the facilities over time. Under this approach, the city would have to issue bonds to pay initial costs and bear the fiscal burden of excess service capacity until new developments came on line to use and help pay for the regional facilities. In contrast, the Ashley model assumed a change in city policy to allow establishment of reimbursement districts, so the developer of the initial project triggering the need for new facilities would put up all of the money to pay for them; then, as subsequent projects were approved, those developers would reimburse the initial developer for their project's share of the capital costs. Given this assumption about funding relationships, the Ashley model could predict no capital cost burden for the city, while the city's FIM identified an initial heavy public burden associated with a project's capital expenditures.

When the planners drafted the background memo on the Bauer Ranch for the planning commission's November meeting, they included an explanation of the discrepancies between the different fiscal impact analyses. A day before they planned to submit the memo to the commissioner,

Kaufman and Broad produced a revised version of the Ashley analysis. The planners hurriedly incorporated these revisions into their memo, but inadvertently left the actual revised analysis out of the information packets that went to the commissioners on Friday, November 18.

At Monday's meeting, fiscal impacts were a major discussion topic, and a major source of confusion. During the public hearing several opponents of the Bauer Ranch argued against project approval, using the information from the city's analysis. Dinndorf charged that approval of so costly a project would constitute an irresponsible act, endangering the health, safety and welfare of the entire community because of the need to spread existing city services so thin. City Council member Kott, appearing before the commission as a citizen and taxpayer, expressed his outrage over the magnitude of the project's fiscal impacts and challenged the commission that approval would violate the spirit of Proposition 13. Although he cited the FIM's results in his comments, he discredited both fiscal impact analyses. Kott depicted city staffers as being in the pocket of developers, since the staff memo contained numerous qualifiers indicating where estimates of impact were uncertain or unknown.

Kott's testimony infuriated the commissioners, who openly resented his attempt to exert political influence at the commission and thereby subvert its independence as an advisory body. Several commissioners defended the integrity of the city's planning staff and its efforts to provide information objectively, even to the point of identifying where information was shaky or non-existent. And to contend with Kott's attacks on the credibility of the Ashley study, the commission questioned Kelly McDermott, the consultant who had prepared that fiscal analysis.

McDermott spent the first portion of her testimony establishing her credentials in the field of land economics, listing her educational training and analytic experience. She asserted that her analysis was: "a complex, theoretical document based on empirical relationships"; "a fair accounting of all direct and indirect costs and revenues associated with new development"; and "a reflection, not a cause of growth"; and that it was not "a political document" or "a biased document." Finally, she lectured for nearly an hour on how her methodology differed from the city's and why her approach captured true cost burdens for the project.

This presentation left the commissioners even more confused about which fiscal analysis was "right"; several wanted to defer a decision on the Bauer Ranch project until they'd had a chance to actually read the Ashley and city analyses. The city attorney intervened, however, reminding the commission that the city charter specifically delineates the planning commission's authority over land use and land-use development, but not over fiscal issues. Fiscal matters fell under the exclusive jurisdiction of the council. Additionally, because the commission had already postponed the Bauer Ranch decision since June, it could not legally continue that postponement without the consent of the developer. When Kaufman and Broad stated that a new continuance would constitute a hardship, the commission was forced to act on the EIR and the zone change.

The commissioners voted to certify the adequacy of the EIR. (One commissioner, Amin David, voted against it to underscore his concern that certification might undermine the incorporation effort for Vista del Rio which was then still unresolved at LAFCO.) The zoning reclassification resolution failed to carry: Commissioner Gerald Bushore proposed to deny it because of the development's probable costs to the city. Taking the opposing position, Chairman Lewis Herbst argued that since the Bauer Ranch plan and zone change conformed to the Canyon General Plan and since the planning commission lacked authority to consider fiscal impacts, he saw no reason to deny the developer his right to develop his property. When the vote to deny reclassification failed to carry, however, the matter was automatically continued to the next meeting date. This gave the officials time to read the fiscal impact reports.

Bauer Ranch—Round Three

This delay also allowed the Anaheim staffers time to revise their own analyses, taking into account another set of assumptions about developer-provision of capital improvements. They drafted a new memo highlighting the differences between the Ashley estimates and the two city projections thus:

(1) *Ashley Analysis*

Assumes change in city policy to allow full payment for capital expenditures by developer, with repayment for costs beyond that project's "fair share" by means of reimbursement districts.

11-year *surplus* = $1.3 million

(2) *FIM Analyses*

(A) Assumes change in city policy to require developer to front money for the project's "fair share" portion of costs of capital improvements that must be constructed to larger-than-project service capacity at time of project development.

11-year *deficit* = $3.9 million

(B) Assumes no change in city policy, where city provides all capital improvements except project's circulation system.

11-year *deficit* = $15.7 million

These new figures further complicated the task of the commissioners when they reconvened on December 4. Most of them wanted to support a project that conformed substantially with the Canyon General Plan, but many also felt compelled to oppose one that could not "pay its own way," given the constraints on public spending imposed by the enactment of Proposition 13. All of the valuable fiscal impact analyses indicated tremendous costs, the magnitude of which depended upon which analysis was believed and the burden of which could be mitigated only by sophisticated financing arrangements. The commissioners' discussion at the meeting indicated the decision-making bind they felt in regard to the Bauer Ranch.

Commissioner Bushore reoffered his old resolution to deny that zoning reclassification, because of its adverse fiscal impacts. Chairman Herbst reminded the commission of its lack of authority over fiscal matters. Commissioner David questioned how the members could ignore information on fiscal impact, given that they had requested it and were now aware of it. Moreover, he questioned the project's consistency with the Canyon General Plan, which called for locating development where services and facilities could be provided economically. In the end, this resolution failed to carry once again.

There was another attempt to break the impasse. Commissioner Tolar began to speculate about ways to tip the balance of revenues and costs into the black. Tolar believed that one section of the Bauer Ranch site might be appropriate for a regional shopping center, given its flat topography and its location at the junction of a freeway and a major planned thoroughfare. Reasoning that this area was one of the remaining sites within Anaheim's sphere of influence that could reasonably support a regional shopping center, and that a commercial use might help the Bauer Ranch "pay for itself," Tolar asked the commissioners, developers and planning staff to consider his proposal. It quickly gathered support, especially after Kaufman and Broad indicated its concurrence with the proposal. The planning director lent his general support to the idea, although he indicated that a larger, flatter site just on the other side of the freeway—the SAVI property, outside the city limits in unincorporated land—had already been identified as more suitable according to standard planning criteria. The problem with the SAVI site was that its owner might not want to develop it that way at all, or it could be annexed to the city of Yorba Linda (or Vista del Rio, yet to be reviewed at that date).

With this information, Tolar offered a new resolution to approve the Bauer Ranch zoning reclassification, with the condition of reserving 50 acres of land near the freeway for major commercial development, and requiring the developer's provision of capital improvements through reimbursement districts. At last, the commission approved. The commission's approval of this resolution did not, however, signify an end to the review process. The city attorney immediately informed the commission that it must somehow reconcile this decision with the General Plan requirements and with the EIR approved only two weeks before (which allowed only 20 acres of commercial development). The planning director and city attorney recommended a way to resolve the inconsistencies. The commission could rescind its vote on the conditional reclassification, approve the original zone change, and then independently direct the staff to accomplish the following: determine the best site for the regional center, draft a general plan amendment and zone change, and prepare an EIR and fiscal impact analysis. The commission followed this advice, eager to approve a strategy that meant allowing development to occur at no cost to the city. The council concurred, approving the zone change on January 23, 1979, with the condition that the developer prepare a precise public facilities plan.

Regional Shopping Center

In the months that followed, Anaheim planners took on the task of analyzing the fiscal impacts of a regional shopping center, located somewhere in the vicinity of the juncture of the Riverside Freeway and the Weir Canyon Road. They used FIM to project public revenues and costs of four alternative sizes of shopping centers, located on a non-specific 70-acre site. The overall conclusion of the analysis was that each of the four options could produce an annual positive cash flow to the city, the amount of which would depend upon the size of the center and the success of the shops. The range of projected net benefits went from a "conservative" $207,000 per year, for a small center with a relatively low market capture, to an "optimistic" $791,600, for a large center with 100% market capture. A staff memo explaining these results cautioned against complete reliance on optimistic figures as the ticket to unconditional approval of residential development in the canyon. The high market-success rate of a large regional population in the Canyon region; but even the highest net benefit estimates would not by themselves be large enough to counterbalance the net negative fiscal impacts of this level of residential growth.

Despite this caveat, news of the fiscal benefits of a regional center was received gladly by city officials, eager to find a means for the proposed residential development to pay its own way. The staff's fiscal analysis gave the Bauer Ranch a new lease on life in September when it came before the planning commission for a general plan amendment. During the summer, Kaufman and Broad had joined with the Taubman Company, a shopping center developer from Michigan. They submitted a request to change 72 acres of land south of the freeway from residential to commercial designation on the Canyon Plan. At almost the same time, another developer came in with an application for a general plan amendment in the immediate vicinity: the owners of the SAVI Ranch, the 275-acre property located on the other side of the Bauer Ranch on the north side of the freeway, requested a reclassification from existing open space to general commercial, office, and industrial uses. Because both the SAVI and Bauer Ranch applications included a 70-acre site for a shopping center, the developers were in competition with one another and the planning commission considered the two matters together on September 24, 1979.

Testimony at this meeting focused on the developers' arguments about why their site was the one best suited for a shopping center. Kaufman and Broad emphasized that their land was already part of the city, and that they were ready to proceed with the development. SAVI argued that its larger site would allow for a unique mixture of retail, office, and light industry, thereby increasing its potential to draw more business to the Canyon.

The commissioners clearly enjoyed the "win/win" choice they had, and voted unanimously to allow the regional shopping center on the Bauer Ranch site. This could then legitimately support the rest of Bauer Ranch's residential development plans. Also, the Bauer Ranch center could be in operation long before a project could get underway on the unincorporated SAVI land. The commission approved a version of the SAVI general plan amendment removing the regional center, but keeping the other planned uses.

When the matter went before the city council a month later, the council members expressed similar concerns over fiscal balance for the entire Bauer Ranch project and over the timing of development. Mayor Seymour gave expression to the dilemma the council faced: if the city approved the SAVI proposal, which was perhaps three to five years away from completion, how could the city finance the costs of the residential Bauer Ranch project, then ready to get underway? Seymour reiterated a promise the council had made months before when, in the face of public opposition, it agreed to annex the Bauer Ranch: thereafter, the city no longer asked current residents to pay the costs of new development. The council felt obliged to approve only fiscally balanced development. This meant that if the council wanted to support the Bauer Ranch housing project, which it did, it needed to find a way to tie it directly to a revenue-generator like the regional shopping center. Design and development of the Bauer Ranch center could be timed with the larger residential project. The council unanimously approved the regional shopping center on the Bauer Ranch location and adopted the SAVI plan amendment without a shopping center. This marked the end of a successful strategy to encourage development at no cost—political or fiscal—to the city.

NOTES

1. Interview with Murdoch, September 5, 1980. For example, Murdoch had involved Anaheim in NSAS's "Four Cities Program," a program designed to facilitate the transfer and implementation of space-age technological developments to local governments.
2. Minutes of the Anaheim City Council, November 7, 1972.
3. County of Orange, Grant Application for H.U.D. Funding (§701 Comprehensive Planning Assistance) for the Environmental Cost/Benefit Joint Study, September 28, 1973.
4. Before 1974, all council members were elected at large, with the mayor selected by the council.
5. Minutes of the Anaheim City Council, July 29, 1978, pp. 74–75.
6. Minutes of the Anaheim City Council, May 15, 1974.
7. Minutes of the Anaheim City Council, July 29, 1974.
8. County of Orange, Cities of Anaheim, Orange and Yorba Linda. Preliminary Grant Application, Comprehensive Planning Assistance (§ 701), Office of Planning and Research, for the Joint Environmental Cost/Benefit Study Phase III, January 17, 1975.
9. The major assumptions of the land-use decision model are: (a) The model measures incremental impacts of alternative development configurations (including commercial, industrial, residential, and open-space land uses) on public costs and revenues, and public safety, environmental, and socioeconomic factors; (b) Each measurement factor is independent of the others; (c) No secondary or indirect impacts are taken into account in the model; (d) When development begins in a planning unit located outside city limits but inside the project area, annexation takes place immediately at the start of development; (e) In a planning unit, development begins at the start of a time segment and continues in equal annual increments to the end of the segment; (f) The model reflects current technological and legislative changes; (g) When a jurisdiction purchases land for open space use, property tax revenue ceases (County of Orange, 1973, pp. 23–24).
10. Only five alternatives were actually analyzed by the Land Use Decision Model. Two options (#3 and #3A, which consisted of high-density clusterings in the staff on the basis of lack of interest by the Task Force. The five remaining alternatives (#1, #2, #2A, #2B, and #4) were analyzed.
11. The planning commission made a slight change in the location of low/medium density housing along Weir Canyon Road and Santa Ana Canyon Road.
12. Minutes of the Anaheim City Council, March 8, 1977, pp. 77–288–293.
13. See City of Anaheim and Ultrasystems, Inc. *User's Manual on Economic And Environmental Growth Impact Analysis: Computerized/Manual Methodology for Use by Local Governmental Jurisdictions,* June 30, 1977.
14. See: Ashley Economic Services, "The Bauer Ranch Fiscal Impact Analysis," prepared for Kaufman and Broad, Inc., Irvine, Calif., November 1978, pp. II: 12–15.

15. FIM results for Bauer Ranch November 1978:

Costs (over 10 years)	−$20,427,808
Revenues (over 10 years)	+ 11,249,403
10-year DEFICIT	$ 9,178,405

This analysis assumes that the city pays for all capital costs associated with the project.

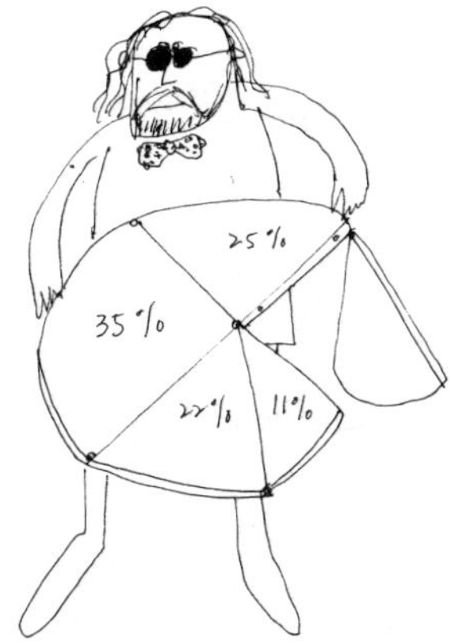

6.
Negotiating Through the Modeling Process

As the foregoing case studies illustrate, modeling is a dynamic process involving a myriad of actors and a constant flow of decisions that shape the implementation, use and impact of computer-based models in the policy process. But who participates in the process? Who influences decisions? And more broadly, who controls the modeling process by virtue of their participation and influence?

The case studies provided examples of how certain actors can, and sometimes do, control the modeling process, shaping who participates, the alternatives they consider, the assumptions and data used in the models, and the ways in which the model results are used in policy making. The cases provide strong support for the view that certain participants will attempt to shape modeling outcomes by their decisions and actions. But, the cases also support the view that no one participant or set of participants fully controls the modeling process. Rather, they negotiate their way through the modeling process.

In this chapter, therefore, we attempt to assess whether one set of participants controls the modeling process or whether control is more pluralistic and negotiated. In order to do so, we begin with a discussion of the major participants. Each participant's primary interests are specified and linked to one or more of our general perspectives about modeling. We then assess the level of participation and the extent of influence of the participants at each stage of the modeling process as a means of making an overall assessment of "who controls." Although primary attention is paid to evidence of direct participation and influence from the cases and survey data, we shall also be aware of instances where certain actors seem to have powerful *indirect* influence in the modeling process.

PRINCIPAL PARTICIPANTS IN THE MODELING PROCESS

The use of computer-based fiscal impact modeling by local governments in their planning and budgeting decisions involves a diverse set of participants who vary widely in regard to their interests in the modeling effort. Almost every participant has some interest that can be classified as personal, professional, political or public. Indeed, any individual or group may be characterized by a mix of these interests and, consequently, our analysis will focus on *dominant* interests in order to make sharper distinctions among the participants. Table 6.1 classifies the participants according to variations in their scope of interests (macro-level or micro-level) and nature of interests (political or technical) in the modeling process. The major participants are partisan groups, political elites, modeling supporters and policy analysts.

TABLE 6.1. Classification of Participants in the Modeling Process

Nature of Primary Interest in the Modeling Effort	Primary Scope of Interest in the Modeling Effort: Macro-level	Primary Scope of Interest in the Modeling Effort: Micro-level
Political	A. *Partisan Groups:* Periodic but intensive involvement in land use decisions. Includes citizen groups, developers, business groups, homeowners, and industrial groups.	B. *Political Elites:* Continuous, but not usually intensive, involvement in both land use and budget decisions. Includes mayors, city managers, legislators, department heads and planning commissioners.
Technical	C. *Modeling Supporters:* Periodic involvement in provision of infrastructure for modeling. Includes federal or state agencies, regional planning agencies and the model consultants.	D. *Policy Analysts:* Continuous, intensive involvement in both the infrastructure and in substantive land use and budget decisions. Includes planners, budget analysts, management analysts and computer experts.

Partisan Groups

Partisans include those groups in the local community, or the region, who can have intensive involvement in land-use decisions by virtue of their position as homeowners, landowners, or businessowners and by virtue of their mobilization of others with interests similar to their own. These groups include homeowner associations, chambers of commerce, good government groups, downtown businessmen's association, developers, building industry associations and combinations of such groups.

Homeowner groups, even though geographically separated, tend to share an interest in the preservation of the rural character of urbanizing areas and in limiting development to achieve those ends. Their interest in limiting development is shared with good government groups who seek a more equitable distribution of the benefits and burdens of government expenditure—particularly that new development pay its fair share of the capital, operating and maintenance costs of government. Consequently, homeowners and good government groups share an interest in fiscal impact modeling because they believe that any objective analysis will reveal the fiscal liabilities of development generally, and of certain development patterns in particular (e.g., sprawl, high density residential development, extensive mixed-use development).

Developers and the building industry share an interest in profits from the development of land for its "highest and best use." Their interest in promoting development is shared by downtown businessmen, suburban businessmen, and the chamber of commerce (usually dominated by downtown business interests) who believe that development will bring new people and new business and industry who, in turn, will become their customers, promote their economic prosperity and, indirectly, promote the prosperity of the community. Although generally opposed to fiscal impact modeling, these groups tend to accept it because they view it as one price they must pay for "growth," they believe that the model results will demonstrate the fiscal wisdom of development, and they know that the modeling process will allow them to exercise additional influence in their own interests.

Political Elites

Political elites include those within the government who owing to their positions of formal leadership, can have direct involvement in fiscal impact modeling and can exert substantial influence to maintain their interests. This group includes local legislators (i.e., city councils and county supervisors), chief executives (mayors, city managers), and department heads. Usually, political elites are periodically involved rather than continuously involved in the modeling process. But when they do become involved, they tend to focus on "big" decisions about modeling, such as the adoption of a model, the allocation of funds for modeling, the use of the model for evaluating large development projects, and continuation of the modeling effort.

More than any other of the political elites, local legislators and elected chief executives (mayors) are concerned with fiscal impact modeling because of personal, partisan, and public interests. The land-use decisions for which fiscal impact modeling is used tend to have large financial consequences for private interests and to involve considerable controversy. Therefore, legislators and elected executives must be sensitive to the partisan interests involved, particularly those important to their partisan election and re-election. As managers of government and community affairs, local legislators and elected executives also are concerned with public interests: the financial consequences of development for the government and the distribution of the benefits and costs of development.

Appointed chief executives (e.g., city managers) tend to see fiscal impact models as management tools, serving personal and professional goals of organizational efficiency, modernization, and leverage. Like the legislators, these managers are interested in how use of the models might help to increase the fiscal profitability of the government. But, they also are interested in the models for what they symbolize about themselves as managers and what they symbolize about their administration (i.e., innovativeness, professionalism, modernity). Finally, managers are interested in the models for the leverage they provide in dealing with partisan groups, the legislature and department heads in the managers' efforts to acquire, husband, or control resources. Department heads, like the appointed chief executives, are interested in the fiscal impact models because of their general professional beliefs in the benefits of modern management techniques and because of the leverage the model might provide them in acquiring additional resources for their department.

Thus it is clear that these actors have different interests and motives regarding fiscal impact modeling, and particular individuals probably have their own unique patterns of interests. But it is generally the case that personal and partisan interests are of central concern to elected officials, and professional interests to chief executives and to department heads.

Modeling Supporters

Modeling supporters are those individuals and organizations outside the government who can and do influence the modeling process by building the models, supplying consultant services, or providing technical or financial resources for the effort. Such supporters include planning consultants, model consultants, federal and state agencies, regional planning agencies, and professional associations. With the exception of modeling or planning consultants, supporters are only periodically involved in local modeling efforts and tend to concentrate on the provision of infrastructure or resources for modeling rather than actually participate in the modeling process. The interests of such supporters are primarily professional and public—they are concerned with the development, promotion, and use of modern planning and management techniques as a means of improving decision making and operational performance of local governments. Modeling and planning consultants of course have personal interests in addition to professional ones. They seek to develop, promote and have *their* model and services used for economic and other personal interests as well as for professional recognition and sense of accomplishment. Because of their initial monopoly of expertise, model consultants tend to be especially involved and influential in the adoption decision and throughout the adaptation phase; but their influence is largely limited to direct modeling activities.

Policy Analysts

Policy analysts have continuous, intensive involvement in both the infrastructure for modeling and in the use of models for substantive land-use and budget decisions. Because of the extent of their involvement, their interests in the perpetuation of modeling, and their monopoly of expertise, policy analysts could even dominate the modeling process. Such analysts include planners, budget analysts, management analysts and computer experts in their information services role. As a group, the policy analysts are distinguished from the other major participants in modeling by their role as providers of information to political elites. They share basic technical skills and values, but are dispersed among different organizational units and, consequently, they usually have operational agendas and interests aligned with the goals of those units. However, since the modeling process brings them together and keeps them more or less continuously involved, they develop certain common interests. Decisions about computer support for the modeling effort, about centralization and routinization of data collection and about the adoption of sophisticated analytical applications are important to their personal performance, their careers, their control over information, and their influence with political elites. They will advocate centralized data systems that cross departmental boundaries because they need such systems for the model and because they view such systems as a means of gaining control over information channels vital to all operating departments. They advocate the development of sophisticated analytical applications such as fiscal impact models because they view the reduction of their analytical uncertainty as the technical key to the legitimacy and influence of their policy advice. When they can combine data and technical sophistication with knowledge about policy issues, they can influence their superiors and the actions of operating departments. They also will advance professionally, gain peer recognition, and achieve some measure of independence within their domain.

EXPLANATIONS FOR THE PARTICIPANTS' INVOLVEMENT

Each of the basic perspectives outlined in Chapter 1 suggests an explanation for the activities and influence of the participants in the modeling process. From the rational perspective, the government's political leaders are concerned with control of new urban development to insure that each development project pays its fair share of government capital and operating costs, and/or that the overall pattern of urban development is fiscally sound; in short, that development is in the broad public interest. Given the complexity of determining fiscal impact, especially in the politically charged context of land-use decision making, the political leaders adopt modeling as a means of more accurately and objectively determining the fiscal impacts of urban development. Since the models are "scientific" tools, the technical experts are provided a great deal of autonomy to employ them in the public interest. Thus, this approach predicts active involvement by political leadership in the decision to adopt fiscal impact modeling but not in the evaluation of specific plans and projects for urban development and not in the details of the modeling process itself. These are left to the technical experts.

According to the partisan perspective, the modeling process is controlled by political leaders who get the technical experts to incorporate partisan preferences in the information, the models, and the process. That is, the dominant coalition among political leaders, usually in coalition with one or another partisan interest groups in the community, dominates the modeling process and controls its outcomes. Here, modeling is a political tool to be used for propaganda and persuasion as its results are shaped to agree with the partisans. From this perspective, the modeling process will tend to be dominated by partisan elected officials, the model experts controlled or at least carefully monitored by them, and the model parameters massaged to produce results favorable to their preferred policy outcomes.

The technocratic perspective posits that technical experts with a relative monopoly of expertise will exert substantial influence and control over the modeling process for personal and professional interests. Given the technical nature of computer-based fiscal impact modeling, it is reasonable to assume that policy analysts could dominate decisions about the development and use of modeling generally and could further dominate detailed decisions about the assumptions, alternatives, criteria and data employed in specific uses of the model for plan and project evaluation. Thus, they could ultimately control the outcomes of the modeling process either by the choice of model used, or by the way in which any particular model is used for specific decisions, or both.

PARTICIPANTS' INFLUENCE IN THE MODELING PROCESS

Each of the foregoing explanations for the participants' involvement, and the related predictions about the participants control, can be assessed by examining the activities and influence of the participants at each stage of the modeling process. Both the case studies and the data from the field survey provide a rich base of information that is best examined by looking at the key activities and the participant's influence in them at each phase of the modeling process: introduction, adaptation, and incorporation. In doing so, we examine activities and influences in both the macro- and the micro-environment of modeling, as shown in Table 6.2. But, we concentrate on the micro-environment for our overall assessment of "who controls" the modeling process.

Model Introduction

The introduction phase of modeling centered around several key activities: perception of the need for fiscal impact modeling, creation of support of modeling, and selection of a modeling consultant. Macro-level forces, particularly the political and economic environment, provided the general impetus for modeling and indirectly influences these key activities. But micro-level forces, particularly the differential influence of participants, were more central.

Three macro-environmental factors appear to have been important in our local governments' decisions to adopt a fiscal impact model: local political concern over development issues, the availability of outside support for model implementation, and/or the promotional efforts of model vendors.

As illustrated in the case studies, citizen dissatisfaction over existing development patterns and citizen-developer conflict over the direction or rate of future growth focused attention on planning as a means of better directing growth. Moreover, the fiscal condition of cities, affected by national economic trends and regional factors such as California's Proposition 13, made the consideration of fiscal impacts a political necessity in planning for future growth.[1] The principal sets of actors giving expression to the

TABLE 6.2. *Activities and Influences in the Modeling Process*

Level in the Environment	Phase of the Modeling Process		
	Introduction	**Adaptation**	**Incorporation**
Macro-Level	Political and economic forces in the environment provide *impetus* for modeling.	Partisan political groups provide definition of alternatives, participation, and support for the *process* of adopting and using the model for a specific decision.	Political competition, the pace of community development and strained government finances keep up pressure for attention to costs and revenues of development.
Micro-Level	Politicians and bureaucrats respond to political impetus, add their own agendas, and procure a model—usually without real understanding of the differences among models.	Staff experts, usually planners, adapt the model for local use; politicians and bureaucrats create organizational and political arrangements for involving key partisans in the modeling process; the city uses the model for one or more plan/project evaluations; conflict, competition and negotiation occurs among participants in the modeling process; decision results which satisfies enough participants to end the current cycle; most participants satisfied with either the process or the outcomes.	Bureaucrats and staff experts perceive modeling as a general tool applicable to other decision situations and a leverage for increased resources and, therefore, likely politicians to incorporate modeling into ongoing government processes; politicians assent because they stand to gain leverage, particularly with developers, and because they gain symbolic benefit vis-à-vis citizens.

need for planning and to consideration of fiscal impacts were two: (a) citizen groups, which were dissatisfied with current development patterns and concerned about future growth; and (b) developers, who perceived planning as a better alternative to development moratoria and sought planning as a means of legitimating current trends or redirecting public investments toward their development interests.

The political salience of such development issues is suggested by several objective features of the macro-environment of the modeling sites. Our field survey indicates that most of the governments that adopted a fiscal model were in rapidly growing suburban areas experiencing spillover growth from neighboring urban centers. Only five were central cities, and three of these (San Diego, Tulsa, Phoenix) were growing central cities of the Sunbelt with large undeveloped areas within their boundaries. All of the local governments experienced considerable population growth during the 1970–1980 decade. And growth management was an important issue in over three-fourths of the governments, with most (11 sites) oriented towards controlled growth, four towards promotion of growth, and one towards restraint of growth.

Outside funding for model adoption also appears to have been an influential factor for nearly one-half of the local governments. Most of the fiscal impact model implementation efforts (14) were funded, in whole or part, by the local governments themselves.[2] But at least eight modeling efforts received some federal funding and one received state funding support. It is likely that the availability of such outside funding provided an impetus or an additional rationale for the local effort on the grounds that the local government need not bear the full costs of the model's implementation.

Promotion by model vendors was another macro-level influence on model adoption. According to the users of the models in our cities, model vendors were the most frequent source of information about fiscal impact models used by the governments. About 75 percent of the respondents indicated that the vendor was "often" a source (Table 6.3). The next most frequent sources of information were other local governments: 59 percent of the respondents indicated that county officials or staff were often a source; and 44 percent indicated that another city's officials or staff were "often" a source. Interestingly, federal and state agencies, which sometimes provided financial support for fiscal impact modeling, were the least likely to be rated as a frequent source of information.

Whereas the general impetus for model adoption stemmed from macro-level forces and actors in the macro-environment, that impetus was operationalized at the micro-level by actors and activities centered mainly within the government bureaucracy. The perception that fiscal impact modeling might constitute an appropriate tool in the planning process, the

TABLE 6.3. External Sources of Information About the Model

"Rate each of the following groups or agencies in terms of how frequently they were a source of information about the fiscal impact model used by your local government."	Proportion of respondents indicating this agency was a source of information			
	Never or Seldom	Often or Very Often	Total	*N*
Agency of the federal government	88%	12%	100%	90
Agency of the state government	70	30	100	98
Regional agency	63	37	100	101
County officials or staff	41	59	100	100
Another city's officials or staff	56	44	100	103
Vendor of the model	25	75	100	100

creation of support for model adoption, and the subsequent search for a model consultant involved a pluralistic mix of elected officials, managers and planners. The mayor and a consultant perceived the need for fiscal impact modeling and initiated action in Tulsa and San Diego; planners and the city manager led the action in Anaheim; and planners, the city manager, the administrative services staff and two council members took the lead in Irvine. In each instance, these individuals also took the lead in generating support for the modeling effort among other elected officials and city staff. And, they generally remained involved with adoption of the model through the selection of a model consultant even though the bulk of this activity fell to the planners.

The individuals most frequently identified in our field survey as influential in the adoption decision were planners: 16 out of 19 sites indicated that the planning department was influential in the decision to adopt a model (Table 6.4). The next most frequently identified individuals were the chief appointed and elected officials, the local legislators, and management and budget staff. About 7–8 sites identified these individuals as influential in the adoption decision. Generally, the finance and data processing departments, interdepartmental boards, and regional planning agencies were seldom identified as influential.

The apparent dominance of planners in the introduction phase is not surprising. Planners have primary responsibility for analyses in support of the kinds of decisions aided by fiscal impact models; they tend to have the technical expertise required for using such models; they have the

TABLE 6.4. Influentials in Adoption of the Model and in Design of Analyses

Type of individual or agency	Number of sites indicating this individual or agency was influential[a]	
	In the decision to adopt the model (*N* = 19)	In designing model analyses (*N* = 19)
Planning department	16	14
Chief appointed official	8	4
Local legislative body	8	4
Chief elected official	7	3
Budget and management office	7	6
Interdepartmental board or committee	5	2
Finance department	4	5
Data processing department	2	4
Regional planning agency	2	2

[a]Respondents were asked to indicate *all* categories that apply rather than one or the primary one.

greatest interest in applying sophisticated techniques to bolster their analyses and recommendations on development issues; and they stand to gain the most, in terms of political/bureaucratic influence and legitimacy, by the use of rational analytic techniques. Thus, it is likely that the planners are the primary internal advocates for model adoption, generally, and that they are influential because of their advocacy role. The case studies support this conclusion and further suggest that the primary roles of other actors in model adoption are "gate-keeping" and oversight of the planners recommendations. However, the cases also suggest that these are not perfunctory roles. The Irvine, Tulsa, and San Diego cases indicate that the involvement and influence of other actors, particularly political elites, in the decision to adopt modeling and to select a specific fiscal impact model can be substantial.

Both the cases and the field survey suggest that the key individuals in the introduction phase, and those whose support they eventually marshalled, were influenced in their adoption decision more by a general faith in technology than by knowledge about the models or the experience of other cities with them. For example, the four case studies show that the process of actually selecting a model and a consultant was a relatively straightforward procurement process. And in all instances, there was uniform agreement among the key participants over the ultimate choice of a model and a consultant. But, the choice was influenced more by confidence in the consultant than by understanding of differences in the models or by understanding of what model adoption implied. None of the participants in model selection understood these things. In addition, the key actors' decision to adopt was influenced by the expectation that the model would support their preferred policy positions on planning, development and growth issues. These expectations were logically flawed: the models' results could not simultaneously support the progrowth and antigrowth factions which usually contended. Yet, these factions gave support to model adoption because they *believed* that their policy position would be vindicated by the model.

Model Adaptation

Once a model was adopted, the real work began. The technical features of the chosen model has to be adapted to local conditions. Technical adaptation was a complex process that involved: detailed examination of how well the model's structure fit local conditions, and change as required; step-by-step review of the suitability of the model's assumptions and operation, and modification for local conditions; department-by-department collection of historical data on the costs and revenues associated with land-use, population and economic activity; year-by-year development of estimates for future land-use development and population growth; careful conversion of the assumptions, data and forecasts for input to the model; preparation of the model and data to run on a computer; preliminary testing of the adapted model in operational runs; repeated operation of the model to evaluate multiple development alternatives; and, iteration through the foregoing steps as experience was gained with the model and its results. Generally, technical adaptation involved $50,000 in direct cost for consultant services, took 18 person-months of city and consultant time, and was spread over a twelve month period.[3]

In addition to these technical tasks, the adaptation phase involved political and organizational tasks: establishing a locus of responsibility for the model within the government; hiring new staff or training existing staff to operate and use the model; providing orientation and training to public officials and others involved with the model; bringing representatives of the various interest groups into the modeling process; meeting with these representatives and with local government officials and staff to obtain agreement on the assumptions, data and forecasts; securing commitment to abide by the model results produced by these processes; and negotiating and bargaining over the assumptions, data, and alternatives when the model's results were clearly unacceptable to the parties at interest.

As suggested by these technical and behavioral tasks, the adaptation phase mainly centered around micro-level processes internal to the government bureaucracy. But it also involved interface with the broader political environment through the participation of representatives of the major parties at interest, and through involved, intensive, and prolonged bargaining and negotiation among these representatives, among planning officials and, ultimately, among politicians. Macro-level forces played an important role in the adaptation phase through influences of both the previous and the continuing play of community politics. The previous play of community politics determined which interests would be represented and which development alternatives would be considered in the modeling process. Citizens, developers, businessmen, politicians, bureaucrats and planners were all represented. So were the development alternatives preferred by these groups; and, new alternatives that provided for mutual gains among all the actors and interests were invented as the modeling process played out during the adaptation phase.[4]

The continuing play of community politics also influenced adaptation through the provision or withdrawal of support for planning and modeling, and through use of the model's results in the selection of a general plan or the approval of a specific development project. In all of the cases studied, the dominant political coalition in the government was fragile; the dominant coalition shifted back and forth between pro- and anti-development interests in planning commissions and city councils; and this continual pulling and hauling affected both support for the modeling effort and how the model results were used. When the model's results fit the preferences of the dominant political coalition, the results tended to be used as objective evidence of the merits of their policy position. When the results failed to support the dominant coalition's preferences, attempts were made to change or discredit the model and its results.

Despite these uses by changing political actors and coalitions, they eventually were constrained in their decision making by the modeling process that had been set in motion. No single actor or political coalition could long sustain efforts to completely override the model results or to use them when consistent with their preferences if the results were inconsistent with agreements evolving from the participatory modeling process. Consequently, the main feature of model use by political decision makers was a shying away from extreme development alternatives and an evolution toward middle ground alternatives and policy positions that gave some advantages to all major parties at interest.

This macro-level negotiation toward middle-ground positions was influenced by micro-level processes of the adaptation phase. The model itself was important in that it set the framework within which development alternatives were considered and set fiscal impact as a primary decision criteria. But, the processes employed in the modeling effort were more influential than the model itself.

The critical micro-level feature of the adaptation phase was the setting up of a process whereby agreement could be reached on assumptions, data, methods, and alternatives in advance of model use so that commitment to abide by the model's results was more-or-less assured. Such a process was essential because while the model provided a general framework, many individual features of the framework involved matters of judgment that had to be agreed to by the participants if they were to accept the model results as credible. Moreover, model use itself had to iterative. It was only by considering the results of their judgments (in the model's outputs) that the participants could begin to understand the reasonableness of various assumptions and thereby change and refine them. And because the model results helped to clarify "what was at stake for whom," as well as how the assumptions affected the outcomes, bargaining and negotiation over outcomes shifted to bargaining and negotiation over the assumptions, data, and alternatives. Such bargaining was essential to arriving at agreement on the reasonableness of assumptions, data, and alternatives. More importantly, it was essential to the step-by-step development of commitment among the participants to the entire modeling effort and, hence, to the eventual acceptance of the model results. And, not surprisingly, it frequently led to agreement on acceptable alternatives before the final model results were run. Since the modeling process involved multiple iterations of the model results, by the time the final model results were ready to be run, previous iterations had set the boundaries within which results would be achieved and had formed the basis for defining the final development alternative, or the range of such alternatives, upon which they could all agree. It is this iterative bargaining and negotiation, in which the range of acceptable alternatives was set, which probably accounts for the overwhelming perception of participants in the modeling process that the modeling efforts were successful.

From a substantive standpoint, the models could be used for evaluating the fiscal impact of development, and for budget making. But, generally, the former purpose dominated model use in our survey sites. Seventeen used the model for impact analysis of new development projects, 13 used the model for analysis of general plans or growth management plans, and two used the model for analysis of development in surrounding jurisdictions. Generally, the models also were used more than once. Fourteen sites indicated they had produced two or more reports using the model; only four sites indicated they had produced a single report.

The individuals responsible for conducting model analyses and for guiding the modeling process overall were most frequently the planners. In turn, the planners often worked with department heads and top management staff in collecting data and reviewing model assumptions, and with computer staff in actually completing the model runs. And as the fieldwork illustrates, the planners were highly dependent on these individuals for cooperation and reliable performance.

Although the planners had operational responsibility for the model, they reported directly to the top political/executive officials (mayor, manager, council) in one-half the sites, and reported to them indirectly, through the planning director, in the other half. The relatively large proportion of staffs reporting to top officials suggests the generally high policy importance given to the modeling effort by many governments. Moreover, as all the cases illustrate, these top officials usually were partisan about the potential model outcomes and, as a consequence, highly scrutinous of the model adaptation effort. Sometimes, they became directly involved; sometimes they assigned a citizen advisory committee as "watchdogs"; and sometimes they did both.

Although top officials monitored and ultimately controlled the modeling effort, generally they were not influential in designing *specific* model analyses. For example, Table 6.4 (discussed earlier) shows that one-half as many sites indicated that top officials (elected or appointed chief executive and local legislative body) were influential in designing specific model analyses as indicated these officials were influential in adopting the model. That is, only 11 sites indicated that top officials were influential in design of analyses whereas 23 sites indicated they were influential in adoption. In contrast, 14 sites indicated the planning department was influential in designing analyses. In part, this might reflect the fact that top officials seldom become directly involved in design of specific model analyses while they more often get directly involved in adoption of modeling. However, the influence of top officials appears to extend to the design of specific analyses through the anticipation of their reactions by planning staff. Such indirect influence clearly appeared in the San Diego and Tulsa cases.

Other participants that were influential, usually in concert with the planners, included budget and management analysts, finance experts, and data processing experts. The influence of these other information service providers is hardly surprising since they frequently are a source of data, assumptions of computing capability for the model, as well as analyst-users who have a stake in the model's results.

Model Incorporation

Once a model had been made operational and used for at least one decision, the adaptation phase was more or less complete. In some cases, the model implementation effort ended here because the model was originally adopted with the intention of using it only for a specific decision, or, because the adaptation phase was unsuccessful. The former situation was illustrated by the San Diego case and the latter by the Tulsa case; other illustrations also were present in our general survey. In fact, less than one-half of the sites in our survey incorporated a model into their ongoing planning processes. Of the 21 sites, nine sites have incorporated a model; seven sites adapted and used a model but never incorporated it; four sites adapted the model but never used it; and one site adopted the model but never adapted it (Table 6.5).

From a macro-level perspective, the incorporation phase seems anticlimatic. In three of the cases studied, by the time the model was incorporated, the planning issues that modeling was meant to inform had been settled. And, they had been shaped as much by events in the broad political environments as by the results of the model or the modeling process. In both Irvine and Anaheim, community sentiment and changing political coalitions led to the elimination of certain development alternatives from further consideration long before the model results indicated they were not fiscally profitable; political sentiment was overwhelmingly against their continued consideration. In San Diego, the mayor and downtown developers struck a political compromise with North City West developers and their council supporters that new suburban development could continue if it largely paid its own way; the model results merely spelled out the developer and public expenditures required. Even in Tulsa, where modeling was terminated, the failure to incorporate modeling was foreshadowed by the gradual erosion of political support for regional planning—a process of which modeling had been a part. The significance of these macro-level political forces was underscored by the fact that the results of Tulsa's modeling effort had lent support to the laissez-faire development policy preferred by the dominant political coalition.

Given all of these conditions set by macro-level forces in the adaptation phase, what then is the macro-level significance of model incorporation for who controls the modeling process? Basically it is that, *when a model is incorporated*, the criteria, methods and processes of political bargaining, negotiation and decision making about land-use development issues in the local governments studied have been *permanently changed.* Fiscal impact has become an established criteria for evaluation of development plans and projects; fiscal impact models have become an accepted method of determining fiscal impact; and modeling has become a routine part of the planning process. In the future, politicians, planning commissioners, developers, and citizens must reckon with this *new force which is only partially controllable*—even when modeling is no longer broadly participatory but conducted largely by planning staff.

The practical significance of this fact is illustrated by the Anaheim and Irvine cases where city officials require that major proposals from developers be evaluated by fiscal impact analysis. The significance is also

TABLE 6.5. Summary of Model Implementation Status, for the 21 Study Sites

Site	Name of Model	Year Model Purchased	Year First Report Produced with the Model	Year Last Report Produced with the Model	Summary Status[a]
Incorporated					
Anaheim, CA	FISCOM	75	76	80	6
Montgomery Co., MD	MUNIES	75	75	79	6
Prince Georges Co., MD	MUNIES	77	76	80	6
Ann Arundel Co., MD	MUNIES	77	78	79	6
Lexington-Fayette Co., KY	MUNIES	78	79	80	6
Greece, NY	MUNIES	80	81	81	6
Irvine, CA	FIM	76	76	80	6
Huntington Beach, CA	FIM	79	79	81	6
San Juan Capistrano, CA	FIM	78	78	80	6
Corona, CA	FIM	78	78	79	6
Not Incorporated					
Phoenix, AZ	MUNIES	78	78	78	5
San Diego, CA	MUNIES	76	77	78	5
Hudson, OH	MUNIES	76	77	77	5
Green Co., NY	MUNIES	78	79	79	5
Washington, DC	MUNIES	78	79	79	5
Norfolk, VA	MUNIES	78	80	80	4
Greenwich, CT	MUNIES	75	76	...	5
Washoe, Co., NV	MUNIES	79	80	81	5
Rancho Cucamonga, CA	FISCOM	80	81	81	4
Orange Co., CA	FIAS	77	...	...	3
Tulsa, OK	FIAS	78	...	...	4

[a]*Code:* 3 Adopted, but never adapted.
4 Adopted, adapted but never used.
5 Adopted, adapted, and used but not routinized.
6 Adopted, adapted, used, and routinized (i.e., incorporated).

underscored by the Bauer Ranch project in Anaheim where the developers hired their own consultant to conduct their own fiscal analysis on terms favorable to their preferred development plans. Although the developers had hoped that their fiscal analysis would be accepted as grounds for approval, in fact, the city's fiscal impact model and analysis was used as the standard against which to judge both the developer's proposal and his fiscal impact analysis. Similarly, although only alluded to in the Irvine case study, the city's model and analyses have come to be the standard for judging fiscal impact analyses prepared by the Company's consultants. Indeed, the extensive reliance of the City of Irvine on its model has led Company officials to hire private consultants to study limitations of the model as a means of discrediting it, or at least, changing it to reflect assumptions, methods and data potentially more favorable to the Company's interests.

At the micro-level, the main feature of model incorporation is that it leads to further innovation. Whereas most academic conceptions of modeling view incorporation as the end of the innovation cycle, our analysis indicates that incorporation is marked by a process of continuous innovation in which the model, the modeling process, the planning process, and other related local government processes (financial reporting, data collection, municipal automation) evolve and change. In Irvine and Anaheim, model incorporation led to new efforts to bring the model in-house, hire staff, train city officials, obtain data, refine assumptions, and improve ease of model use. In Irvine, it also led to an effort to develop a new model, which would better facilitate the assessment of fiscal impact at multiple levels and units of analysis, and to the development of new information systems that would support the modeling effort. Moreover, in Anaheim, model incorporation led to adoption of the technique for other planning issues than the issue for which the model had been adopted, thereby causing a partial recycling of the implementation process for each new issue; and it further led to the introduction of countermodeling by developers.

As a by-product, these micro-level features of the incorporation phase also increased the resources and influence of city planners, financial analysts, and management officials. Additional resources were provided in line with the additional responsibility created by repeated use of the model. Repeated use, which was routine in the sense of being similar to previous uses, was left largely in the hands of the planners without extensive community participation or oversight by politicians and managers. When new uses evolved, the modeling effort was also entrusted to the planners and analysts, but the politicians provided oversight themselves or delegated the task to representatives.

Like the decision to adopt the model, the decision to incorporate its use into the on-going operations of the government had many participants. Usually, the decision was a classic example of staff recommendation, chief executive endorsement and legislative approval. There was little controversy over the decision because the model had proven itself useful, the decision participants had prior personal experience or knowledge of it, and the participants believed in the ultimate superiority of decision making with the aid of such technique. Responsibility for continued operation of the model was given to the planners who continued to need the cooperation of central management staff and the operating departments. As throughout earlier phases of the modeling effort, both the chief executive and the legislative body retained oversight responsibility—the executive through normal management processes (budgeting, reporting, evaluating), and the legislative body through assignment of the task to some of its members.

But, as the foregoing also suggests, the number of participants in the modeling process was reduced from what it had been during adaptation. This was especially the case for uses of the model which were more or less routine in the sense that they represented uses which had been worked through previously. Usually, the participants included the planners, the chief executive or a representative, and the council or its model subcommittee. Partisans such as citizen groups and developers seldom remained a part of the modeling process, except when the model's results were presented and discussed at public meetings of the planning commission and/or the legislative body.

Although the pattern of participation after incorporation became focused around a smaller circle of influentials, control of the modeling process remained diffuse. The planners had responsibility for model operation, but they required the cooperation of management staff and the departments in updating the data and setting the assumptions for the model; they also required agreement of the chief executive and the legislature to the assumptions and the alternatives to be evaluated. These elected officials, in turn, generally were constrained by the process and the data, assumptions and alternatives that evolved from it. No one individual or group was able to control the model process or its outcomes by themselves. Thus, although confined to an elite group of politicians, managers and technicians the modeling process remained pluralistic within this narrowed scope of participation.

ASSESSING OVERALL CONTROL

Our assessment of control by participants during the incorporation phase of modeling presages our overall conclusions in this chapter. No one individual or group systematically and uniformly dominates all activities and decision processes. Rather, there are several relatively independent elites that appear to dominate different decision processes. But none of these elites are fully autonomous. They are interdependent.

Actors and events in the macro-environment nearly always influence the micro-level actors and events. Sometimes they overshadow the micro-environment in the sense that overwhelming community sentiment or other factors simply predetermine the decision outcomes independent of and in advance of completion of the modeling process. But, macro-level actors such as citizen groups and developers do not control the modeling process. Indeed, their participation and involvement in the process varies widely from community to community and further varies within a specific community, depending upon the phase of implementation of modeling in the government. Consequently, we focus our overall assessment of control on micro-level actors, activities and decisions. And we consider each of the explanations for the participants' involvement and control in turn.

There is very little evidence in support of the rational perspective, which predicts that the government's political elite will select a model and then give great autonomy to the policy analysts to apply the model in scientific fashion to the evaluation of specific plans and projects for development in the broad public interest. While elected officials give the analysts considerable responsibility and, correspondingly, authority over technical matters and over conduct of the modeling process, they constrain the analysts by requiring them to cooperate with other analysts, with department heads and with partisan groups in the community. Moreover, elected officials themselves participate in the modeling process, monitor the process when not participating directly, and reserve to themselves ultimate decisions about the use of specific model results and about continued use of modeling per se.

Similarly, there is little support for the partisan perspective which posits that a political elite controls the process by getting the analysts to incorporate their partisan preferences in the information, the models and the process. It is true that the analysts consider the policy preferences of elected officials, to the extent that they are known, and include them in the set of alternatives to be evaluated in the modeling process. But it is seldom the case that elected officials agree on preferences; usually there are at least two sets of preferences because usually there are at least two political factions in the legislative body. Moreover, the analysts also consider the preferences of other participants—including other analysts, the chief executive, community groups, and their own preferences as professionals.

There is also little support for the technocratic perspective which posits that the analysts will control the modeling process for personal and professional interests. The assumption that the analysts promote a particular model because it is their creation or reflects their point of view is unsupported by the evidence. The analysts almost never build their own models; most often they use a model developed elsewhere; thus they generally have no reason to promote their own invention. The analysts seldom understand the differences among competing models; even the developers of the models do not fully understand the differences. And, the analysts seldom understand the biases and limitations of the model they do use—at least not until they have had considerable experience with it. Consequently, it is difficult for the analysis to control the modeling process through choice of one or another model or through manipulation of technical features of a chosen model. As discussed above with regard to the rational perspective, it also is difficult for the analysts to control the modeling process behaviorally; they are considerably constrained by other participants, by legislative oversight, and by the broader decision processes of which modeling is a part.

NATURE OF THE MODELING PROCESS

Most early studies of modeling focused on model development. Indeed, most of the literature tends to define modeling as the technical activities involved in building a model.[5] Only recently has attention begun to focus on implementation and use as a neglected part of the modeling process. We chose to focus on developed models in this study precisely because we wanted to gain a clearer understanding of modeling as implementation and use rather than development, and from the user's perspective rather than the modeler's. Our field work and survey supports the utility of this approach and also underscores the complexity and dynamism of the modeling process. Within a small number of cities, we witnessed so many twists and turns and iterations that the modeling process appeared more labyrinthian than the straightforward, linear process depicted in the literature. For example, Tulsa adopted a model which had already been developed and used in other cities; the model was redeveloped by the vendor to meet the specific needs of Tulsa; the model was physically transferred to Tulsa and during the process of adaptation a series of local fiscal impact models were reinvented; both the original and the local models were then utilized for plan evaluation; and, ultimately, both sets of models were rejected. In Anaheim and Irvine, a cyclical process emerged in which each new development issues began a new cycle of adaptation and utilization of a model that had been successfully incorporated into ongoing planning processes.

Modeling is labyrinthian also in the sense that there are multiple actors whose participation varies from stage to stage, and within stages, and whose participation can substantially influence the process and the outcomes. Modeling is not simply an activity of the model builders and consultants. These modelers were joined, and eventually, replaced, by in-house analysts from finance, budgeting, and planning and by in-house computing experts who helped to implement and use the models. These analysts in turn were joined by a variety of managers (chief executive, planning director, modeling director) responsible for monitoring the implementation process, coordinating the activities of participating units, linking the modeling effort to the general planning process, and facilitating technical tasks (such as marshalling input data from operating departments and agencies) at various stages of the modeling process. Technocrats and bureaucrats further were joined by a heterogenous group of political actors including elected officials, politically appointed advisory groups, politically appointed officials) and representatives of community groups and interests (the media, developers, business people and homeowners).

Not surprisingly, then, the modeling process also tended to be characterized by multiple goals and agendas, reflecting the array of participants, their shifting involvements and their interests. Sometimes these goals and agendas coalesced—as when independent and competing actors agreed to support the introduction of a fiscal impact model. Sometimes, goals and agendas were in direct conflict—as when competing actors and interest groups each sought to have the model results support their preferred development plans. Moreover, these agendas were dynamic, changing as new participants and new events impinged upon the modeling process.

The dynamism of the implementation process was manifested in a variety of other ways as well. For example, in Irvine and in Tulsa, extensive changes in features of the model package were instituted during the adaptation phase. These changes included alteration of the mathematics of the models, their physical and organizational location, their operators, and the character of their database. In Irvine we also saw changes in the computing support for the models as well as the data handling operations. And, in Tulsa there were radical changes in the lines of authority and responsibility for the modeling effort and dramatic narrowing of the kinds of scenarios or policy alternatives that were evaluated.

In many respects, these micro-level changes in the modeling process reflected macro-level changes in the political environment. This was best illustrated in Tulsa where shifts in the fortunes of principal political actors severely impacted bureaucratic actors and key processes of model adaptation. Such dramatic changes in the broader political environment were important in the other cities as well.

Finally, it is likely that these foregoing features of the modeling process contribute to the fact that modeling occupies such a tenuous place in most local governments. Incorporation of fiscal impact models appears to be the exception rather than the rule among the governments we studied and among local governments generally. So does incorporation of other planning and operational models (Lee, 1973; Pack & Pack, 1977b; Wright, Hall & Hatry, 1978; Chaiken, 1978). While the technical characteristics of a particular model influence its implementability, and hence its likely incorporation, other factors appear more prominent. One factor is the original intent of model adoptions. Some models were adopted to aid a single decision situation and then no longer used. While their adaptation and use was successful, they were not incorporated by the government. Another factor is the political advantage derived from the model's use. Incorporated models were more likely to give political advantage to chief executives and staff rather than to local legislatures or to citizen groups. Since all of the governments where this occurred were characterized by the strong executive form of government, the models can be viewed as essentially reinforcing the influence of the dominant, stable political influence in the government.

But the development policy environment also seems to have a strong influence in governments that incorporated a model. These governments were characterized by certainty over the course of urban growth and development and by the adoption of growth management policy in recent years. In contrast, governments that did not incorporate a model were characterized by uncertainty about future growth and the lack of a growth management policy (Table 6.6). Thus it appears that a major difference between incorporated and non-incorporated sites is the extent to which the model was used to decide development policy versus to work out the details of development policy that had already been decided. Sites that incorporated a model, appear to have used fiscal analysis primarily as a tool for scheduling the amount, kind and timing of urban development, whereas sites that did not incorporate a model appear to have used fiscal analysis primarily for deciding whether development should occur, or, for deciding the overall pattern of development.

While conflict over development policy might be high in either instance, and indeed appears to have been high in all the sites studied (Table 6.6), the political stakes involved in deciding development policy are likely to be considerably higher than those involved in growth management within established policy. Consequently, the information produced by fiscal analysis is likely to be only one input to development policy-making—and a minor one at that. It might be that in such instances, fiscal analysis simply was found to be an inadequate aid to decision making and was abandoned rather than incorporated into the local government's decision processes.

TABLE 6.6. Agreement Over Development Policy in the Government, By Incorporated and Nonincorporated Sites

Development Policy Environment	Mean Score Indicating Agreement with the Statement					
	Incorporated A Model		Did Not Incorporate A Model		F Statistic	Significance Level
	Mean Score	*N*	Mean Score	*N*		
Overall, there is more consensus than conflict over development issues among the planning bodies in the government.	1.72	9	1.70	11	.02	.89
In general, future course of urban growth and development during the period of time in which fiscal impact analyses were being conducted was more certain than uncertain.	1.63	9	1.34	11	3.94	.06*
This government had adopted growth management policies in the last few years.	1.83	9	1.45	11	4.72	.04*

NOTES

1. All of the models in our study were adopted in the mid-late 1970s, with the most frequent number of adoptions (eight) occurring in 1978—the year that California's Proposition 13 was enacted. Only three of the eight cities that adopted fiscal impact models in 1978 were in California. However, Proposition 13 received much national publicity and attention and, therefore, might have provided a stimulus for other local governments to pay increasing attention to the costs and revenues of urban development.
   At the time, in 1978, fiscal impact models appeared to be "taking off" as an innovation. The enactment of Proposition 13 in California and similar measures in other states was viewed positively by model developers as an impetus to more carefully conducted cost and revenue studies. Yet, the growth of modeling, like most other local government activities, was dampened in the wake of the budget cutbacks that ensued from the tax limitation measures. By 1980, only 21 governments had adopted one of the four models in our study, and each government adopted one model.
2. This pattern of primarily local funding is consistent with the pattern of funding for other local efforts involving the introduction of computerized systems (Perry & Kraemer, 1978; Danziger & Dutton, 1977) and, generally, with the adoption of other management and planning innovations by local governments (Lambright, 1977; Yin et al., 1976).
3. In considering these resource expenditures, it is important to recall that, generally, the models were already developed—they were more or less "packaged products" that could be transferred without the costs of developing them anew. Of course, the transfer costs might include a purchase price for the model, but this price tends to be small proportion of the total transfer cost. On this basis, the direct dollar cost of acquiring a fiscal impact model and making it ready for an operational run in our sites ranged from less than $10,000 to over $100,000. Ten of the models were transferred for between $25,000 and $100,000; seven were transferred for under $25,000; and one for over $100,000.
   These direct costs usually consisted mainly of the model vendor's time for assisting in adaptation of the model, but also could include travel, the purchase price of the model, and administrative expenses. The model vendors' time for adaptation was generally around five person-months. However, the vendor's time usually represented only 1/4 to 1/3 of the total person-months devoted to model adaptation. Local government staff spent from 12 to 14 person-months working with the model vendor, getting data for the model, participating in training on operation and use of the model, and otherwise preparing the model for its first operational runs.
4. Although the characteristics of their preferred development vary over time and in different locations, generally it tends to be the kind of development most current decision participants prefer: higher income (higher social class) housing, open space, retail commercial/office activity, and light (preferably high-technology) industry. Thus the models tend to be supported by politicians, planners, current residents, and developers. The only question for

most of these participants is how much of the various land-use activities should be provided. Developers might prefer one mix; residents usually another; planners and politicians usually line up on one side or the other, or in between. Sometimes politicians, planners or residents might want to throw in "inclusionary housing" requirements and to balance off the other land use activities to pay for such subsidized housing.

5. For example, two relatively recent and significant scholarly books define modeling in this narrow technical fashion. William Ascher (1978, p. 210) does so in passing:

> Future developments in forecast methodology in all areas will be influenced by "modeling," the mathematical expression of structural relationships between the forecasted trend and other factors.

Greenberger, Crenson and Crissey (1976, p. 47) give the subject more extensive but similar treatment:

> Having discussed the setting for policy modeling in the last chapter, we will now proceed to consider the modeling process itself. Here the model is the thing. Taking a tutorial approach, we will inspect the model on a most basic level, beginning with the fundamental question,"What is it?" In attempting to answer this question, we will review a wide variety of different kinds of models.
>
> A model is like a tripod. The three legs on which it depends for its support, balance, and soundness are theory, data and methodology. We will examine the vital roles played by each of these three elements in determining how models are conceived and put together. [Actually discussed in a section entitled: "The modeling process: theory, data and methodology." Note the similarity to the use of the term by Ascher.]
>
> Last in our consideration of the modeling process, yet first in importance, is the modeler and his relationship to the model. The modeler not only builds and runs the model, he affects the way it is received by emphasizing its strengths and points of interest and by compensating for its weaknesses and vulnerabilities.

7. Consensus as an Impact of Modeling

Modeling appears to be far more a political process than is portrayed in a literature more often focused on model building than model use. The preceding chapters have described the frequent conflicts—differences of opinions, beliefs, and interests—among the wide array of participants involved with the introduction, adaptation, and incorporation of models into the policy arena. These conflicts tend to require a level of bargaining and compromise that contrasts with many of the stereotypes of a technical, analytical process.

That modeling is often a highly political process, however, does not mean that it is necessarily a partisan process. At times, modeling has been a political tool used to reinforce a particular partisan position. It is, as Chapter 6 indicates, a more pluralistic, and hence somewhat less narrowly partisan, process than is suggested by most journalistic accounts and behavioral studies of policy modeling. It's a process that is seldom controlled by a particular group of elites because the implementation of policy models offers multiple points of access to groups and interests. There exist such a multitude of points at which participants can block or delay the progress of the modeling effort that one group or individual is seldom able to dominate and single-handedly control the process.

An adequate characterization of the politics of modeling requires an answer to the question "who is served" as well as a consideration of who controls the modeling process. Pluralistic control over the modeling process doesn't necessarily indicate that a pluralistic array of groups and interests will be served.[1] In fact, the pluralism of the modeling process might lead to its failure as a technical, analytical aid to decision making; and, in that sense, modeling might serve no one but those interested in blocking or delaying action.[2] Alternatively, some groups might be ineffectual. Also, if many groups and interests are left out of the modeling process, as in the case of North City West development, their interests might or might not be affected by the outcomes. Finally, the modeling process or a particular class of models might be biased towards the interests of particular political elites, policy analysts, or community groups.

This chapter describes the consequences of fiscal impact modeling in an attempt to more broadly define whose interests are served. Admittedly, this assessment must be less direct than a description of participants in the modeling process: the interests of groups and individuals are neither clear nor simple. Nevertheless, by describing the major consequences of computer-based fiscal impact models in American cities, alternative perspectives on the modeling process can be assessed because each perspective implies different outcomes. Here these expectations are briefly reviewed. Then, the impacts of modeling, based on the preceptions of participants, will be described in order to reflect back on these perspectives in light of the empirical findings.

PERSPECTIVES ON INTEREST SERVED

The alternative political perspectives on the role of models in the policy process suggest that different groups and interests are likely to be served by models. Since models as information are a potential political resource much like expertise, status, or positional authority, they might be used to frustrate or support the policy and professional objectives of various participants in both the bureaucracy and larger community. From the *rational perspective,* modeling is expected to serve the organizations' and community's interest because the technology is not used as a political resource. Instead, it is used as a neutral, analytical tool for providing better access to new and qualitatively improved information. Modeling is controlled by modelers—policy analysts, planners, and other experts assigned the technical task of implementing the model. The rational perspective suggests that modeling will not systematically favor any narrow group or interest either within the bureaucracy or the larger community affected by the results of modeling.

The *partisan perspective* suggests a substantially different set of expectations. From this perspective, modeling is expected to be a political tool in the most traditional sense. That is, models will be used to support and to reinforce the interests of the dominant coalition of interests within the organization and community. If this is the case, modeling should tend to systematically favor the interests of certain powerful groups. A bias will, however, be difficult to discern because the influence of various groups and interests is likely to differ across cities in ways that are difficult to anticipate. Hence, the analysis will identify particular interests served by modeling within a particular city or across the communities in our study. In local governments, the partisan perspective suggests that modeling will tend to favor and to reinforce the interests of the most powerful groups. In the bureaucracy, modeling would be likely to serve the interests of the chief executive, top managers, and their staff rather than those of the local legislators, technical experts, and policy analysts in the various operating and administrative departments. In the broader community, modeling would serve the interests of higher socioeconomic groups such as upper-income homeowners over the interests of low-income renters.

From the technocratic perspective, modeling is controlled by the modelers, those who understand how to use models. This perspective views models as a political resource, one dominated by technical experts and used to support and reinforce their interests and opinions. Models will tend to shift more power and influence to the information elite. In the case of urban fiscal impact models, the technocratic perspective suggests that urban planners, analysts, and administrative staff charged with implementing the models will be systematically benefitted by the modeling effort.

The *consensual perspective* suggests that modeling will be used to support negotiations among a pluralistic array of participants in the policy process. Therefore, modeling should not tend to systematically favor any special interest group in the bureaucracy or community. Instead, the interests served by modeling should vary with the balance of power among competing interests both over time and across communities. Both directly and indirectly, models should tend to facilitate negotiation, compromise, and bargaining among contestants in the policy process. This chapter suggests exactly that. Modeling tends to support consensual decision making by defining problems, informing participants, setting criteria of choice, setting decision agendas, constraining the scope of conflict, legitimating decisions, symbolizing rationality, and involving contestants.

ASSESSING INTERESTS SERVED

This chapter assessed the interests served by modeling by examining the perceptions, opinions, and attitudes of the local elected and appointed officials, managers, and staff surveyed in the 21 jurisdictions that had adopted one of the four selected fiscal impact models. User perceptions are likely to vary from an objective observer's account. Participants' images are formed by advertisements, claims, counter-claims, and rumors. Moreover, these images are colored by their political interests and preferences as much as by the actual structure, dynamics, and performance

TABLE 7.1. Perceived Success of Modeling Process[a]

Question: Overall, the use of this computer-based fiscal impact analysis was a success.	Politicians (%)[b]	Bureaucrats (%)[c]	Technocrats (%)[d]	All Respondents(%)
Strongly disagree	6	0	7	5
Disagree	12	16	11	13
Undecided	19	12	17	16
Agree	49	60	51	52
Strongly agree	14	12	14	14
Total	100%	100%	100%	100%
N	49	25	43	117

[a]Chi-square not significant at .05 level.

[b]Politicians include elected officials and politically appointed citizen and interest group representatives.

[c]Bureaucrats include department heads, managers, and administrators.

[d]Technocrats include planners, budget analysts, and model specialists.

of a model. Yet, perceptions of models and their impacts are likely to have a major influence on the role of models in the policy process. As an early study of modeling suggests:

> The image of models, especially their technical image, has been as important as their technical characteristics and performance record in determining their role in policy. (Greenberger, Crenson & Crissey, 1976, p. 92)

This is an especially useful observation for this study, where the performance record of computer-based fiscal impact models appeared rather poor. While such models generally are appropriate technical solutions to the problems of fiscal impact analysis, few local governments have actually introduced them. And even fewer governments had successfully incorporated them into their ongoing planning process.

Despite some objective indications of failure, most participants (citizens, developers, elected officials, managers, analysts) in the field survey judged their modeling efforts to be successful. The users of computer-based fiscal impact models were asked if, "overall, the use of [this] computer-based fiscal impact analysis was a success." About two-thirds of the respondents (66%) generally believed that the use of computer-based fiscal analyses in their jurisdiction was a success (Table 7.1). While there is a significant variation in perceived success, fewer than one in ten respondents strongly disagreed with the view that modeling was successful. Although bureaucrats are somewhat more likely to perceive models a success, this general support for the value of fiscal impact modeling is shared by politicians, bureaucrats, and technocrats alike.

This positive view of computer-based fiscal impact models is reflected in other responses. Nearly three-fourths (73%) of the users believed that the jurisdiction's fiscal impact analyses should be continued (Table 7.2). Only one of ten respondents believed the model should be "discontinued." Fully 92 percent of the respondents believed that fiscal analysis should be a routine function of the local government. This general support is reinforced by the view that the cost of the analyses is justified in the minds of most users. Only 15 percent of the respondents believed computer-based fiscal analyses "cost too much" (Table 7.2).

This perceived success of the modeling efforts in particular led to the search for a new perspective on the politics of modeling. Current perspectives on modeling in the policy process fail to describe adequately the role of modeling, and thereby create the perception that modeling has failed to contribute to the policy process, when in fact, participants view this contribution positively.

This chapter shows that models are perceived to be a rather influential force in resolving conflicts over public policy. Also, the perceptions of participants regarding the impacts of models are described. In doing so, the impacts of modeling are described in relation to the interests of various community groups. The politics of the bureaucracy are then explored as it affects the interests of executives, legislators, managers, and analysts.

THE INFLUENCE OF MODELING

Models are expected to affect the politics of the community and bureaucracy because modeling seems to resolve conflict over the nature and consequences of public policy. As discussed in relation to North City West and San Diego's growth management plan, modeling can have a powerful role in resolving conflict by virtue of its use in negotiating decisions as well as nondecisions. Are such impacts limited to a few unusual cases, or are these impacts more generally perceived?

The following tables present the survey responses grouped by the perceived quality of data and forecasts, their comprehensibility, and their information benefits. In most cases, respondents recorded their agreement with each statement as it is related to their personal experience in their own city. As the tables illustrate, the perceived characteristics of fiscal

TABLE 7.2 Support for Fiscal Analyses and Modeling

	Item	Strongly Disagree	Disagree	Undecided	Agree	Strongly Agree	Total	*N*
17.	The use of this computer based fiscal impact analysis model should be discontinued by this local government.	36	37	15	6	6	100%	120
18.	Fiscal analysis should be a routine function within this local government.	0	3	5	50	42	100%	123
19.	Computer-based fiscal analyses cost too much.	17	36	32	10	5	100%	122

impact models vary across respondents. This disparity is itself an important finding, but there are notable tendencies that can be discerned in respect to each attribute. Overall, most respondents viewed models as credible sources of information even though the process itself is seen as political rather than purely analytical.

Quality of Data and Forecasts

Most respondents believed that the input data required for model implementation were more or less accurate, as were the output data or forecasts. The old cliche "garbage in, garbage out" doesn't seem to be the verdict of most respondents. Table 7.3 shows that on a scale from one through seven, ranging from accurate to inaccurate, most respondents rated the input data for the fiscal impact models in the highest three categories of accuracy. However, a significant (and recurring) minority of about one-third of the respondents disagreed and rated the data as more or less inaccurate. Perceptions of accuracy were mixed, rather than uniformly positive.

There is little difference in perceived accuracy with the exception of one category among the categories of input data. Input data about the "costs" of services were perceived to be somewhat less accurate than input data about revenues, population, or land-use. While this difference is small, it reflects the fact that local governments routinely record data about revenues, population, and land-use. In contrast, cost accounting and program budgeting are widely advocated and are becoming more widespread practices. Still, few governments currently record cost-data concerning the cost of sprawl, or growth, or increased population density.[3]

The value attached to model forecasts is somewhat mixed as well (Table 7.3). In fact, more respondents were wary of model forecasts than of the original input data. Almost two-thirds (61–63%) of the respondents tended to rate the model forecasts as useful, complete, believable, and reliable (rating them in the top three categories on the seven-point scale). Perceptions were more mixed regarding the clarity and realism of the forecasts. The forecasts were rated least positively in terms of their bias and accuracy. Less than half (45%) of the respondents rated the models as "unbiased." Only about one-third (35%) rated the models as accurate (again, defined as the top three categories of response). Fifty-eight percent of the respondents rated the models in the lowest three categories of accuracy. These perceptions suggest that lay policy officials and professional staff have educated or intuitive doubts about the accuracy and bias of forecasts, and yet, they are generally supportive of the analysis.

For the most part, the analyses were credible enough that they were neither hotly contested nor disregarded. Generally people seemed to have

TABLE 7.3. ***Perceived Quality of Input Data and Forecasts***

Quality of Information	Lowest 1	2	3	4	5	6	Highest 7	Total	*N*
39. Quality of input data:									
a. Input data about *costs of services*	3	5	16	12	26	30	8	100%	123
b. Input data about *revenues*	2	4	7	11	28	32	16	100%	123
c. Input data about *population*	2	2	6	8	26	40	16	100%	124
d. Input data about *land use*	2	3	5	11	24	40	15	100%	124
40. Quality of forecasts:									
a. Accuracy[a]	7	26	25	7	21	12	2	100%	122
b. Clarity[a]	1	11	20	14	22	18	14	100%	122
c. Usefulness	4	7	7	19	21	30	12	100%	122
d. Completeness[a]	2	11	11	15	29	23	9	100%	122
e. Believability[a]	3	7	14	15	29	23	9	100%	122
f. Reliability	3	8	10	16	31	27	5	100%	122
g. Realism	4	6	8	23	25	29	5	100%	122
h. Unbiased[a]	3	8	20	24	8	18	19	100%	121

[a]Question wording and scoring has been reflected.

accepted the forecasts generated (Table 7.4). This said, a full third of the respondents (30%) noted that the analyses were hotly contested. A bare majority (53%) believed that many people accepted these forecasts as their view of reality. Still, they were generally not ignored. Less than one-fifth (17%) of the respondents believed that the forecasts were disregarded by policy makers.

Given that most local government decisions are relatively routine, incremental, and non-controversial, the fact that 29 percent of the respondents believed that the results of model analyses were "hotly contested" might indicate a relatively high level of controversy. While only 17 percent of the respondents believed that the findings of analyses were disregarded by policy makers, another 24 percent were undecided. Likewise, only about 54 percent of the respondents believed that people accepted the model's forecasts "as their view of reality." Almost as many respondents were undecided or of the opposite opinion. Thus, on the one hand, computer-based fiscal impact analyses were judged to be a success and are perceived as credible to most respondents. The forecasts could not be or were not disregarded. On the other hand, from one-half to one-third believed that the model lacked credibility, accuracy, or neutrality. In short, questionable forecasts became a force and a rather legitimate force to contend with in the minds of most respondents.

Comprehensibility

The influence of computer models might be contingent on their comprehensibility. People would be unlikely to be guided by an incomprehensible model unless they held a great deal of faith in the modelers, the process, or the outcomes of the analysis. Certainly, comprehensibility has been a concern to those designing and using models as well as other computer-based information systems (Brewer, 1973; Greenberger, Crenson and Crissey, 1976; Wiezenbaum, 1976). Ironically, computers permit incomprehensible models to be built, in that computer programs can handle more variables, calculations, and data elements than any single person could fully comprehend. Also, the difficulties and urgencies of model development can focus early modeling efforts on programming rather than on clearly documenting systems. In some cases, clear and readable documentation becomes a luxury to invest in after the model development process winds down. Many respondents believed that model analyses were not well understood (Table 7.4). Less than half of the respondents (42%) believed that elected officials understood the assumptions underlying the analyses. Less than one-third (30%) believed that community groups understood these assumptions. More generally, half of our respondents (50%) believed that the analyses were "incomprehensible to many people"

TABLE 7.4. ***Beliefs and Attitudes About Modeling***

Question: **Please indicate the degree to which you agree or disagree with each of the following statements.**	**Strongly Disagree**	**Disagree**	**Undecided**	**Agree**	**Strongly Agree**	**Total**	***N***
Credibility of Analyses							
2. The results of this model analysis were hotly contested.	10	52	8	23	7	100%	119
10. Many people accepted the forecasts generated by this model as their view of reality	2	27	18	44	9	100%	119
6c. Generally, the findings of analyses conducted with this model were disregarded by the policy makers.	16	43	24	11	6	100%	121
Comprehensibility							
14. Elected officials understood the assumptions underlying these analyses.	9	30	19	36	6	100%	117
16. Community groups understood the assumptions underlying these analyses.	8	30	32	23	7	100%	118
1g. Generally, analyses conducted with this model were incomprehensible to many people.	6	29	15	37	13	100%	123

(Table 7.4). The fact that many participants lack a full understanding of models might undermine the credibility of the analyses and help explain some reservations about the model data and forecasts.

Information Benefits

Models were expected to make better information available to decision-makers. In most of the case study sites, this was a common perception. Generally, most respondents attributed a number of information benefits to the models (Table 7.5). Specifically, almost three-fourths (70%) of our respondents believed that the model analyses answered important questions: only 15 percent disagreed with such a claim. Fewer people, but still most (59%), believed the model challenged preconceived notions about the fiscal impacts of development. For example, in several cities, developers were surprised by the fiscal deficits of development. Whether or not people's perceptions were challenged, the models clearly stimulated discussion, according to 86 percent of the respondents. In addition, they were perceived useful to experts as well as non-experts and were thought to have taught people more about the conduct of fiscal analyses. In these ways, modeling was perceived to provide a qualitatively better base of information for decision makers (still, in other respects, such as the accuracy of forecasts, the information is called into question). In doing so, they might lead to more agreement over the likely fiscal impacts of development and help clarify differences of opinion (Table 7.5). At least this was the opinion of most respondents. Here again, however, about one-fifth disagreed, suggesting that the models were not associated with more agreement or a clarification of differences of opinion. These informational benefits are consistent with the perceptions of the usefulness of the model forecasts and the general credibility of the analysis in that attitudes were somewhat mixed but more often positive than negative.

The informational benefits are important because they might facilitate consensus among contestants in the policy process and thereby support decision making. These benefits derive from the tendency for models to *define problems* as well as *inform participants*.

Models tend to define and structure problems. Indeed, models are sought by planners because urban planning problems tend to be relatively nonroutine and unstructured. Models provide structure to urban planning problems in two ways. First, they structure the choice process; that is, they necessitate development of a working definition of the current "state-of-nature," the exact alternatives being considered, a forecast of future conditions, a forecast of the consequences of the alternatives, and a set of specific criteria for assessing the alternatives. While substantial, this choice structure imposed by models is not new to the planning process.

TABLE 7.5. Perceived Informational Consequences

Question: **Please indicate the degree to which you agree or disagree with each of the following statements.**	**Strongly Disagree**	**Disagree**	**Undecided**	**Agree**	**Strongly Agree**	**Total**	***N***
6a. Generally, the findings of analyses conducted with this model answered important questions.	4	11	15	56	14	100%	122
6b. Generally, the findings of analyses conducted with this model challenged preconceived notions about the fiscal impacts of development.	4	20	17	47	12	100%	121
5b. Overall, the use of this model stimulated discussion over development policies.	2	7	5	63	23	100%	120
1e. Generally, the analyses conducted with this model were useful to those with expertise in local government fiscal matters.	4	10	10	53	23	100%	122

1f.	Generally, the analyses conducted with this model were useful to those with *no* expertise in local government fiscal matters.	7	10	22	51	10	100%	120
5e.	Overall, the use of this model taught people more about how fiscal impact analyses are conducted.	8	12	11	51	18	100%	123
4.	After using this model, there was much more agreement about the probable fiscal impacts of a development being studied.	4	12	13	57	14	100%	115
5a.	Overall, the use of this model helped to clarify differences of opinion surrounding development issues.	4	18	19	51	8	100%	118

It has always characterized planning—with or without models and computers. However, the second way in which models give structure to planning problems *is new* (since the 1950s), and important. Models provide a theoretical and substantive framework to planning problems. In particular, fiscal impact models systematically specify quantitative relationships between land-use and governmental costs and revenues and, when supplied with empirical data, simulate the year-to-year fiscal profitability of development alternatives. Because their structure is explicit, such models facilitate understanding of the general problem and the particular definition embedded in the model. By giving structure to planning problems, models concretize problems and relevant policy alternatives and, thereby, might simplify policy making for many participants.

Models inform participants in policy making beyond the understanding provided by the model's structure of a problem. By improving the accuracy of data, and speeding-up calculating tasks, models can provide an improved base of decision information and facilitate the participants' comparison of the fiscal impacts of development alternatives. Such information consistently affected policy deliberations in the cases studied. Information supplied by Anaheim's modeling effort was instrumental in leading to the proposal for inclusion of a shopping center in the Bauer Ranch project as a means of making the development profitable to the City. In San Diego, the modeling process informed participants about the practical limits on the City's ability to redirect or manage growth. That is, it showed earlier assumptions about the effectiveness of growth management strategies were unrealistic because they forecast the development of land whose topography or ownership patterns made in-fill (development of vacant land areas close-in to the central city) impossible or unlikely. And in Tulsa, final analyses of alternative growth strategies indicated that there were only marginal differences in their overall fiscal impacts. In every case study site, fiscal impact modeling generated information that was either unknown or unexpected prior to the modeling effort. Considered cumulatively, the information provided to participants educated them about modeling and about the planning problem they sought to resolve. Consistent with this thrust of the case studies, most users perceived the models to have been informative, despite some reservations regarding their accuracy and bias.

Such educational impacts have been noted in other modeling studies. For example, Brewer (1973) suggested that the educational functions of modeling were among the most important outcomes of the process. Similarly, our survey found that the most common perception was that model analysis stimulated discussion over development policies. In this way models might have indirect as well as direct informational benefits by encouraging more information seeking. Also, there was only a slight tendency for fiscal impact models to be perceived as more useful to those with expertise in local government fiscal matters than to those without such expertise. Generally, models were perceived as informative to both groups of users.

These perceptions of the information benefits of models tended to support the notion of consensus-building, a political function of models that was suggested by the case studies. Models might help participants arrive at a broader consensus by reducing conflict and uncertainty over some informational issues. Models structure problems and questions, answer some questions, lead to more agreement over fiscal impacts, and clarify differences of opinion. This consensus-building, conflict-resolution role of computer models might well describe the perceived uses and impacts of computer-based fiscal impact models. Models might play this role by virtue of their use to persuade contestants and legitimate policies to the general public.

Persuasion

In several case studies, models were successfully used in persuading people to form or change their position on development policy. Certainly, more, better, or even contradictory information does not necessarily affect policy positions or choices. Such choices are shaped by a variety of non-informational factors such as the values and interests of decision makers. We cannot expect better information regarding the fiscal impacts of development to necessarily shape or alter development policies since other factors play important roles in shaping policy choices. Yet, this is an intended impact of models and potentially a factor contributing to their political relevance. Models are more likely to be persuasive if they are perceived to be accurate, credible, comprehensible, and informative. Most users did perceive them to have such qualities, although opinions were mixed.

Despite such reservations and the mixed opinions regarding the value of particular models, the respondents perceived the models to be influential in persuading people to form or change their position on development policy (Table 7.6). Over 60 percent believed that results of the model analyses directly affected development decisions. This does not mean that the models necessarily changed decisions; less than half (42%) of the respondents believed the analyses persuaded people to *change* their position on an important issue (Table 7.6).

The pattern of responses suggests an interesting paradox. On the one hand, there is uncertainty across users regarding the quality of these models. On the other hand, there is a general belief that these models played an influential role in the policy process—clarifying differences of opinion, and affecting decision.

TABLE 7.6. Perceived Impacts of Models

Question: **Please indicate the degree to which you agree or disagree with each of the following statements:**	**Strongly Disagree**	**Disagree**	**Undecided**	**Agree**	**Strongly Agree**	**Total**	***N***
1a. Generally, the analyses conducted with this model persuaded people to change their position on an important issue.	5	35	18	32	10	100%	116
11a. The results of the model analyses directly affected development decisions of this local government.	4	18	16	52	10	100%	115
Legitimation							
1b. Generally, the analyses conducted with this model substantiated the claims of some public officials and staff.	4	8	7	68	13	100%	120
1c. Generally, the analyses conducted with this model reinforced the views of the most influential policy makers in this local government.	4	17	22	48	9	100%	118
11b. The results of the model analyses directly supported development decisions that already had been made.	5	19	28	42	6	100%	114
8. Some public officials used the results of this model analysis to persuade others.	2	9	16	61	12	100%	115

Legitimation

In several cases, such as in promoting San Diego's growth management plan, models are used in an information campaign to legitimate the policy preferences of a dominant coalition of public officials and interest groups. Several perceptions of the survey respondents lend support to this expectation. About 80 percent of the respondents believed the analyses "substantiated the claims of some public officials and staff" and a majority (57%) believed the findings reinforced the views of the most influential policy makers (Table 7.6).[4]

The legitimation of dominant policy positions is reflected also in the fact that 48 percent of respondents agreed that the models supported decisions that had already been made. Moreover, when models were perceived to reinforce decisions, such effects were viewed as intentional. About three-fourths of the respondents believed the models were used by some officials to persuade others (Table 7.6).

The modeling process tends to be iterative and interactive (Chapter 6). Seldom does the first run of a model provide an adequate basis for understanding or negotiating policy agreement. Rather, agreement evolves through the use of multiple model runs that sequentially narrow the alternatives to a range acceptable to the participants. As a result, policy agreement occurs prior to the final model analyses being completed. In this respect, final model analyses tend to legitimate decisions that have already been made. This is not to say, however, that models fail to help officials decide among alternatives. Rather, it suggest that models tend to have subtle persuasive effects and that modeling is itself affected by negotiation and bargaining among the participants and by the broader political environment of the policy making process.

The results of model analyses tend to legitimate non-decisions as well as decisions. Non-decisions are illustrated by explicit decisions not to decide something, and by implicit choice of what things to include or exclude in decision making (Bachrach & Baratz, 1970). They are decisions nevertheless in that failure to decide something usually means continuation of current policies, practices, or trends; similarly, consistent inclusion (or exclusion) of certain participants, criteria, or alternatives in decision making constitutes an implicit choice favoring what is included over what is excluded. Such non-decisions abounded in our fiscal impact modeling cases. For example, the decision to develop North City West was indirectly supported by the fact that the growth management study incorporated North City West development in every growth scenario that was examined. Similarly, every scenario examined in San Diego assumed a continuing high rate of growth; the prospect of alternative growth rates was never considered. Thus, growth was legitimated as a non-decision by the growth management study.

In many respects, the legitimation of non-decisions is a natural outcome of any process that simplifies decision making. In structuring and defining problems, as models tend to do, there is a natural tendency to hold constant those factors about which there is broad consensus. As a consequence, important non-decisions are frequently built into the modeling process and into the models themselves.

POLICY IMPACTS AND COMMUNITY INTERESTS

Most respondents perceive models to be credible, informative, and persuasive in the public policy process. What difference has this made on the outcomes of the policy process? Have simply better decisions been made? Or, have some groups and interests been systematically and differentially affected?

Some policy positions appear to fare better than others with respect to their fiscal impacts and therefore tend to be systematically reinforced by the use of such computer models. In this way, some groups and interests generally gain while others tend to lose as a consequence of the use of computer models.

The conventional wisdom is that fiscal impact models are partisan political tools. More concretely, the use of fiscal impact models is said to block development that is subsidized by public expenditures for roads and other infrastructures. Used in this way, fiscal analyses might promote exclusionary zoning policies. That is, modeling serves the preferences and interests of homeowner groups that wish to block the development of low-income rental housing. Those who pay as a consequence are the low-income groups and renters competing for less housing and the neighboring jurisdictions likely to absorb a disproportionate share of the costs of subsidizing more low-income housing.[5]

However, the case studies cast some doubt into these expectations of a uniform bias. The cases suggested that models were malleable tools in that local implementation decisions seemed to shape the outcome of the analyses. Fiscal impact models were found to support a variety of positions. Models supported growth managers in San Diego, environmentalists in Anaheim, and developers in Tulsa. Maybe there are not systematic biases tied to the use of these models independent of the values and interests of those that use these tools.

In several respects, the survey responses endorsed the rather malleable role of computer-based fiscal impact models in the politics of growth policy. A somewhat larger proportion of respondents indicated a pro-growth versus anti-growth orientation of the models, which counters prevailing expectations. This pro-growth outcome is by no means uniform. About one-third of the respondents indicated that analyses did not support the fiscal profitability of a proposed development, while about half (53%) of the respondents indicated that analyses supported the profitability of a proposed development (Table 7.7).[6] What is important—more so than the majority position—is the variation across respondents and cities as well. The models appear malleable.

A more pronounced impact on growth politics might be the kinds of development that are supported by the models. Respondents believed the models tended to support industrial and commercial developments, and not support low-rent housing developments (Table 7.8). Whether they support population growth or greater population density seems to depend on the nature of the development. In short, fiscal impact models have been implemented for the most part in ways that support a variety of growth policies, but also, and more importantly, more fiscally profitable growth patterns, which tend to be exclusionary in their social impacts.

This support for exclusionary policies is critical because most local governments tend to follow the most fiscally profitable course of action. In nearly every city, fiscal impact analyses tend to show one alternative to be more fiscally profitable. Tulsa, of course, represents one of the possible exceptions. And, according to our respondents, this fiscally profitable alternative is the course that either has been taken or is most likely to be taken.

So, in general, a political bias of fiscal impact analyses is evidenced in the results of modeling. Lower-income residents and renters might be systematically disadvantaged by the use of computer-based fiscal impact models. In this way, models might affect the distribution of benefits.

There might also be less direct and less intentional ways in which modeling will differentially affect the outcomes of interest group politics in local communities. Generally, models might further disadvantage citizen-based interest groups vis-a-vis the government, and resource-poor versus resource-rich interest groups that cannot marshall the resources and expertise to contest the results of governmental analyses (Lupo, Colcord & Fowler, 1971).[7] Indeed, the case studies suggest that models are primarily a government-owned and -controlled medium. They generally are not citizen-group technologies, unless such groups are supporters of the local government position. In Tulsa, for example, the Chamber of Commerce began to see the city's model as a potential resource to promote their own preferences for more balanced growth.

In this respect, computer models might be a potent resource because the credibility of such analyses could make it more difficult for opposition groups to dispute.[8] However, our survey respondents' perceptions were mixed in this regard. First, nearly three-fourths (71%) of the respondents noted that some community groups were able to use the analyses to strengthen their position (Table 7.9). Second, only about one-third believed that model analysis made it more difficult for community groups to dispute

TABLE 7.7. ***The Perceived Results of Analyses***

Question: **Please indicate the degree to which you agree or disagree with the following statement:**	**Role of Respondent**			**All respondents**
	Politicians	**Bureaucrats**	**Technocrats**	
1d. Generally, the analyses conducted with this model indicated that a proposed development would be fiscally profitable for this local government.				
Strongly disagree	16	4	11	12
Disagree	18	35	14	20
Undecided	13	13	17	15
Agree	46	26	30	36
Strongly Agree	7	22	28	17
Total	100%	100%	100%	100%
N	43	23	36	104

TABLE 7.8. Impacts on Development Policy

Question: **Please indicate the degree to which you agree or disagree with the following statement:**	**Discouraged**	**Somewhat Discouraged**	**Neither**	**Somewhat Encouraged**	**Encouraged**	**Total**	***N***
42. Did the analyses conducted with this model encourage or discourage any of the following kinds of development?							
A. Industrial development	4	6	42	28	20	100%	109
B. Commercial development	2	4	27	26	41	100%	112
C. Higher density development	5	17	33	33	12	100%	113
D. Low-rent housing development	16	22	51	10	1	100%	106
E. Population growth	10	20	47	18	5	100%	111

TABLE 7.9. Model Utilization and Interest Group Politics

Question: **Please indicate the degree to which you agree or disagree with the following statement.**	**Strongly Disagree**	**Disagree**	**Undecided**	**Agree**	**Strongly Agree**	**Total**	***N***
Interest Group Politics							
3. This model was used by some community groups to strengthen their position.	2	15	12	55	16	100%	113
5c. Overall, the use of this model made it difficult for community groups to dispute the findings.	4	38	25	27	6	100%	112
5d. Overall, the use of this model lowered the credibility of emotional appeals about development.	9	25	22	42	2	100%	116
Agenda Setting							
7a. Since this model was adopted, this local government has focused more attention on the fiscal impacts of development.	3	16	15	50	16	100%	123
7b. Since this model was adopted, fiscal impact analyses are conducted more often.	4	21	21	38	16	100%	120

5f.	The use of computer-based fiscal analyses deflected attention from social or environmental issues that are not fiscal in nature.	5	49	22	16	8	100%	115
	Legitimate Technique							
9.	Since this model was used, people are less likely to accept the findings of less sophisticated analyses.	3	36	24	31	6	100%	116
	Legitimate Technicians							
12a.	The use of computer-based fiscal analyses has made us more dependent on experts.	6	49	24	20	1	100%	119
12b.	The use of computer-based fiscal analyses led to hiring more people with technical expertise.	10	43	16	29	2	100%	117
	Inter-Departmental Cooperation							
13.	In general, the use of computer-based fiscal impact analysis led several departments to work more closely together.	3	18	21	43	15	100%	117

the findings (Table 8.9). Yet almost half (44%) of the respondents believed that the use of this model lowered the credibility of emotional appeals about development. In part, these mixed views might be due to the mixed nature of these impacts. That is, such impacts might truly vary across jurisdictions and groups within communities. San Diego's analyses strengthened the city's position and the eventual position of the development community while the analyses weakened the position and emotional appeals of North City West and Del Mar residents opposed to nearby high density development. Community groups and interests were differently affected.

In this respect, models affect interest group politics by tending to constrain the scope of conflict in several ways. First, models create new "standards of evidence." The impact of emotional appeals and back-of-the-envelope calculations can be easily discredited or their impacts lessened by the explicit, rigorous quantitative results of large-scale modeling studies. While few survey participants (who took part in the modeling process) perceived that the models were used to undermine emotional appeals and less sophisticated analyses, the case studies provide evidence that this occurred. In Anaheim, modeling was used to quash the Vista del Rio incorporation attempt by 40 homeowners; it also was used to beat down a counter-modeling effort by the developer of Anaheim Hills. In all of the cases studied, there generally were no alternative analyses to compete with the city's modeling efforts; therefore, discussion and debate had to occur on the city's terms.

Models constrain the scope of conflict in a second way: namely, they set the "credentials for influence" in policy making. By altering the techniques used for analyzing the impacts of planning alternatives, modeling affects which participants are involved and which participants are left out of final policy making over planning issues. Participants get credentials from the act of participation; they know and understand the techniques; they know what went on in the modeling process. Non-participants do not. Thus, influence in the policy making process seems to require prior participation in the adaptation phase of model implementation. Those left out of the adaptation phase are not only left out of influencing the outcomes of the model analyses, but they are also likely to be at a much greater disadvantage in supporting their policy positions in various forums.

Much of the literature critical of modeling predicts that it will centralize control over decision making in the hands of small groups of technical experts who are influential because they determine what information is supplied to policy makers. However, we found that technical experts were seldom the sole participants in the modeling process; participants included developers, citizens, politicians, managers, and many others. While certain technical tasks and overall coordination of the participatory process might be centralized in the hands of technical experts, control over decision making was not. Moreover, the experts frequently sought to broaden the basis of participation and to anticipate the reactions of proximate and other participants. They employed citizen committees to test the reactions of various groups and interests to their decisions and recommendations. They also consulted broadly with various departmental bureaucrats and elected officials to assure that their decisions were sensitive to a broad array of people concerned with the outcome of the analyses. Thus, by virtue of the experts' anticipatory actions and widespread participatory involvement in the modeling process, control over the modeling process tended to be more decentralized than it otherwise might be. This is not to say that all participants in the policy debates were equal, however. Citizen/developer, central city/suburban and similar interests tended to be more or less evenly represented.

A more subtle impact of modeling on the outcome of interest group politics is *agenda-setting*. In San Diego, it seemed that fiscal analyses focused more attention on fiscal issues and deflected some attention from social and environmental issues. By influencing what people think about, fiscal impact models might alter the outcome of decision making processes. Most participants agreed. Almost two-thirds of our respondents (66%) believed that their local government has focused more attention on the fiscal impacts of development since a model was adopted. Consistent with this new focus on fiscal impacts, a majority of respondents (54%), by no means all, indicated that fiscal impact analyses were now conducted more often than before a model was adopted. However, the attention accorded fiscal issues was not perceived to have deflected attention from other issues. Few respondents (24%) believed that models had deflected attention from social to environmental issues that were not fiscal in nature (Table 7.9). Users believed that fiscal impact models enabled or lead more attention to be placed on fiscal issues without over-shadowing social and environmental issues. The case studies highlight the highly political and long-term nature of land-use decision making. This process leads to extensive and prolonged debates, study, and more study and debate. Few groups and viewpoints are unheard from and, in this perspective, a computer model might not exclude old concerns from continuing, while heightening the visibility of fiscal issues.

In defining the problem and informing participants, models tend to shape both what people think about and what they ignore in policy making. But, they might focus thinking even more by altering the criteria for choice. We saw this effect clearly manifested in San Diego, Irvine, and Tulsa. The use of computer-based fiscal impact models in these cities tended to focus attention and debate on the results of the fiscal impact analysis as opposed to social, environmental, or other impacts that might well receive equal attention. Moreover, these systems focused on a particular kind of fiscal impact—not the impacts of development on the community's economic base, the generation of jobs, or the total economy. If the models had examined these broader economic impacts, or considered nonfiscal impacts, the nature of public discussion and debate and the outcomes of modeling might have been different.

Only the Anaheim case involved consideration of choice criteria other than fiscal impact (narrowly defined in all the cases as net cost/revenue to the city). In Anaheim's evaluation of the Santa Ana Canyon General Plan, fiscal considerations were one of four sets of factors used to evaluate development alternatives: revenue/cost, public safety, environmental, and socioeconomic. As it turned out, the alternatives were ranked similarly under fiscal and the other considerations, but the potential for different rankings existed because multiple criteria were used. In Anaheim's evaluation of the Bauer Ranch Project, considerations of the broader economic impacts from development were brought into the debate by a developer-sponsored fiscal impact analysis. While this new criterion temporarily led to confusion and gave an edge to the developer in the debate, the City's narrower criterion of net cost/revenue eventually decided the issue.

Finally, the modeling process invariably operated to narrow the decision agenda by narrowing both the number of development alternatives considered and the substantive differences among the alternatives. During the adaptation phase of nearly every case examined, development alternatives were sequentially narrowed to a small number (often two), all of which were within a range acceptable to the direct participants in the modeling process. This usually led to development alternatives that varied little in their forecasted impacts, as clearly was the case in Tulsa. Thus, by sequentially narrowing the number of alternatives and variations between each alternative evaluated, the modeling process usually yielded a small set of financially and politically viable planning alternatives. This outcome had a strong influence on the broader political agenda because it determined the alternatives that would be debated in public forums (such as planning commission and council meetings) and reported in the media.

DECISION MAKING IMPACTS AND BUREAUCRATIC INTERESTS

Models are central to the bureaucratic reform of local government. Modeling is a sophisticated, analytical technique that encourages the use of other such techniques and technicians. And the huge and diverse data requirements of models are likely to promote interdepartmental cooperation and coordination. In the long term, such bureaucratic impacts of institutionalizing computer models might be of great significance. Alterations in bureaucratic structures and processes might have important continuing and indirect effects on the relative influence of different kinds of public officials, and, thereby, to a series of future policy choices.

The legitimation of sophisticated analytical techniques and criteria in decision making is one expected effect of the institutionalization of computer models. The use of sophisticated computer models might undermine the use and credibility of less sophisticated analytical strategies, such as paper and pencil estimates or common experience. The evidence in support of this expectation is weak, but that is to be expected given the subtle nature of these impacts as described in Anaheim, for example, where computer-based fiscal analysis became standard input into major land-use decisions.

However, fully one-third of our respondents believed that since computer models were introduced, people were less likely to accept the findings of less sophisticated analyses (Table 7.9). Moreoever, computer models might not have been perceived to undermine the credibility of less sophisticated analyses but the use of such models seems to have convinced users of their value. In short, experience with modeling seems to support the legitimacy of such analyses without consciously threatening other analytical approaches.

Models do change the work of planning, budget, and management analysts. In each case studied, the fiscal impact models were a new tool for the analysts; one that had not been used before, and, therefore, one that required the analysts to learn about the model's structure and operation. In each case, the models were computerized, requiring the analysts to become familiar with the preparation of input data and making of computer runs with the model. In each case, the models also required the analysts to collect and organize data that had not previously been part of the city's information systems. But most importantly, the models established new and demanding standards for the analytical process. While modeling might not undermine less sophisticated studies and analyses, the use of models makes less sophisticated analyses far less likely to gain attention and credibility.

A second expectation, linked to the technocratic perspective is that the use of computer-based models might enhance the importance of technical expertise, and thereby, promote what some have called a "skill bureaucracy" (Danziger, et al., 1982) or "algorithmic thinkers" (Mendelson, 1982). This is not reflected directly in the perceptions of our respondents or in the case studies. It is reflected indirectly in the importance of planners to the design of fiscal analyses and in the historical emergence of chief executives who understand the use of modeling, cost-benefit studies, and policy analysis. Still, less than one-fourth (21 percent) of the respondents believed that the use of fiscal analyses made their local government more dependent on technical experts (Table 7.9). And less than one-third (30 percent) believed that model use led to hiring more people with technical expertise (Table 7.9). This infrequent perception of a technocratic bias might be explained in the case of these models by the common reliance on outside consulting support available from model vendors. However, the case studies suggested that such perceptions have a more general basis that could extend to other kinds of models. Technical experts in our case study sites seldom exercised critical influence over the policy process. Their work was closely scrutinized, monitored, and guided by higher elected and appointed officials. In some cases, analysts actually lost influence and status if they were positioned at odds with dominant policy makers, whose opinions and reactions they sought to anticipate.

A related impact is expected to be the encouragement of greater interdepartmental cooperation, which might also weaken the autonomy of technical experts in a particular department. A majority of respondents (57 percent) believed that computer-based fiscal impact analysis led several departments to work more closely together (Table 7.9). The mixed perceptions of respondents, together with the case studies, did not suggest this as a major impact of modeling. However, data requirements often led to repeated visits to data-rich departments, but they seldom led to smooth collaborative relations. Cooperation was often temporary and competitive attitudes were often more prominent than cooperative attitudes toward such joint endeavors. For example, conflicts developed between planning and financial management units in San Diego over model selection and the design of the analysis. Given the fragmented fiefdoms of Tulsa's commission form of government, operating departments were concerned over the centralization of data. Still, such interdepartmental activity did diminish the autonomy of modelers who might be centralized in a single organizational unit. They must present and defend their approach and objectives in other departments and agencies to gain their cooperation and to avoid their launching of various organizational torpedoes aimed at sinking the modeling effort.

The use of computer-based fiscal impact models enhances the resources and importance of technical modeling experts within the organization. It does not, however, seem to enhance their influence over the content and direction of public policy. In fact, the maintenance and enhancement of the modelers' resources might be dependent on their ability to anticipate and react to the preferences and interests of influential actors in the public policy process.

The process of anticipatory reactions might lead to a particular kind of official being more influential. We asked respondents to indicate whether the fiscally profitable alternative (as determined by modeling) was in agreement or disagreement with the policy positions held by a variety of public officials and interests. The aggregate responses suggest that no single class of officials were systematically advantaged or disadvantaged. To the contrary, the beneficiaries of these modeling efforts were notably widespread. Only in one-fourth to one-third of the cities did the results of the modeling effort identify a fiscally profitable alternative that did not agree with the position of any single type of public official (Table 7.10). Generally, models identify a fiscally profitable alternative fitting the policy preference of most public officials. In other words, models support and reinforce (and help to mold) a policy consensus.

It is important to note some exceptions to this generalization. First, the finance department most often agrees with the most fiscally profitable alternative, which reflects its revenue-generating mission. The regional planning agency is least often in agreement with the fiscally profitable alternative. This might reflect its limited influence in each city's policy deliberations. But, it also is likely to reflect those biases of fiscal analysis that create spillover effects for neighboring jurisdictions that must bear the costs of exclusionary zoning. Within these two extremes, the preferences of most public officials are generally supported by the results of fiscal impact models. Rather than supporting a particular partisan interest, models appear more often to support a negotiated policy consensus among a pluralistic array of public officials.

Users in sites that incorporated a model were more likely to feel that the fiscal analyses supported the claims of some public officials and staff over others. More often than not, the model sustained the views of the local legislative majority or those of the planning commission in incorporated sites (Table 7.11). More often yet, the model supported the views of the chief elected or appointed official—the chief administrative officer in counties and the city manager in cities—and their staffs (finance, budget and management, planning). Although non-incorporated sites demonstrated this latter tendency even more strongly, they also tended to show that the fiscally profitable alternative was more often in agreement with the local legislative majority than with any other group. Thus, it seems that the model reinforced the views of key administrators and staff over legislative bodies in the incorporated sites—a potentially significant political impact.

As statistically weak as it may be, this pattern of relationships suggests that there might be groups disadvantaged within the bureaucracy as well as within the broader community in relation to the modeling process. At the community level, there is a likelihood that powerless groups will be disadvantaged by the modeling process. Even though the process may conform to a consensual pattern, powerless groups are likely to be left out. We saw this in the case of North City West in San Diego, where some groups opposed to North City West development were not involved

TABLE 7.10. ***Reinforcement of Existing Positions of Public Officials***

Question:	Disagreement	Agreement	Total	*N*
46. Was the fiscally profitable alternative in agreement or disagreement with positions of each of the public officials listed below? (CIRCLE ONE CODE FOR EACH OFFICIAL OR AGENCY.)				
Public Officials				
A. Chief elected official	30	70	100%	64
B. Chief appointed official	34	66	100%	53
C. Local legislative body (majority)	34	66	100%	71
D. Planning commission	31	69	100%	67
E. Planning department	24	76	100%	74
F. Finance department	18	82	100%	44
G. Budget and management office	26	74	100%	39
H. Urban renewal agency	29	71	100%	17
I. Regional planning agency	45	55	100%	20

TABLE 7.11. Perceived Political Impacts, By Incorporated and Nonincorporated Sites

Political Impacts	Mean score indicating agreement with the statement					
	Incorporated a Model		Did Not Incorporate a Model			
	Mean Score	*N*	Mean Score	*N*	F Statistic	Significance Level
Was this fiscally profitable alternative in agreement with the positions of each of the public officials listed below?						
Chief elected official	1.61	7	1.78	6	.46	.51
Chief appointed official	1.65	8	1.75	6	.18	.68
Local legislative body majority	1.42	9	1.94	6	7.78	.02
Planning commission	1.60	8	1.77	5	.47	.51
Planning department	1.68	9	1.92	8	2.15	.16
Finance department	1.75	7	1.90	5	.64	.44
Budget and management office	1.61	5	1.80	5	.75	.41
Urban renewal agency	1.60	4	1.89	3	1.12	.34
Regional planning agency	1.45	4	1.89	3	.92	.38

in the modeling process. Further, this pattern was reflected in the survey data, indicating that fiscal impact models might tend to disadvantage the interests of lower-income groups.

At the bureaucratic level, there is some likelihood that legislators or elected lay policy officials might be disadvantaged relative to top bureaucrats and technocrats because their involvement in the modeling process can be more episodic, short-term, and marginal. There are a variety of explanations. One is that legislative bodies are more likely to represent extreme policy positions on development issues. Their ability to achieve a majority coalition on one or another policy position is strained, and their ability to maintain a majority coalition is highly tenuous due to frequent turnover of their members. Given tenuous coalitions, even a legislative majority might be persuaded by the results of fiscal analyses that indicate their preferred alternative is not in the government's best interest. Both the Irvine and Anaheim cases illustrated this tendency.

Another explanation is that chief executives and staff, whose tenure outlasts that of most elected officials, are more likely to favor continuity in development policy and, therefore, favor only marginal adjustments to existing development policy rather than wholesale change. And the results of fiscal impact analyses are more likely to favor such marginal adjustments in development policy over the large changes that might accompany pro-growth or anti-growth alternatives. Again, the case studies clearly illustrate that extreme development alternatives usually fared worse in terms of fiscal impact than middle-ground policies. Politically, middle-ground policies also fared better since they offered opportunities for compromise.

Finally, chief executives and city staff are more likely to be more influential with individual legislators than are other legislators when the legislative body is divided on development issues. In such instances, the legislators are more likely to look to the local government staff and to objective evidence in support of development alternatives than to simply adhere to a predetermined policy position. Evidence such as that provided by fiscal analyses can take individual legislators "off the hook" with their constituencies and help to legitimize the policy position they finally adopt.

CONCLUSIONS

In this chapter, we have described the impacts of modeling in an effort to define whose interests are served by the process and outcomes of the analysis. In many respects, our analysis is highly dependent on the particular class of models we have studied. Fiscal impact models have systematic biases different from other kinds of models. Therefore, it is important to separate our conclusions about modeling *per se* from those tied to fiscal impact models in particular.

Fiscal impact models appear to systematically advantage those community groups and interests supportive of exclusionary, fiscal zoning policies. Lower-income renters and their advocates are disadvantaged by the use of fiscal impact models because the taxing and spending structures of most American cities and counties make high-income housing, commercial, and industrial development more fiscally profitable than low-income housing.

The development biases of fiscal impact models are neither as dramatic nor as one-sided as might be expected, given the logic that drives fiscal analysis. Surprisingly, the models appeared flexible in that the outcomes of analysis supported development in one city, growth management in another, no growth in another, and so on. The outcomes of fiscal impact modeling seem to depend importantly on the decisions made by local modelers and public officials regarding the assumptions, data, and scenarios that governed the analysis. Fiscal impact models, and models more generally, are usefully viewed as tools that facilitate negotiation and bargaining over policy alternatives and preferences rather than as a tool that has a deterministic influence on the outcomes of the policy process.

The view of models as bargaining tools is supported by our analysis of the impacts of models. First, it is clear that models have the potential to influence policy formation and deliberation. Our respondents believed that models were successful, useful, believable, and credible sources of information even though they recognized limits in their accuracy and objectivity. For those involved in the modeling process, the models structure and define the policy problem, aid the determination and specification of what data and assumptions are to be accepted as "reality," provide a reason for and precision to the specification of alternative policy positions, and establish one of several important criteria for determining the preferred alternative.

This process is influential both in persuading some participants to change their position and in legitimating the position of other participants. More generally, models seem to resolve conflict over policy issues. They aid the development of a consensus over the preferred policy option, one tending to reflect broad rather than a narrow partisan views, and representative of a pluralistic array of political, bureaucratic, and community interests involved with the modeling effort.

For those left out of the modeling process, this consensus might be less benign. In fact, here is the critical problem: Who represents the interests of powerless groups that are likely to be left out of the modeling effort? In the case of fiscal impact models, who represents low-income residents that desire more rental housing? Who represents neighboring jurisdictions that might suffer the consequences of an exclusionary zoning policy or nearby development? In large part, it is the role of planners, mayors, legislators and state and regional agencies charged with representing the public interest. However, other groups and interests such as developers and industrial leaders are often directly and influentially involved in the modeling process through their staffs or appointed representatives. Modeling reflects fundamental problems of representation in a pluralistic society—but to a greater degree. These are greater problems because modeling constrains participation in the policy making process to a greater degree than many other political processes.

Whose interests are served by modeling? What is the most insightful perspective on the politics of modeling?

The utility of the rational, technocratic, and partisan perspectives has already been questioned by the pluralistic array of interests participating in the modeling process. The uses and impacts of modeling also vary markedly from expectations indicated by the rational perspective. A rational approach to problem solving suggests a sequence of discovering a problem, gathering relevant information, and then determining a solution based on that information. This problem–information–decision sequence is to be distinguished from a partisan perspective. From that perspective, we would expect political elites to determine policy on the basis of their self-interests and then generate information that supports and reinforces that decision. A decision-propaganda-conformity sequence reverses the expectations of the rational perspective.

Neither sequence fits well with our findings. Policy makers seldom begin with a clear formulation of the problem. The information gathered is at times rather objective but often based on negotiation and compromise among contestants regarding the data and assumptions to be accepted as valid for the modeling effort. That is, information is generated by a political process. Finally, the decision is not simply based on the final outcome of the analysis. In fact, prior to the final analyses, the decision or policy preference is usually an already agreed outcome. In this respect, the analysis often appears to simply legitimate decisions already made by the participants.

In contrast with the partisan perspective, policy makers seldom begin with a clear policy decision. More often, they begin with a vague conception of a policy issue and a need to generate an approach that is politically viable for their community. The information generated by the modeling process is not simply propaganda, either. Some participants are influenced by this information. The process of generating this information is critical to building a political consensus around a definition of the problem, viable alternatives, credible and relevant information, and criteria for judging among the alternatives.

Models can be influential in the policy process by defining problems, informing participants, setting the decision agenda, legitimating decisions and non-decisions, and involving contestants. As such, models might serve as tools for facilitating conflict resolution and consensus. In doing so, they are not neutral tools. Rather, they are powerful tools of bargaining and negotiation.

Such a potentially powerful technology is not monopolized by technical experts (modelers, planners, computer specialists, budget and management analysts). Quite to the contrary. Technical experts do play the major role in adapting models for local use, but the technical aspects of modeling are overlaid by a broadly participative process. Thus, technical experts seek agreement from major parties at interest for the judgmental aspects of the model and for technical aspects that importantly influence model results.

Finally, both the technical and the participatory aspects are overlaid by the broader political environment. Thus, the modeling process is a virtual labyrinth of actors and interests that must be sensitively negotiated by the technical experts who anticipate the reactions of multiple participants with sometimes shifting and conflicting agendas. The multiple points at which implementation can be blocked, delayed, or defeated tends to force responsiveness on the part of the technical experts. In this way, the modeling process becomes a process of negotiation and bargaining among proximate participants in the modeling effort and ultimately among political decision makers. Rather than pathological, such a labyrinthine process is functional to the goal of conflict resolution.

Our analysis suggests that the uses and impacts of models tend to facilitate conflict resolution and consensus among a relatively pluralistic array of interests in the policy process. The modeling process is far more political than suggested by the rational perspective. Modelers have far less influence over the outcomes of this process than suggested by the technocratic perspective. And, the process necessitates the involvement and support of a much more inclusive array of groups and interests than suggested by the partisan perspective. In such ways, our study suggests a new perspective on the modeling process that we label consensus modeling.

NOTES

1. Early research on the political process in the United States tended to focus on who participates in what aspects of policy making (i.e., Dahl, 1961). Later studies directed more attention to who pays and who benefits from particular policies and decisions, in part, as a means for determining who really controls the policy making process (Crenson, 1971). Critics of the early pluralists argued that participation in decision making is not at all equivalent with influence and control (Bachrach & Baratz, 1970; Hayes, 1972). Some groups might be co-opted by participation and the political

system itself might be biased such that the outcomes of the process tend to favor certain groups and interests over others, even if that process was pluralistic rather than overtly dominated by particular groups.

2. Of course, this is a common and important strategy of groups, especially those benefited by the status quo. We described such a strategy in Tulsa. However, the American political system has long been characterized by the multitude of institutional barriers and hurdles that permit intense minorities (and majorities) many opportunities to block and delay action.
3. This is because services are not parceled out neatly by demand categories. The staff of a water department, for example, would find it difficult to specify the costs of servicing a new single family detached home, while they could more easily estimate the costs of running a new water main into a specific planned subdivision with relative accuracy.
4. The substantial investments of time and resources required of local government officials by the modeling process tended to commit them to its results, and/or to continuation of the modeling effort. However, this certainly was not always the case: city officials in Anaheim chose to ignore the results of the Santa Ana Canyon analyses, but they retained the modeling effort and subsequently followed its results more closely. Officials in Tulsa and San Diego abided by the model results but terminated the modeling effort. Only the City of Irvine showed consistent commitment both to the model results and to modeling. These cases and the broader survey data indicate that although the investments in modeling are relatively large, commitment to modeling is fragile and more strongly influenced by external conditions (e.g., California's Proposition 13) and the broader political environment than by sunk costs.
5. These impacts are tied to the specific class of models that we have focused on. Computer models *per se* are not argued to have any policy content at all.
6. An argument could be made that any proportion of studies that suggests development is not profitable is a conservative influence on urban development policy. In an earlier era, the wisdom of publicly subsidizing urban development was unquestioned. By even posing questions concerning their fiscal impacts, the viability of new development is lessened.
7. An excellent case study of a resource-poor group of homeowners contesting a governmental modeling study in the transportation policy arena is provided by Lupo et al., 1971.
8. Modeling might affect interest group politics by constraining political interpretation. Contemporary modeling is somewhat analogous to forecasting techniques that had been used throughout history. For example, the Delphi process is a modern forecasting technique that takes its name from the Delphi oracle of ancient Greece. However, models are markedly different from previous forecasing techniques in one critical respect: they often leave little margin for political interpretation of their results. For example, in forecasting the net revenue/cost differences between alternative planning options, fiscal impact models leave few conclusions for people to draw regarding the preferred alternative, given their earlier acceptance of the assumptions of the

model. One must either discredit the model and/or the criteria upon which it is based, or draw the explicit conclusion that the model forecast indicates the preferred alternative. In contrast, the striking feature of the Delphi oracle and many other forecasting techniques is the ambiguity of the forecasts which, because of their ambiguity, are typically interpreted by the highest ranking political officials. With contemporary models, such political interpretations are more highly constrained. If the results of the models do not fit the desires of the politicians, the results might be ignored as was the case in Anaheim's evaluation of the Santa Ana Canyon General Plan (but not in its Bauer Ranch and other uses of the model); but they are seldom capable of being easily reinterpreted.

35%
20%
25%
10%
20%
FIBS
MODELS

8. Negotiation in the Information Society

Two opposing themes are increasingly prevalent in discussions of technology in modern society. At once, Americans are said to be in the midst of a new information age—an age in which knowledge is the primary resource and computers are the primary means for mining and refining this resource. It is an age characterized by an explosion of information and rapid innovation in the tools used to process information. The thrust of this age could hardly be characterized better than it has been by Herman Kahn as the era of C^4I^2—"Command, Control, Communications, Computing/Information and Intelligence" (Kahn, 1982). Yet, while we are undoubtedly the beneficiaries of new information technologies, still, we are said to be overloaded with information in an increasing complex society that we are growing less capable of fully comprehending. In an information age, both the public and the experts are expressing grave doubts about their ability to fully understand the behavior of the social and economic systems of the day.[1]

The emergence of the information age is manifested daily as we read of new computer-based techniques to forecast everything from the economy to the weather.[2] Even the forecasting of political crises is considered within the range of current techniques. Efforts to accurately predict political instability in other nations became a major political issue after the collapse of the Shah's regime in Iran and has long been sponsored by the Department of Defense. One report suggests that such efforts are near completion (Zientara, 1979). In short, new forecasting and modeling techniques are being called to the service of an increasing variety of tasks that appear to focus on areas in which we have little increased understanding.

Computer models represent an important class of these new information technologies that compose the infrastructure of this emerging post-industrial society (Ascher, 1978). The use of models reflects the paradoxical nature of the age. The art, science, and application of modeling has been advancing at a rapid pace at the same time that the use of computer models in the policy-making process has often resulted in failure.

Examples abound of "poor models" and problems of implementation and use in such well-traveled areas as economic and fiscal forecasting at the national and local level.[3] Among these cases, it is appropriate to return to an example with which we began this study—the projections of a budget surplus of the Office of Management and Budget. Faced with huge, countervailing predictions from Wall Street forecasters, the Office of Management and Budget (OMB) began revising its models and projections soon after the enactment of the Administration's budget. Nearly one year after OMB had projected a 1984 surplus if the Administration's budget plans were enacted, Congress was to learn that the deficit for that year could reach as high as $124 billion (*The New York Times,* April 3, 1982, p. 1). Later, budget deficits were estimated as reaching $182 billion by 1983 and $233 billion by 1985 (*Time,* May 10, 1982, p. 11). By the latter part of 1982, there was a growing consensus among a variety of forecasters on the overall impacts of the Administration's tax cuts and military spending increases on employment, deficits, and interest rates. Still, debate continued between OMB and other forecasters, such as the Congressional Budget Office (CBO), which projected higher deficits than OMB. Differences among forecasters had narrowed and OMB forecasts had fluctuated dramatically since OMB first projected budget surpluses. Stockman's use of OMB models appeared to be classic example of partisan modeling and the pulling and hauling among various forecasters reinforced what appeared to be a highly political modeling process despite the narrowing gaps in alternative forecasts.

The stakes and resources are seldom as awesome at the state and local level, yet the growing prevalence of models in the state and local political process appears equally significant and equally as central to the formulation of public policy. At the same time that OMB and the CBO were debating forecasts of the national debt, state and local officials were debating forecasts of budget deficits, land use, and transportation needs. In Washington, D.C., Patricia Roberts Harris was leading a lively mayoral campaign against the incumbent mayor, Marion Bradley, by taking issue with the projected surplus by the end of the D.C. fiscal year. Harris was unpersuaded by such information and disputed this positive fiscal forecast, telling reporters:

> I don't believe the figures. . . . The problem is we cannot get the truth because of deliberate efforts to obscure the truth by this administration (*The Washington Post,* July 23, 1982, B1).

On the opposite coast, the Southern California Association of Governments (SCAG) circulated a major set of reports based on sophisticated and relatively non-controversial population forecasts.[4] The reports called into question the capacity of Southern California to absorb an estimated increase of 3.4 million residents between 1982 and the year 2000, moving the six-county region from 11.5 million to 14.9 million people. SCAG circulated its forecasts and reports on the same day that "area political leaders heard that big obstacles [faced] the Metrorail Wilshire subway plan," a new mass transit system evisioned for the Los Angeles area (*Los Angeles Times*, August 2, 1982, p. 3). The SCAG reports claimed that the forecasted growth would strain existing transportation systems, nearly doubling congestion especially in Los Angeles and Orange counties. However, SCAG claimed that the planned Wilshire subway would contribute to relieving this increased congestion (*Los Angeles Times*, August 2, 1982, p. 3).

Clearly, computer-based models and forecasts are becoming a prominent feature of politics in the dawning information age. Whether such forecasts are contested as partisan ploys or summoned as non-partisan instruments of policy analysis, they are realities with which public officials must increasingly contend. This growing importance and varied role of models in the policy-making process was clearly supported by our case studies and field surveys of computer-based fiscal impact models. Fiscal impact models are occasionally used as partisan tools, for example, as ways of legitimizing exclusionary fiscal zoning policies.[5] In other cases, fiscal impact models are used to delay development and to raise the costs borne by developers that are then passed on to new home buyers. But, in some cases, models are used to help resolve conflicts among groups with different opinions, interests, and beliefs about development policies. When used in this way, models tend to serve a relatively more pluralistic array of interests than is portrayed by the highly partisan perspective on the modeling process which tends to dominate both journalistic and behavioral research on the use of computer models in the policy process (Lupo, et al., 1971).

Clearly, models are becoming an increasingly visible and important part of the American political landscape (Ascher, 1978). There are several reasons: the increasing complexity of modern society; the growing availability of models and model builders; and the rise of politicians and managers who understand how to use and manage new information technologies in the policy process.

The phenomenal growth of modeling has generated great expectations of benefits among those who view modeling from a rational perspective. Yet, behavioral research, including the present study, casts serious doubts on such expectations. New computer models do not necessarily generate better information (Freedman, 1981). Even when they do, such information is not necessarily utilized to inform policy decisions (Brewer, 1973). And, even when so used, the information from computer models is only one decision input to the policy process. Such observations strike at the heart of positive views concerning the new information age.

This study used these findings as a starting point, examining a fundamental question about the role of computer models in public policy: "To what extent are computer models merely minor influences in the established play of power in public policy making versus new analytical tools that change the nature of public policy making and, hence, change policy outcomes?"

Our conclusion is that while computer models are only one of several influences in the policy making process, they introduce new features that importantly influence public policy making and, hence, shape policy outcomes. These features introduce changes in policy making, shape the analytic framework of policy debate, the criteria for choice, the extent to which model results will be binding on the participants, and the limits of negotiation and compromise over policy outcomes. Once accepted and institutionalized as part of the policy process, these features of modeling change the way in which policy debates are carried out, and thereby fundamentally change the nature of policy making and policy outcomes in the long run.

Our research, carried out in American cities, focused on fiscal impact models. Increasingly, officials are computerizing fiscal impact models in order to allow for more complex and flexible analyses of the fiscal impacts of alternative development patterns. These models are marketed as aids to urban planning and land-use decision making. They are also suggested as aids to urban budgeting and policy decisions that fall outside the boundaries of planning departments.

This study was based on a mix of qualitative and quantitative research methods, and triangulation among the methods. Case studies were carried out in four cities. In addition, a survey of all cities using computer-based fiscal impact models was conducted. Both research methods were critical to the conclusions of this study: neither in isolation would have led us to the same conclusions.

The focus and methods of this study place modest limits on the generalizability of our findings. That is, there are risks in generalizing beyond the kinds of organizations we researched, the models we examined and the period in which our research was conducted. Specifically, our study focused on the early adopters of a relatively new family of computer-based models in local governments. Early adopters might differ from later adopters in their motivations and approach to modeling. Also, the models are constantly being modified by their vendors, so that the technology is changing over time. For example, many of the vendors are in a continuing process of simplifying the models, providing them on a time-shared basis, and rewriting documentation. And, local government experiences with model use might vary from that in state and federal agencies.

Given these limits on the generalizability of this study, its value will depend upon the degree to which analogous settings exist. In this respect, we are encouraged by the reactions of our colleagues and practitioners who have responded to early drafts and presentations of our findings. We also are encouraged by corresponding results from studies of modeling in federal agencies (Weimer, forthcoming; King, 1983, 1984; Fallows, forthcoming; and Greenberger, 1983). All this informal and formal feedback suggests to us that implications of this study extend beyond the early adopters of computer-based fiscal impact models.

Despite our reservations concerning overgeneralization, we could not completely report on this study without moving away from the restrictions of our data to suggest several more general implications of our research for modeling in the policy process. We began this book by discussing William Grieder's interviews with David Stockman about the use of computer models in the U.S. Office of Management and Budget. This case suggested that major issues revolve around the role of models in public policy. We, therefore, conclude this book by returning to the issues posed in that introductory chapter.

EXPECTATIONS

The Stockman case clearly raised an issue of expectations. How are computer models expected to affect the policy-making process? The major theme of this study has been that the dominant expectations regarding the role of models in the policy process can be summarized by four competing perspectives, which we have called the rational, partisan, and technocratic perspectives (Table 8.1).

The primary proponents of modeling hold what we have called a rational perspective. Models are tools for scientific management and policy analysis according to this view, tools that provide new and better information to assist in the policy making process (Freedman, 1981; Kahn, 1982). In contrast, the major critics of modeling hold a partisan perspective (Lupo, et al., 1971). They view models as tools for propaganda and persuasion. To the critics, models are adopted to legitimize choices that have already been made, and, therefore, provide new tools to support the policy initiatives of the dominant coalition of interests within an organization or society. Other critics hold a technocratic perspective. They view models as tools of the high priests of the emerging information society—the in-

TABLE 8.1. Comparison of Four Political Perspectives on Modeling

	Model Impact		Modeling Process	
Alternative Perspectives	**Manifest Role**	**Latent Role**	**Most Critical Phase of the Modeling Process**	**Critical Relations Between Modelers and Other Contestants**
Rational: Models are tools of ''scientific'' management and analysis	Adopted to analyze the merits of alternative policy choices	Provide information about implications of policy alternatives	*Incorporation:* ongoing use of models for analysis	Independence and autonomy of modelers
Technocratic: Models are tools of a new information elite	Promoted to further position of modeler	Explicate the rationale of a policy argument	*Incorporation:* ongoing use of models for analysis	Modelers promoted or discredited by politicians
Partisan: Models are tools to propaganda and persuasion	Adopted to legitimate choices made on basis of power or influence	Provide support for a policy initiative	*Introduction:* adoption of models that reinforce dominant coalition's interests	Modelers lack independence, assuring support for dominant coalition's
Consensual: Models are tools of interactive decision making, negotiation and bargaining	Adopted to serve multiple and shifting interests of different contestants	Provide a process for resolving conflict and achieving consensus	*Adaptation:* mutual adjustments of models to take account of competing beliefs	Modelers consult broadly, anticipating reactions of various groups and interests

formation elite, the modelers, and policy analysts. According to this last perspective, modelers use information technology to baffle policy makers, impress the public, promote their own views, defeat their opponents, and seal their position as authorities on the issues of the day (Greenberger, et al., 1976).

Expectations of each perspective are especially apparent in the widely purveyed rhetoric about whether modeling is benign or harmful, revolutionary or incidental, in its impact on policy making. Visionaries of the new information society take a rational perspective and view models as information resources which can be used to greatly improve policy making. They see models as offering solutions to problems of information overload and incomprehensibility of complex systems and, therefore, a benign force for coping with the complexity of modern society. The critics of the new information technology view modeling as potentially harmful in its effects on policy making. Those with a technocratic perspective view models skeptically as overly complicated representations of a particular modeler's theory and biases which might not be apparent to analysts or to policy makers. Those with a partisan perspective, such as political commentators and journalists, view models almost cynically, as new tools for political manipulation, a new twist to a routine of partisan deception.

Expectations about the extent of modeling's impact are equally varied depending upon these perspectives. Those who hold the rational perspective view models as almost revolutionary in their impacts. Models are expected to fundamentally change the way in which policies are formulated and chosen. Scientific models of reality will now become the accepted basis for decision making by all participants, the scientific arbiter of the public interest. What is revolutionary, then, is that technique, rather than actors (analysts and policy makers), will become the driving force behind politics and policy making in the information society. To those who hold a technocratic perspective, models are equally as revolutionary in their potential impact on policy making. In this view, technocrats will gain political power as a result of their monopoly on expertise and will become the central actors in the policy process, thereby constituting a threat to democracy. To those who hold a partisan perspective, models are not at all revolutionary in their impacts. They are merely "old wine in new bottles." Politics, in the sense of personal power and influence taking precedence over rational weighing of the merits of an argument, will continue as usual. Politicians will continue to control the policy-making process. Experts will continue to be merely experts with new tools. Large-scale computer models will merely replace hand calculators just as hand calculators earlier replaced slide rules. While revolutionizing the analytical process, such changes in techniques will have no demonstrable effects on decision processes. Politicians and analysts have simply updated their techniques to respond to the new language and new technology of the era. Little will be revolutionary.

PERFORMANCE

How does the performance of computer models compare with expectations? While the three dominant perspectives on the modeling process have been reflected in our case studies and survey findings, we have uncovered subtle but numerous exceptions and deviations from the expectations of each. Neither the rational, the technocratic, nor the partisan perspective adequately describes the experiences of most agencies that have been relatively successful in utilizing computer-based forecasting models in local government. At least, we found this to be the case for one class of models—fiscal impact models. We did find that the use of fiscal impact models in some cities more closely approximated a partisan than a rational perspective. However, we found the experiences of cities to be better accounted for and described by an entirely different perspective on the modeling process. We have called this perspective "consensus modeling."

We did not expect to discover the patterns we refer to as consensus modeling (Table 8.1). These patterns emerged inductively from the cases and survey and our efforts to unravel seemingly contradictory findings. For example, we found computer models to be rather consistently perceived as political tools and yet also perceived to be informative and accurate. "Accurate propaganda" is certainly a paradoxical expression if viewed from the traditional perspectives. We had inadvertently accepted a positivistic view of science, according to which the facts must speak for themselves. Scientifically sound information, according to this view, is based on scientific method, which might involve communciation among peers and the judgment of peers (scientists), but would not involve an active responsiveness to the political opinions and interests of various clientele that are not trained or skilled in accepted methods of inquiry. We discovered instead that policy analyses which are accepted as legitimate and informative are driven towards their conclusions through a process that has been referred to in the literature on persuasion as "consensual validation" (DeFleur & Ball-Rokeach, 1982, p. 226). In this view, reality—in terms of the appropriate data, assumptions, and techniques—is a social rather than a positivistic scientific construction, decided on by group decision making processes.

Consensus modeling suggests that models tend to be used as tools to facilitate negotiation and bargaining in a process of interactive decision making (Fisher and Ury, 1981). While models are adopted to serve multiple and often competing and shifting interests of a variety of contestants in the policy process, their broader function seems to be the provision of a process for resolving conflict and achieving consensus on controversial issues. These issues include the assumptions, alternatives, data, and criteria for choice. Agreement on these issues in turn creates a commitment among participants to abide by the outcomes of the process. As a result, models can be more appropriately viewed as tools for negotiation and bargaining than as tools for scientific policy analyses or for partisan propaganda and persuasion.

Still, models *do* serve some of the functions suggested by each of the alternative perspectives. As predicted by the rational perspective, models *do* provide information about the implications of policy alternatives. However, this information is more often important because it is derived through a series of negotiations over the state-of-nature, the most reasonable modeling assumptions, and the most reasonable construction of alternative policy scenarios than because it is the result of independent analysis by experts. Similarly, as predicted by the partisan perspective, models are often used to legitimate choices that have already been made. However, we also find in such instances that processes of negotiation and bargaining, or interactive decision making occurred throughout the modeling process and resulted in a general consensus over policy alternatives *before* the final results of the analytical process indicated the preferred policy. Finally, as suggested by the technocratic perspective, models are sometimes used to promote the interests of modelers. However, if influential groups are not involved, their interests not anticipated, and their representatives not informed, it is common for the legitimacy of the modeling effort to be questioned.

While modeling does not always conform to what we have labeled a consensus modeling process, our cases and field survey do suggest that successful modeling (not necessarily good models) tends to conform to a consensual perspective. Indeed, we found that the rejection of models can be accounted for in large part by the failure to use models as tools for negotiation and bargaining. When the modeling process is carried on as an isolated technical exercise or as an obvious partisan maneuver, the models tend to lack relevance or credibility, respectively, in the decision-making process.

Of course, the generalizability of the consensual perspective is an interesting empirical question that, at this point, is open to debate. Several factors support and detract from the validity of this perspective when applied to other forms of expertise in the policy process, other policy arenas, and other levels and jurisdictions of government.

On the one hand, consensual modeling is a plausible perspective on modeling at other levels of government because the policy making process remains often as unstructured, conflictual, and pluralistic as at the local level. Also, the inherent attributes of models that might lead them to be natural facilitators of a negotiating process are not necessarily different across policy areas or levels of government.

On the other hand, there are differences we would expect to find outside the local arena and outside the politics of urban land use decision making. These stem from the larger scale and greater resources at the state and federal level and in policy arenas (e.g., energy policy making) that are often capable of marshalling more attention and resources than urban planning problems. A larger scale process is likely to generate more modeling efforts. For example, economic modeling at the federal level is characterized by a sizeable number of counter modeling efforts by heavily financed modeling organizations. John King of the University of California at Irvine has described the rise to prominence of Data Resources, Incorporated's (DRI) large-scale macro-economic models of the United States economy, for example. The DRI case suggests that the differences of scale between the local and national level are great indeed and might, in fact, create qualitative differences in the entire process of modeling (King, 1983, 1984).

Moreoever, the DRI models compete with other large-scale macroeconomic models to add further complexity to the modeling process at the national level. Multiple and competing models characterize other policy areas such as the energy policy studies, which have been carefully examined by Martin Greenberger and his associates (Greenberger, 1983). This is in marked contrast to most local government fiscal impact modeling efforts that are characterized by a modestly funded effort. Perhaps the availability of a single model is one driving force behind the consensual modeling process. The availability of multiple models supported by competing firms employed by competing partisan groups and interests in federal economic and energy policy arenas might drive the modeling process toward a more partisan process. In this kind of setting, modeling firms might develop reputations for supporting different partisan positions, again facilitating a process in which partisan interests can shop for modeling resources to support and reinforce their policy preferences (Ascher, 1978).

However, consensual modeling might characterize the modeling process even in these situations, but it would take place through a process of bargaining and negotiation among multiple models and modelers. In fact, the consensual validation of reality strikes us as a promising perspective on the ongoing debate among competing modelers of the national economy and national energy policy, and, in that respect, reinforces rather than detracts from our thesis that the consensual perspective will find support by other investigators looking at other models in other policy areas.

The diffusion of microcomputer systems within local governments could even change the character of fiscal impact modeling at the local arena such that far more participants and groups in the planning process have their own models and data bases. Even the modest scale of local government might then nourish multiple models and adversary or counter modeling in the near-future.

Likewise, the greater scale of the modeling process at the state and federal levels is likely to create more situations in which institutional modeling gives way to celebrity modeling. National economic modeling, for example, is commonly personified by celebrities or near-celebrities associated with models or their results. Arthur Laffer and David Stockman, for example, became closely linked to early economic forecasts of the Reagan administration. Jay Forester rose to celebrity status with his world systems model (Greenberger, 1976). Our review of the literature suggests that as modeling becomes more tied to celebrities, it will be more characterized by the partisan and technocratic perspectives.

Different perspectives on the modeling process might help in understanding and explaining the role of experts and analysis in the policy process in different political and organizational settings. Stated differently, each of the simplified perspectives on the modeling process shed some light on many concrete cases. To the degree others find these perspectives to be useful conceptual lenses, then future research might begin to specify the contingencies or factors that push the modeling process toward one direction or another across our cross-cutting dimensions of (a) who controls, and (b) who is served by the modeling process.

WHY CONSENSUS MODELING IS EFFECTIVE

Consensus modeling sometimes reflects the actual modeling process better than other theories because it takes into account the logic of persuasion in a way that the other theories do not. The rational perspective on the modeling process is based on a rational theory of persuasion. From this perspective, models generate information that alters or reinforces the beliefs or opinions of individuals in order to persuade them to support a policy position or interpretation of reality. Modeling is simply the provision of new information. From the technocratic perspective, persuasion is based on the authority of expertise that is vested in the technical expert or modeler. In contrast, the partisan perspective represents modeling as a purposive effort to persuade people by invoking the name of science over models laden with partisan assumptions.

The consensual perspective depends on a different theory of persuasion. Consensual modeling is based on the notion that groups serve to define reality for their members through interaction and communication. As DeFleur and Ball-Rokeach suggest:

> Realities are defined and interpreted within social frameworks. This generalization has often been called the reality principle, and the interactional process by means of which such definitions are achieved has been referred to as consensual validation. (DeFleur and Ball-Rokeach, 1982, p. 226)

Thus, it is both the process of interaction itself and the social definition of reality which results from this interaction that persuade the participants in the modeling process more than it is the provision of objective, scientific information. Such social definitions of reality and their persuasive impacts are the theme of Watzlawick (1976), Shibutani (1967), and other social scientists.

POLITICAL ANALYSIS

Are models primarily political or analytical tools? From the perspective of consensus modeling, models are *both* political and analytical tools. Modeling can be used as an analytical process that facilitates and organizes political negotiation and bargaining.

In some respects, however, models are neither political nor analytical tools in the sense that the question assumes. The basic rationale for the adoption of models is to improve the rationality of decision making. And such a goal is more or less an objective of most participants in the modeling process. At the same time, most contestants in the policy process are not content to rely on modelers or other technical experts to conduct analyses independently that might have important ramifications for public policy. For this reason, the analytical process itself becomes a focus of political oversight, negotiation, and bargaining. Contestants as participants in the modeling process negotiate over the appropriate data, assumptions, policies, and alternatives—factors that might often be considered to be the purview of the technical experts. Such an involvement can compromise the views and recommendations of modelers. Yet, such involvement seems to be important to understanding, supporting, and utilizing models as tools for policy negotiations.

Again, however, modeling does not always conform to a consensus perspective. In cases where modeling is closer to the rational or technocratic perspectives, the analytical process might be governed more by technical expertise.

THE FUNCTIONS OF MODELING

What are the broader organizational and political functions of models as used in the policy process? Clearly, the functions of models are not limited to only those intended by analysts and politicians. The broader, often latent, and often unintended consequences of modeling are among the most dramatic of the themes identified by our case studies. These impacts are best characterized by way of two general observations.

First, modeling can serve a broad function in resolving conflict and achieving consensus in the policy-making process. In this respect, modeling can serve an important role, politically and analytically. Conflict resolution is one major function of government, albeit one that is oftentimes not in the interests of dissatisfied groups and proponents of change.

Modeling can support the function of consensus-building by directing debate and discussion away from the people and groups involved in conflict, towards the implementation and use of a computer model. Modeling casts abstract debates over positions and interests into concrete and more precisely defined discussions (sometimes hot debates) of appropriate assumptions, frameworks, and data related to an issue. Modeling facilitates solutions by defining concrete options that tend to be acceptable to most contestants involved in the process. Unacceptable options—options believed to be unrealistic or unacceptable to powerful groups—tend to vanish. And, modeling can provide criteria and a process for assessing the remaining options.

Second, modeling tends to reinforce the biases of those who control the modeling, and broader political process. Early in this study, we characterized modeling as leading to the automation of bias. Nothing we have found subsequently negates that general conclusion. The modeling process, even if it is one of negotiation and compromise among a broad array of contestants, is one which injects the shared interests and goals of particular interests into the decision making process. In this way, the use of models tends to reinforce and legitimate the interests of those who adopt and implement these systems. Models are neither neutral or apolitical nor are they benign to all individuals and groups affected by public policy. Those left out of the modeling process might or might not have their interests supported by that process.

Of course, we have also seen that not all individuals and groups are equal. On the one hand, some groups can be and are left out of the modeling process with little or no impact on outcomes. In San Diego, the opponents of North City West were not involved in the modeling of alternative growth strategies until it was too late: all scenarios in the model involved the *development* of North City West. On the other hand, some groups must have their interests anticipated, reflected, and sometimes directly involved or the modeling process will be likely to falter. The failure of Tulsa's modelers to involve the new laissez-faire growth coalition in the modeling process seems to have been partly responsible for the cancellation of modeling efforts.

THE MODELING ENVIRONMENT

We have documented considerable variation in the use of technologically quite similar computer models. This study and the literature suggest that an important source of variation in the use of models, as in the use of other information technologies, is the social setting: the macro- and micro-levels of the environment of the modeling process. What environmental factors affect the use of computer models?

Features of both the micro- and macro-levels of the environment of modeling seem to have affected the modeling process at its various stages of adoption, adaptation, and incorporation. We found political characteristics of the macro-environment to be extremely influential in the success of the modeling effort. In every case study, modeling appeared to conform to the needs and interests of important political leaders and groups within the community. In those situations where important interests were not involved and supportive of the modeling effort, the effort was unlikely to be successful. Tulsa's rejection of planning *and* the fiscal impact modeling effort is the most vivid example of the failure to obtain the supportive involvement of major interests.

Features of the micro-environment were also found to be critical to the success of modeling. The political-administrative organization of the modeling effort seems to influence the degree to which various public and private groups and interests can be informed about and involved in the modeling effort. Also, their access to key officials affects the modelers' ability to mediate among conflicting interest groups. For example, the success of the modeling efforts in San Diego, Irvine, and Anaheim, was influenced by the fact that the modelers were able to get access to key public officials and their staffs at critical times in order to review preliminary findings and obtain their reactions to critical choices. The nature of communication in the modeling process importantly influences success. The survey findings show that the key variables related to the perceived success of the modeling efforts were the participants' perceptions of the credibility of the consultants and the information they received about the modeling effort.

In addition to accounting for the success of the models we studied, environmental factors might also account for the fact that computer-based models have not been widely used by local governments. Modeling is still a new art in local government with a spotty track record since the 1960s when large-scale urban planning models were widely promoted. The major impetus for model adoption in the sites we studied appears to have been a need to resolve community and intra-governmental disagreements over the rate and direction of development. Development issues were a feature of the macro-environment that was critical to both the adoption and the incorporation of models, but other environmental factors also seemed to play an important role. Slack resources were available to most adopters in the form of outside funding to support either the model's adaptation or the modeling staff.

The initial impetus for adopting a fiscal impact system generally did not stem from top management. Nor was it the result of an extensive search for a model, although some cities did conduct extensive searches. Generally, information about the model was first provided by the model vendor and first considered by each city's planners. In retrospect, given that most local governments of the late 1970s and early 1980s were not rapidly growing or blessed with abundant resources, it is hardly surprising that vendors and planners had so little success in diffusing these models.

The modeling environment also played some role in model adaptation. Adaptation was the direct responsibility of planners and occasionally analysts of other departments who were normally active in involving other officials and groups as advisors and sounding boards for their efforts. The primary problems mentioned by the modelers were technical difficulties in gathering the needed data and converting the model to run on the jurisdiction's computer. A number of cities and counties had problems in getting the necessary staff and time to properly implement the models. Still, these technical problems were not critical in most cities and counties. Technically, adaptation was simply a time-consuming process that was successfully accomplished in every jurisdiction where there was sufficient political support to complete the work. In this respect, the macro-environment of the modeling process was critical.

There are other respects in which the macro-environment played an important role in the incorporation of models. Jurisdictions with long-range growth issues and therefore a continuing need for planning analyses were the major incorporators. Incorporators were also those with somewhat more successful experiences with modeling, although this relationship was not strong and consistent. Users in sites where the models had been incorporated tended to judge the models as somewhat more successful. Both the incorporators and their neighbors (nearby cities and counties) which had also utilized such models were more likely to have the staff capability to conduct analyses.

EFFECTIVE MODELING

The findings of this study offer some rough guidelines for addressing a final issue that was raised in Chapter 1: How might the use of models in the policy process be better organized and more effective?

Modelers typically approach the development and implementation of models from one or more of the traditional perspectives outlined above as rational, technocratic, or partisan modeling. More often than not, it is the rational perspective that guides development and implementation. It is this view of modeling that is most commonly portrayed by management science and operations research texts that treat politics as an exceptional and pathological phenomenon of some modeling efforts. This study suggests that the rational approach to modeling might not only be empirically misleading, but it might also be normatively misleading in the sense that it fails to sensitize modelers to the organizational and political dynamics of successful modeling. If a modeler followed the guidelines of the rational approach, s/he would attempt to maintain distance and independence between his or her work and the beliefs, attitudes, and opinions of various political elites within the policy arena of the modeling effort. The models would be based on the technical expert's best professional judgment of the most appropriate criteria, data, parameters, assumptions, and scenarios necessary for implementing the model.

This is a decidedly different strategy than one would extrapolate from the other modeling perspectives if taken as normative approaches to the modeling process. For example, a technocratic perspective would encourage modelers to be advocates of their approaches and models, letting the marketplace of ideas decide on the relative merits of their approaches. In practice, however, the marketplace is sometimes more sensitive to the personality and style of the modelers than it is to the merits of the models (Greenberger, et al., 1979).

A partisan perspective would encourage modelers to relate their models to the interests of influential elites. A modeler might hook his/her fortunes to a rising political star. In effect, the expert would be the new "hired gun" of the information age. In contrast, a consensual perspective would encourage modelers to become mediators and to use their models deliberately to mediate conflicts among politicians, bureaucrats, and technical experts with differing opinions, beliefs, and interests about the policy environment, options, and implications.

Should modelers be mediators? Many scholars and practitioners would argue that modelers are technical experts and not politicians. Moreover, these scholars and practitioners would point out, modelers would not be successful if they *tried* to be politicians. Modelers should avoid politics. Modelers should not be mediators.

We believe this to be an unrealistic position. We also believe it to be an unsuccessful strategy, if computer models are genuinely hoped to be of value as policy models. We would advocate that modelers play a role which closely approaches what Arnold Meltsner has labeled an "entrepreneur" policy analyst (Meltsner, 1976, p. 48). The entrepreneur views policy analysis as both a poltical and analytical process for influencing policy and uses skills in analysis, communication, and coordination to arrive at policy advice that is acceptable and beneficial to most contestants in the policy process (Meltsner, 1976, p. 48). We would add that the successful policy modeler must not only satisfy his or her immediate client, but must also seek to mediate among contestants in the policy process using modeling to facilitate negotation and bargaining.

Modelers should be mediators and political actors because the results of policy modeling are inherently political—whether they support, undermine, or muddy the position of particular contestants in the policy process. It is unrealistic to expect otherwise because, as we have seen, the careers and efforts of modelers and their models are literally at stake. Modelers must become sensitive, political actors or they risk being irrelevant to, or casualties of, the political process.

More generally, modelers should become mediators because consensus modeling appears to be the most successful approach to the use of models in the policy process. If modelers are to be judged by those who use their models rather than by abstract technical, mathematical, and statistical criteria of modeling elegance, then consensus modeling seems to be a relatively more successful strategy. Such a strategy implies that modelers assume a role as mediators—anticipating, soliciting, and reacting to the diversity of beliefs, attitudes, and opinions of the various participants in the modeling process.

Politically, the mediating role of consensus modeling is relatively more likely to serve a broader, more pluralistic array of interests. All modeling will tend to constrain the number and diversity of people and points of view that are directly incorporated into the policy process. However, consensus modeling seems least likely to be biased in favor of serving narrow, special interests—whether those of developers, homeowners, or the affluent—to the exclusion of other interests.

Modelers can become mediators and move modeling processes toward a consensus perspective. Modelers can attempt to involve all major interests and parties into the modeling process. Modelers can attempt to anticipate the reactions of every group and interest that could be importantly affected by the results of the analyses. Modelers can also try to inform as broad an array of people as possible about the goals, methods, and progress of the modeling effort.

Of course, modelers are normally rather powerless political actors.

They normally lack the authority of a high political office, the legitimacy of elected politicians, the independence of a mediator, or the style and personality of a successful promoter. A review of the modeling literature perhaps said this best in noting that:

> a modeler or implementor of a [Decision Support System (DSS)] . . . would be relatively powerless within the context of their operation. That is, they would be without either reward or coercive power, which are defined as the ability to control behavior by controlling pleasure or pain, either directly or through bestowal or withdrawal of material goods. Nor is it likely that they would have legitimate power, which is conceived of as resulting from the authority conferred on an individual as a result of consensual acceptance of the 'rightness' of that individual's exercise of power. While it is possible that the exercise of expert power might result in the acceptance of modeling or DSS, in most cases this seems unlikely, since expert power derives from the possession of knowledge unavailable elsewhere, and it is difficult to conceive of . . . the application of models or DSS as essential to solving the identified problem. . . . Eliminating these four bases of power leaves only reference power, which is usually defined as the ability to influence behavior as the result of being liked, admired, or a desirable model for others. (Kovaric, 1982, p. 3)

Yet, within the limits of personal influence and ability, the modeler should attempt to bring all participants into the process early on, not simply to review the final analysis at the end. The modeler should communicate with participants so that participants are more likely to understand the purposes and operation of the model in sufficient detail to evaluate its merit and trust its results.

Modelers can also attempt to ensure that all policy positions are represented, even if all major parties are not directly involved in the modeling process. Moreover, modelers can insure that information about the modeling effort is broadly and effectively disseminated; and that appropriate training is available to interested participants (Komsky, 1983). Modelers should move away from a textbook view of modeling as a purely scientific process that will provide *the answer,* to a more realistic view of modeling as a more political process that necessitates negotiation, communication, and compromise and that might arrive at *an acceptable answer.* Such a perspective requires modelers to trust the opinions and intentions of politicians and citizen group representatives relatively untrained in the building and operation of formal mathematical and computer models. This might well be a critical constraint on the role of modeling in societies governed by a pluralistic political process that requires a consensus among a multitude of public and private groups and interests, each of whom can block and delay policies which they strongly oppose.

There are many occasions in which consensus modeling is unlikely to be the preferred strategy. To the degree that there exists a prior consensus on the policy alternatives, data, assumptions, and criteria for assessing outcomes, a more rational approach to the modeling process might well be both successful and realistic. Uncertainty, less structured problems, and conflict seem to be features of the modeling environment that drive modeling towards a consensus process.

There are likely to be models that are not as amenable to consensus modeling as those that we have studied. Fiscal impact models are generally very flexible and permit a variety of assumptions, data, and alternatives to be modeled. This flexibility provides room for negotiation and bargaining. As we noted above, some models are likely to predetermine particular results and to be less amenable to variations in their assumptions, parameters, data requirements, and hence, in their outputs. Such models would be less adaptable to a process that involves negotiation and bargaining (Greenberger, et al., 1976; Keen & Morton, 1978).

THE POLITICS OF AN INFORMATION SOCIETY

Urban policy processes in the United States have long been characterized as pluralistic, depending on bargaining and negotiation among a variety of contestants with different resources and interests (Meyerson & Banfield, 1955; Sayre & Kaufman, 1960; Banfield, 1961; Dahl, 1961). The introduction of master planning in the 1950s did not rationalize this pluralistic political process (Meyerson & Banfield, 1955). Nor has the introduction of computers, communications, command and control, information, and intelligence-oriented technologies into the policy process of the 1970s and 1980s altered its fundamentally pluralistic political character (Danziger, et al., 1982).

Likewise, the early introduction of master planning into cities during the 1950s seldom succeeded when the interests of powerful contestants were not anticipated during the planning process. As pointed out by Floyd Hunter in his seminal study of decision making in Atlanta:

> The under-structure personnel consider it expedient not to press for activity on scores of plans which may already have cost large sums of money and great expenditures of effort in their development. Planning . . . becomes a ritualistic panorama engaged in by reasonably well-paid under-structure personnel whose plans more often than not fail to reach the point of action. Action results when a plan fits the relatively narrow interests of the policy-makers. . . . There is considerable doubt that much of what they learn ever reaches very far if it is contrary to the existing pattern of the balance of power. (Hunter, 1953, pp. 249–250)

This same pattern is reflected in the use of computer-based models in the policy process. When powerful participants are not involved in the modeling process, any consensus that evolves from this negotiating process is far more likely to fail or be ignored by top policy makers. Computer models have not bestowed power on modelers and analysts, the new understructure personnel of the information society.

Of course, American pluralism has seldom been interpreted to imply that all groups and interests are well reflected in the political process. Not all participants are equal in the politics of the policy process. As Duane Lockard noted, American pluralism has long left out the "obscure:"

> Those without money, without organizing skills, without expertise in political activity, and often with weak, divided, or perhaps no real leadership, are in no easy position to mount campaigns—whether rebellious or political—to remedy their ills. (Lockard, 1971, pp. 25–26)

Similarly, policy negotiations of the information society are unlikely to incorporate the interests of those without the expertise, resources, or organization to be involved within the modeling process. While modeling may restrict the scope of participation in the policy process, this is a feature of American politics that long antedates the arrival of computer-based models on the urban scene.

Thus, it is probably wishful thinking to believe that new information technologies will provide better information and therefore fundamentally rationalize the policy making process. Models have been incorporated into the policy process because they can be compatible with the urban policy process in many fundamental respects rather than because models offer the potential to dramatically reform the process. In large part, this compatibility derives from the value of modeling as a tool for negotiation and bargaining among a pluralistic array of contestants in the policy process.

The policy making process in the information society will remain highly political rather than becoming highly rational because the new information technologies will not fundamentally alter differences of opinion, beliefs, and values. Problems in the public sphere often involve conflict over "who gets what, when, where, and how." Public issues and choices are often poorly defined and ill-structured. Public policy issues normally involve controversy and uncertainty over the consequences of alternatives.

However, politics in the information society might be fundamentally different from politics of earlier eras. New people and new techniques might supplant older ones. It seems that those who know and understand the new information technologies will increasingly be involved in the political process and the use of information technologies in the policy process will become ubiquitous, even routine.

This trend does not necessarily empower the technocrats of the information age. We have seen that modelers, analysts, and technical experts are seldom powerful actors on their own, and are seldom successful unless they are unusual individuals, tied to powerful individuals, or skilled mediators who can use modeling as a tool for negotiation and bargaining.

One of the most critical problems that the increasing use of information technology in the political arena poses for a pluralistic society is the increased importance that his technological change places on the organization and political resources of groups and interests in the society. Groups and interests that are unable to marshall the resources and expertise to effectively participate in the process of defining alternative policies and forecasting the consequences of alternative policies are unlikely to be well served by the new politics of the information age. If such is the case, we will be left with a pluralistic political process for the few that will accentuate inequalities between the haves and have-nots of the information society.

NOTES

1. An account of discussions at SRI International in Menlo Park, California, indicated that the growing complexity and incomprehensibility of systems became a general theme of discussions at the think tank. The reporter illustrated this theme noting that someone "recalled a comment by Reagan's Budget Director David Stockman that no one really understands what is going on in the economy" (Moritz, 1981, p. 65).
2. *Time* magazine describes a $16 million "supercomputer" built by Control Data for the Suitland weather center that "is expected to double the accuracy of the weather service's daily forecasts" (*Time,* August 2, 1982, p. 72). The same article quotes the National Weather Service Director Richard Hallgren who claims (not necessarily referring to the supercomputer): "The larger the computer, the better the forecast. . . . As the computer gets bigger, we can get more of the mathematics and physics of the atmosphere into our models." Such arguments are echoes of debates over models in urban fiscal analysis. And, there are similar counter arguments. One forecaster wondered whether computers will "actually improve forecasts or give bad forecasts more frequently" (*Time,* August 2, 1982, p. 72).
3. For a critical assessment of the statistical integrity of an economic model, see Freedman (1982). Implementation issues at the local level have been covered in this book, but are also discussed by Schroeder (1982).
4. These included a memorandum from the SCAG staff dated July 30, 1982 with several attachments, including materials from January, February, and April of 1982 on the growth forecast. See SCAG (1982a, 1982b, 1982c).

5. Fiscal impact models are not the first analytical tool that has been used on occassion to support exclusionary zoning policies. The environmental impact study and impact statement is occassionally used by environmental ''imposters'' to accomplish other political objectives (Hagman, p. 26). Also, see Bernard Frieden (1981).

Appendix. Fiscal Impact Models

This Appendix describes the nature of fiscal impact models. These computerized mathematical models are similar in form to the popular "spreadsheets" (e.g., VISICALC, LOTUS 1-2-3, MULTIPLAN), and are designed to calculate the fiscal impacts of alternative development patterns as well as the fiscal impact of inter-governmental and local policies that might affect local development patterns. Such policy decisions might encompass a proposed general plan, a planned unit development, a major rezoning, a shopping center development, a proposed freeway, a new property tax rate, a California Proposition 13–type of tax limitation, or a new inter-governmental revenue source. The models are designed to produce "what if" budgets. That is, they calculate and print projected fiscal impacts in a form comparable to the local government's actual capital and operating budgets.

FISCAL IMPACT ANALYSES IN LOCAL GOVERNMENTS

A fiscal impact or cost–revenue analysis has been defined as a "projection of the direct, current, public costs and revenues associated with residential or nonresidential growth to the local jurisdiction(s) in which growth is taking place" (Burchell & Listokin, 1978, p. 1). As such, most fiscal impact analyses ignore a wide array of costs and benefits commonly associated with development. These ignored costs and benefits include: many secondary effects of development such as the alteration of neighboring property values; differential impacts inflation might have on revenues and expenditures given the phasing of costs and associated revenues; economic impacts on developers, renters, homeowners, private, commercial, and industrial enterprises; the revenues and expenditures of other governmental jurisdictions; and a host of social, political, and environmental impacts ranging from the segregation of racial and ethnic groups to air quality. In short, fiscal impact analyses provide only a *partial* assessment of developmental impacts. Even so, such analyses require scores of simplifying assumptions and sophisticated estimating techniques to deal with the complexity and uncertainty of the actual relationships. And, such analyses require many arithmetic calculations to sum up all of the pluses and minuses associated with any change.

Considerable literature has been generated on alternative methods for conducting fiscal impact analyses. Most analyses can be accomplished by a few analysts using pencils, paper, and a calculator in about 40 hours *if* they have standardized data and *if* they evaluate very few decision alternatives. So why develop computerized fiscal impact budgeting systems?

First, while some fiscal impact analyses are manageable with a calculator, they are also constrained in several respects. Any useful, cost-revenue analysis involves hundreds of calculations. Not surprisingly, one of the major failures of non-computerized fiscal impact analyses is the large number of arithmetic errors. Given the interdependence of calculations, the cumulative errors of manual calculations are often formidable. Computers, if they are nothing else, can be excellent high-speed calculators and solve a major problem of manually calculated analyses. Moreover, computers can permit analysts to calculate the revenues and expenditures associated with a much larger number of alternatives, introduce far more decision variables, and vary many more assumptions than would be feasible using manual processing.

Second, computer-based fiscal impact analyses share the mystique that so often attaches to computers and models of any flavor or variety. In part, such a mystique has undoubtedly led some public officials to expect these models to solve far more analytical and political issues of fiscal impact analyses than can be realistically expected. While promoters are sometimes guilty of overselling, buyers are sometimes guilty of purchasing on the basis of faith rather than a critical weighing of the costs and benefits of the technology.

Thus a variety of right and wrong reasons have generated an interest in FIBS. To understand the actual pros and cons of adopting such models, it is first necessary to describe them in some detail.

FISCAL IMPACT MODELS

Most broadly, fiscal impact models are mathematical models that have been translated into computer languages. These models are used to forecast local government service needs, expenditure levels, and revenues for the coming fiscal year(s). Such forecasts are based on current and historical expenditure, revenue, and service data; community land use, housing, and demographic data; and projected changes in these characteristics. The models define the relationships among these elements by sets of mathematical equations and instructions. The complexity of these models varies from the automation of what could be done on a hand calculator to a system of urban development and budgeting models that are linked so that the outputs of some component models are inputs to other component models. The projections from the models can be of direct relevance to governmental budgeting decisions given that projections can be made at a level of detail that reflects the budget categories of local government departments and agencies (Figure A.1). The result is a new kind of model that can serve a function much broader than, and different from, the fiscal impact and urban development models used by planners in the past. The more traditional analyses range from back-of-the-envelope methods for estimating the costs and revenues of a projected population change to finely tuned and sophisticated models which project the costs and revenues of new land uses. Such methods are components of some fiscal impact models but fall short of a complete system. Likewise, urban development

INPUTS

Historical revenue and expenditure data

Taxing rates

Governmental characteristics

Intergovernmental relationships

Community land-use, housing, demographic data

Projected changes in the above factors (caused by urban renewal project, zoning ordinance, population growth, new construction, abandoned housing, etc.)

OPERATIONS

Range from automation of hand calculator operations to:

- Population and employment allocation models
- Functional models, including transportation, water and sewer, fiscal impact, budgeting, and planning models

OUTPUTS

Predictions of revenues and expenditures

Departmental and government-wide budgets by expenditure category for both capital and operating expenses

FIGURE A.1 Fiscal Impact Models

TABLE A.1. Four Fiscal Impact Models, Marketing Firms, and Selected Adopters[a]

	FIAS	FIM	FISCOM	MUNIES
System	Fiscal Impact Analysis System	Local Gov't Fiscal Impact Model	Fiscal Impact System for Communities	Municipal Impact Evaluation System
Marketed by	Decision Sciences Corporation	Ultrasystems, Inc.	Marshall Kaplan, Gans and Kahn	Tischler, Montasser and Associates, Inc.
Base	Jenkintown, PA	Irvine, CA	San Francisco, CA	Washington, DC
Selected List of Adopters	Ottawa, Canada Orange County, CA SEMOG, MI (including Detroit) Tulsa, OK	Anaheim, CA San Jose, CA San Juan Capistrano, CA	Irvine, CA Rancho Cucomonga, CA	San Diego, CA Greece, NY Metro-Washington, DC, COG Montgomery County, MD Baltimore Regional Planning Council

[a]The selected lists of adopters are partial. However, these selected lists illustrate the varied kinds of adopters.

models are components of some fiscal impact models but also fall short of a complete system. Urban development models range from regional population and employment allocation models to functional models of transportation, air quality, water, and sewer services. These urban development models sometimes give attention to cost and revenue impacts, but seldom have been linked to budgetary projections. In fact, it is more useful to view fiscal impact models as an outgrowth of large-scale corporate planning models developed for the private sector than as a natural extension of traditional fiscal impact analyses.

Available Fiscal Impact Models

There are a variety of models and suppliers to support and promote the diffusion of fiscal impact models. There are at least ten versions of such models within the U.S. today that can be relatively easily transferred. In order to better understand the use and impact of these models, we chose four of the most generalized software packages for our study. These were the Fiscal Impact Analysis System (FIAS), the Local Government Fiscal Impact Model (FIM), the Fiscal Impact System for Communities (FISCOM), and the Municipal Impact Evaluation System (MUNIES). These packages have strong institutional bases for marketing, are similar in their overall purpose, and are competing models in the local government marketplace (Table A.1).

Each of these models is adaptable to local jurisdictional needs by the developers in consultation with users. After establishing the purpose for the analysis (e.g., fiscal analysis of a development or a broader budgeting system), the consultant will suggest a package for the user that includes options for data collection, model installation, time-sharing facilities, in-house training, urban development forecasting, scenario development, and interpretations of results. Most of the firms place a major emphasis on tailoring their services to the needs of the user in order to increase the usefulness of the impact analyses and the attractiveness of their model.

Inputs

The accuracy, detail, and comprehensiveness of model projections are constrained by the accuracy, detail and comprehensiveness of the input. Thus the database requirements for fiscal impact models can be substantial. In fact, the data gathering stage of fiscal impact analyses can be the most time- and resource-consuming stage of the entire process—potentially the "black hole" of the modeling process. A comprehensive database requires analysts to collect, code, and store both current and historical data on revenues, expenditures, service levels, tax structures, land use, demographic, and economic attributes of the local jurisdiction.

The historical period for which data is collected can vary from two to ten years. Generally, a longer historical database is believed to improve the accuracy of forecasts by providing more information for estimating trends. Moreover, historical data can be used for retrospective projections of current revenues and expenditures. Such retrospective analyses can be helpful in tuning (adjusting) the model and assessing the reasonableness of its forecasts. However, historical trends are not important to all fiscal impact models and could be misleading if there are such dramatic changes in rates of inflation, taxation, growth, or decline that relationships among components of the model actually change.

By necessity, most manually generated fiscal impact analyses leave out many variables, such as minor or growth-insensitive sources of revenue, because of the complexity of calculations. Computer-based analyses can either replicate the manual analyses or include many more variables.

Revenue data could include property, sales, and payroll tax revenues; all license, fee, and user charges; and federal, state, and local subventions, transfers, and contracts. Local governments often rely on 10 to 20 significant sources of revenue and each might be included in a model database. Expenditure data must be as detailed and comprehensive as the predictions desired. Expenditure data could include both capital and operating/maintenance expenses for all government departments and agencies included in the analysis.

Tax structure details must be supplied to correspond with the included revenue sources. For example, to forecast property tax revenues, analysts must identify the property tax rate, rate structure, and boundary limitations (i.e., the property tax rate cannot be raised beyond its current level).

Likewise, other information can be as limited or as comprehensive as desired. Service-level data are key to expenditure projections and require breakdowns by type of department, agency, and function. For example, police service data could include estimates of patrol cars, officers, maintenance costs, overhead, and so on, calculated on a per capita or more sophisticated allocation basis. For example, police service levels might be projected as a function of demographic and economic factors such as population density, income levels, crime rates, and locations of known offenders.

Land-use data requirements vary also with the desired accuracy of estimates. For example, the data could be very fine-grained and coded by blocks rather than by census tracts and coded by any number of land use categories. Generally, residential land-use categories distinguish between single-family detached, multiple-family dwellings, and mobile homes. Yet, some jurisdictions have created elaborate codes for up to 17 different kinds of housing units. The types of information relative to residential usage normally include: the average number of persons per dwelling unit, the average number of units per acre, the average assessed value per unit, and the number of units by type. Commercial land usage data normally includes by type of use: acres of commercial development, square footage per acre, the market value per acre, and average sales per square footage. Industrial data by types of land use include: the number of acres of industrial development, square footage, and market value per acre of developed industrial land.

Finally, demographic and economic data must be collected. Demographic data such as total population are often required to estimate future revenues and expenditures as linear (or more complex) extrapolations of historical relationships. Component factors are population size and density, median age, and service levels. Similarly, economic data such as inflation rates and per capita income are often included. Again, fiscal impact analyses, typically, if desired, can account for inflation and other variables in order to make the analyses more realistic.

The comprehensiveness and detail of the database is flexible for most fiscal impact models. Ultimately, the size of the database will depend on the resources committed to the effort, the availability of data, and the ability of the analysts to find and quantify data from a variety of departments and agencies at a comparable level of analysis.

In addition to the data sets, local officials and analysts must specify a large number of model assumptions. These include multipliers, the capacities of capital facilities, and the appropriate decision scenarios. That is, the ultimate users of the model need to formulate the desired goals along with assumed characteristics of the decision making environment. For example, if a rezoning decision is to be made, the ultimate users must decide on what alternative land uses are considered to be feasible. If the cost of police services is being estimated, will service needs be estimated as a function of the population, population density, median income, or what? If school capital facility costs are being estimated, how many new students will be assumed to be absorbed by schools now in place? Clearly, such assumptions often are subjective and influence the model projections. Thus it is important to develop some consensus among users on the appropriateness of model assumptions.

Most modelers, the private firms that market FIBS, supply standard data collection and entry forms to aid users in the construction of the required database. In addition, the modelers can either be consulted or paid to completely conduct the data collection and data entry process. However, the primary expertise needed at this stage is familiarity with the particular local government's revenues, expenditures, services, and existing databases. The needed expertise plus the large number of person-hours involved with developing the database push most adopters to conduct this stage in-house with the advice of the model developers.

Operations

Fiscal impact models vary in their level of complexity. The least complex models might be likened to "high-speed calculators." These models permit a large number of simple operations to be performed very accurately. For example, according to those who market MUNIES, virtually all of the algorythms of the model could be replicated by a hand calculator. However, if analysts were to use hand calculators, they would be likely to make larger, cumulative arithmetic errors, take a longer period of time, and incorporate fewer variables into the calculations than if they were to use a computerized model.

The FIAS model is one of the most complex, largely because it contains an urban development (econometric) forecasting model. FIM, FISCOM, and MUNIES do not have econometric forecasting models, but generally have capabilities for generating straight-line constant increases in forecasted variables. But complexity is not a value in itself. Generally, the issue of complexity evolves into an issue over the value of urban development models. This will be apparent once we describe the structure of a generalized fiscal impact budgeting system and then show the most significant differences between this generalized system and specific models.

While each model is structured differently, the *generalized* fiscal impact system is most usefully viewed as two subsystems of models (Figure A.2). The first subsystem is composed of *urban development (forecasting)* models. The forecasting models utilize the current and historical input data and projected policy changes such as a hypothetical rate of population growth to calculate characteristics of the community (demographic, land use, economic characteristics) for the next year(s) and the service levels required for these altered community characteristics. The second subsystem is composed of *budgeting* models. The budgeting models utilize the community- and service-level forecasts along with historical revenue and expenditure data to calculate local government revenues and expenditures for the forecasted year(s).

The linkage between the urban development and budgeting models is straightforward and in one direction. The outputs of the forecasting models are fed directly into the budgeting models. For example, once the need for a new high school is projected, a budgeting model would translate this new capital facility need into a set of expenditures over a period of years. Since the flow of information is unidirectional, many secondary

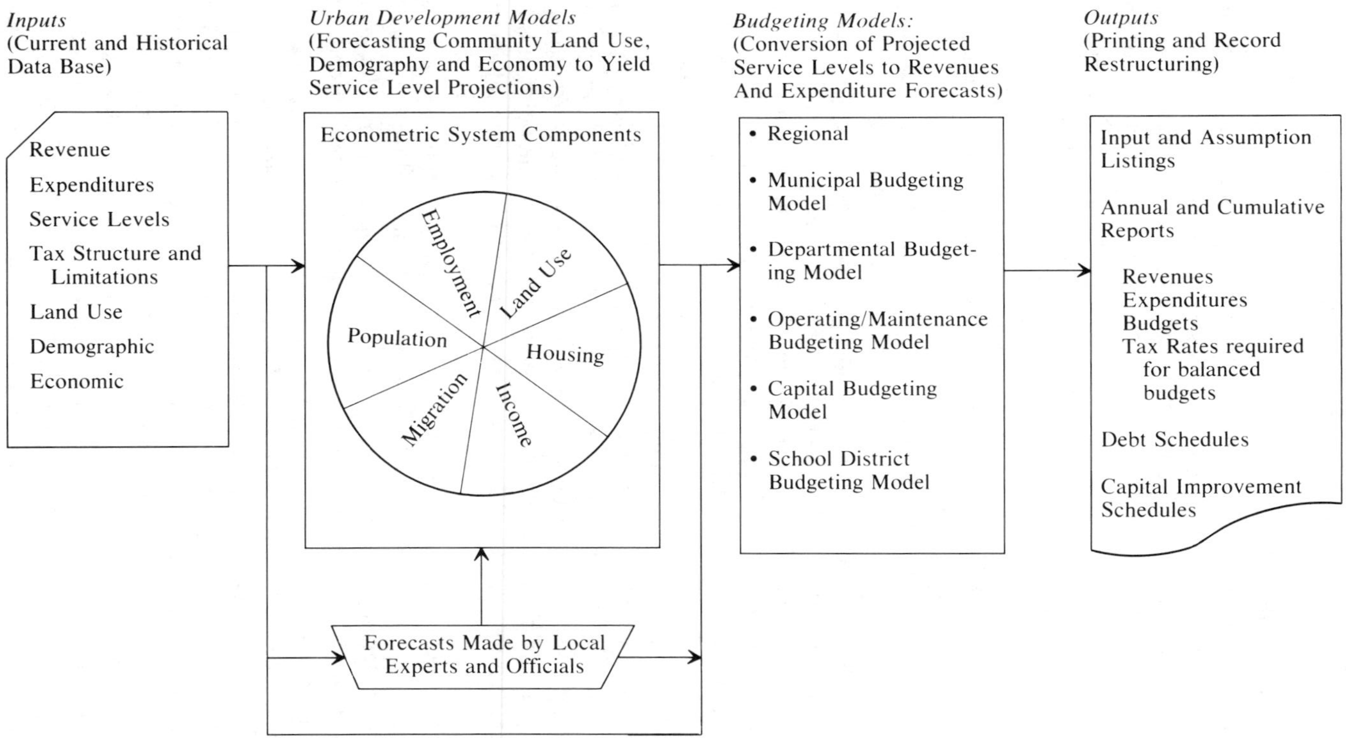

FIGURE A.2. The Components of Fiscal Impact Systems

economic impacts are ignored. For example, the construction of a new high school might affect the migration of additional families to an area. Such interactions can be incorporated, however, if manually reentered to effect changes in the forecasts. This approach allows the user to redefine certain parameters of the model (such as tax rates, housing value forecasts, or service standards) and rerun the analysis to observe changes in the output. Another advantage of a computerized system is that it can accommodate many such changes in a short period of time and at reasonably low costs compared to what would be required with manually generated projections. Over time, the models can be continually refined in this way as new data is gathered.

The forecasting models produce data that is used as input to the budgeting models. FIAS incorporates a full-scale urban development forecasting system for projecting such factors as population by cohorts, employment, sales of retail outlets and shopping centers, income, housing, and land use. This system is based on a series of econometric relationships (including linear regression and gravity models) that forecast employment, population, migration, land use, housing, and income.

The FIAS model is based on the assumption that elaborate demographic and economic projections are required for an accurate fiscal forecast, and that urban development (econometric) modeling is probably the best method available for generating such projections. Other models are based on alternative assumptions. For example, the MUNIES model is based on the assumption that urban development modeling yields forecasts that are no more accurate than the projections of planners and public administrators with an intimate knowledge of the local context. And, since modeling should be a continuing process, rather than a one-point-in-time effort, demographic/economic projections can be refined and updated as new data are collected and relationships better understood. Thus, the MUNIES model has a structure significantly different from the generalized fiscal impact system (Figure A.3). Projections are derived from a variety of sources external to the system (possibly including urban development models), rather than from urban development models linked directly to the larger systems.

Some local governments might prefer to generate their own forecasts because most local government planning departments provide such community forecasts. Most models without a built-in forecasting system will allow the entry of a constant rate of change factor for extrapolation beyond the current year, such as linear regression. Other models permit change factors to differ from year to year. Otherwise forecasts could simply be entered manually for each year in which service, revenue, and expenditure forecasts are to be computed.

Sources of urban development forecasts and standard multipliers

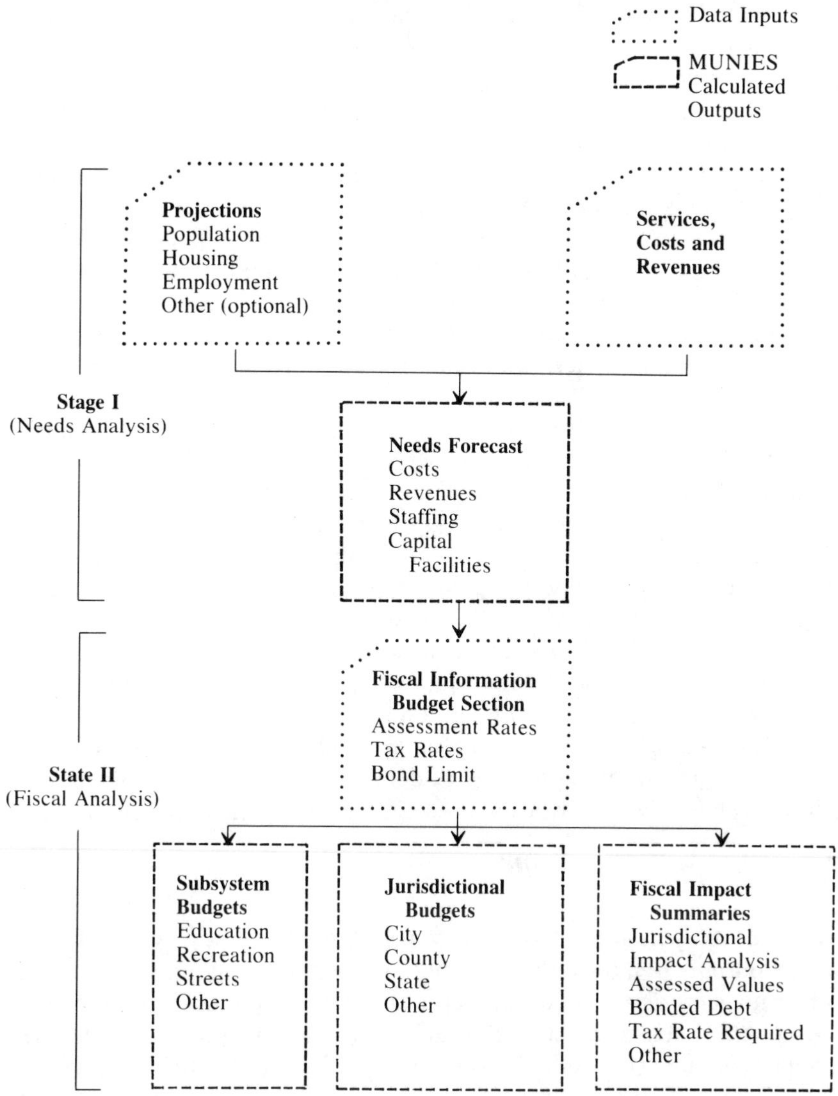

FIGURE A.3. The Munies Process

[a]*Source:* Tischler, Montasser and Associates, Inc.

are available from federal, state, local, and private sources. Local planning departments and councils of governments are likely to have generated forecasts of population, housing, and land use characteristics. Economic projections for regions are frequently available from bank economists. More judgmental forecasts can be obtained from local government officials. Also, a committee of local experts could be employed to obtain consensus forecasts as a kind of delphi approach.

It is possible to test the sensitivity of the model outputs to alternative development forecasts. For example, the effect of a land use change can be measured by rerunning the model with modified input parameters. Outputs based on different sets of forecasts can then be compared in assessing the fiscal impact of land use assumptions and alternative development forecasts.

The budgeting subsystem is composed of regional models, operating/maintenance models, capital budgeting models, and school district models. Two options are available for constructing the analysis. The least prevalent option is a top–down approach. Assumptions regarding expenditures, revenues, and service demands are first established for the largest unit of analysis (typically the city or region). Aggregate totals are then calculated. The analysis progressively moves down to finer levels of detail such as a department (police or fire) and calculates the departmental budget. The analysis could even move across and within departments to the program level (such as crime prevention or community relations). The most prevalent option for analysis is a bottom–up (building-block) approach. This analysis begins with a fine level of detail, such as the department level and proceeds upward towards more aggregated levels of analysis.

Outputs

Model developers have focused a considerable effort into structuring the model outputs in a form that is easily interpreted by administrative staff, top managers, and elected officials. The types of outputs are shown in Figure A.2. Because most municipal budgets vary in appearance but have similar contents, the models permit users to make cosmetic modifications in headings and output formats to suit the local context. The most prevalent report generated is the municipal budget for the current and future years, separated by revenue and expenditure categories. If desired, detailed line-item budgets can be generated by each department and program. The typical output is a summary of the jurisdiction's budget for a given number of years (ranging from 5 to 20 years). Debt structure and expense schedules are available along with schedules of capital improvements and debt service requirements. Tax rates that are required for balancing the generated budget are a typical output. In addition to annual totals, it is not uncommon for cumulative reports to be generated. In order to make explicit the assumptions invoked in each analysis, a listing of input assumptions and scenario descriptions can be printed along with the forecasts.

THE USE OF FISCAL IMPACT MODELS

The Ideal: Rationalizing the Policy Process

Ideally, fiscal impact models represent a management science approach enhancing rational public control of governmental planning and budgeting decisions by leading to improvements in information processing, content, and flows (Figure A.4).

Fiscal impact models are expected to greatly facilitate the work of planning, management, and budget analysts in making service, revenue, and expenditure projections for the coming fiscal year(s). By utilizing the recordkeeping, calculating/printing, record-restructuring, and sophisticated analytical capabilities of the computer, the systems are designed to reduce the workload of menial and exacting tasks involved with fiscal impact analyses and associated budget projections. By automating these information processing tasks, the time of analysts can be more focused on reviewing such decisions as the design of the database and the reasonableness of assumptions rather than the accuracy of routine calculations. In this way, analysts might provide more timely and adequate support to top management and elected officials.

Fiscal impact models might also improve the content of information available to central management, elected officials, and the general public. They are designed to provide more accurate information, permit analysts to explore a wider range of alternative policy decisions, and to free decision

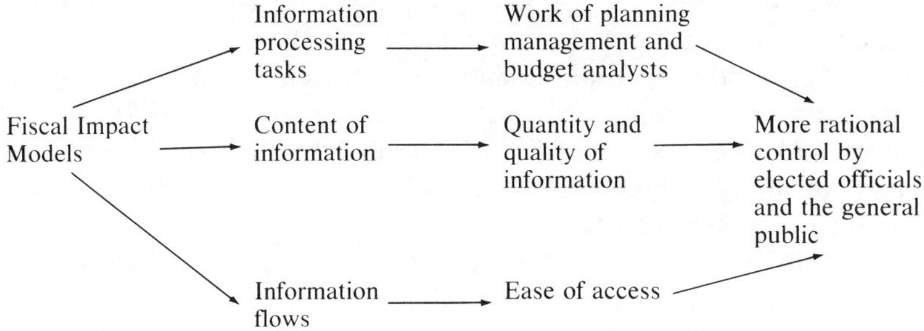

FIGURE A.4. Ideal Impact of Fiscal Impact Models

makers from traditional rules-of-thumb such as basing revenue estimates on the penultimate year plus or minus some major alteration of the community's revenue (e.g., an annexation or population decline).

Also, the models might alter the character of information flows. They might accomplish this, first, by presenting forecasts of the service, revenue, and expenditure implications of alternative policy decisions in a simple format (e.g., comparable to local government budget documents) that is directly interpretable by lay officials. Second, the models might present elected officials with information that is simplified, but otherwise less filtered and distorted than available through the more traditional decentralized and fragmented budgetary process. Third, they might have an educational role by informing elected officials and the public of the fiscal impacts of decisions.

The Practice: A Tool for Planners, Managers and Elected Officials

In practice, the use of fiscal impact models is constrained by characteristics of local government planning and budgeting decision processes. These constraints have prevented the use of the models from approaching their potential utility. They sometimes create work for analysts, sometimes distort projections, and sometimes confuse rather than enlighten lay policy officials.

There are a variety of technical and political–administrative factors that constrain the use and ultimate value of the models. Technically, the most severe constraint is the location, quality, and comprehensiveness of local government databases. Often, local government revenue, expenditure, service, and community data are incomplete, varied in quality, scattered among a variety of departments and agencies, collected and organized in different ways, and thus not easily assessible and comparable over time. As a consequence, the users of the models must devote considerable resources to constructing a satisfactory database—one that analysts and officials believe to be complete and accurate *enough* to make reasonable estimates. On the one hand, this is a limitation on the value of the models. On the other hand, the resulting database is often at least as complete and accurate, if not more so, than that which would be used for manual analyses. And, once constructed, the integrated database represents a potentially valuable resource for planning and management uses other than for implementing fiscal impact analyses.

Even if fiscal impact models were technically easy to implement, a host of political–administrative constraints affect their use and impacts. In practice, local government officials normally place severe constraints on the number of development alternatives to be evaluated. This is because they need to simplify their decision and lessen uncertainty over the outcome of the analysis. Officials are also unlikely to understand and fully trust the results of the models. And, the models are likely to be used selectively as a political tool rather than a rational tool, to gain credibility, publicity, and legitimacy in order to persuade others to support a given policy.

Despite these limiting constraints, a number of local governments have found them to be a useful tool for planners, managers, and elected officials. The most common use by planners has been to conduct traditional fiscal impact analyses of major planned land developments and sometimes general community plans. As such, the models are at times supplanting, but more often enhancing, traditional fiscal impact analysis techniques. Consistent with this use, the main adopters of the models have been councils-of-governments and county and municipal planning departments in some of the developing regions of the country.

The models have been used less frequently for revenue and expenditure forecasting, budgeting, and policy analysis. A variety of factors account for this. First, the models are typecast as a planning tool even though their applicability is potentially broader. Second, local governments have tried and trusted techniques for such functions as revenue and expenditure forecasting. Each analytical function is perceived as specialized and is increasingly performed by separate groups of analysts, each with their own home-grown techniques and practices. Often general purpose and transferred tools are mistrusted in this context.

Yet, because some local governments have envisioned these uses, some of the models have been adopted by the financial management division of some cities, which are taking over the analysis of fiscal impacts from the planning department. This is due in part to the heightened importance of fiscal issues, the growing presence of economists and public finance experts among the central management staff and the desire to bring fiscal analysis under tighter control of top elected and appointed officials. As such issues as development, growth management, and taxing/spending limitations become more paramount as public and highly political issues, control over fiscal analyses is likely to rise to higher levels within the organization.

The least common use of the models has been made by elected officials, community groups, and organizations. On the one hand, elected officials, community groups, and organizations are among the audience to which fiscal impact analyses are addressed. Used in this way, the models have some educational value by providing information regarding the fiscal consequences of policy alternatives. On the other hand, these groups seldom directly participate in the design and conduct of fiscal analyses. Yet, such direct involvement has occurred in some communities, that have experienced intense and protracted debate over community development. If these uses of adversary and counter-modeling became more common, they would be a tremendous educational tool. The models are relatively well-suited for such a function given the relative ease of estimating the consequences of alternative assumptions and policy scenarios.

References

Altschuler, A. A. (1965). *The city planning process: A political analysis.* Ithaca, NY: Cornell University Press.

Anthony, R. N. (1965). *Planning and control systems.* Boston, MA: Graduate School of Business Administration, Harvard University.

Ascher, W. (1978). *Forecasting: An appraisal for policy-makers and planners.* Baltimore, MD: Johns Hopkins University Press.

Ashley Economic Services. (1975). "A proposal for fiscal and economic impact studies." South Laguna, CA, November 10.

Ashley Economic Services. (1977). "Anaheim Hills West 9/19—Fiscal impact analysis." Prepared for Anaheim Hills, Inc., August.

Ashley Economic Services. (1978, November). "The Bauer Ranch fiscal impact analysis." Prepared for Kaufman and Broad, Inc., Newport Beach, CA.

Associated Homebuilders vs. City of Livermore. 17 Cal. Rptr. 5. Associated Homebuilders of the Greater East Bay, Inc., vs. City of Livermore. S.F. 20414, Supreme Court of California, November 16, 1961.

Bachrach, P., and Baratz, M. S. (1970). *Power and poverty: Theory and practice.* New York: Oxford University Press.

Banfield, E. C. (1961). *Political influence: A new theory of urban politics.* New York: The Free Press.

Bardach, E. (1977). *The implementation game.* Cambridge, MA: MIT Press.

Bell, D. (1973). *The coming of post-industrial society.* New York: Basic Books.

Bell, D. (1979). Communications technology—for better or worse. *Harvard Business Review 57*(3), 20–42.

Benveniste, G. (1977). *The politics of expertise,* (2nd Ed.). San Francisco, CA: Boyd & Fraser.

Bettencourt, P. (1977). Anaheim Hills, Inc. Letter to Mayor and City Council, City of Anaheim. RE: GPA #144 and EIR #207A, 12/20.

Bevis, H. W. (1959). A model for predicting urban travel patterns. *Journal of the American Institute of Planners 25* (May), 87–89.

Blumberg, D. F. (1979). *The emerging state of the art in the application of planning models for local government.* Jenkintown, PA: Decision Sciences Corporation.

Boettner, J. (1978a). "Man who guided growth now on the other side." *Los Angeles Times* (July 7), II-1.

Boettner, J. (1978b). "Anaheim to weigh revised ranch plans." *Los Angeles Times* (November 18), II-15.

Boettner, J. (1978c). "Planners approve canyon community." *Los Angeles Times* (December 5).

Boguslaw, R. (1965). *The new utopians.* Englewood Cliffs, NJ: Prentice-Hall.

Boyle, P. (1978). "Goliath Anaheim runs into David: Canyon residents seek new city in path of annexation," *Los Angeles Times* (July 7), II-1.

Brewer, G. D. (1973). *Politicians, bureaucrats, and consultants: A critique of urban problem solving.* New York: Basic Books.

Burby, R. J., and Weiss, S. F. (1976). *New communities U.S.A.* Lexington, MA: Lexington Books.

Burchell, R. W., and Listokin, D. (1978). *The fiscal impact handbook.* New Brunswick, NJ: Center for Urban Policy Research, Rutgers University.

California Building Industry Association. (1979). *Fiscal impact analyses: A broader context.* Prepared by Connery & Associates, April.

Calland, W. B. (1959). Forecasting traffic for freeway planning. *Journal of the American Institute of Planners 25* (May), 82–86.

Caplan, N. S., and Barton, E. (1973). *Social indicators.* Ann Arbor, MI: Center for Research on the Utilization of Scientific Knowledge, University of Michigan Institute for Social Research. (Mimeo)

Chaiken, J. (1978). Transfer of emergency service deployment models to operating agencies. *Management Science 24* (7), 719–731.

Citizens Direction Finding Commission. (1980). "The Impacts of Propositions 13 and 4 on Land Planning and New Developments" (Report and recommendations to the Orange County Board of Supervisors. C.D.F.C., Orange County, February.)

City of Anaheim, Planning Division. (1979). "Canyon general plan," July. October 26, 1977; November 17, 1977; December 4, 1978.

City of Anaheim, Minutes of the City Council Meetings: August 15, 1972; September 19, 1972; November 7, 1972; October 30, 1973; May 15, 1974; July 29, 1974; July 15, 1975; April 20, 1976; March 8, 1977; December 20, 1977; March 20, 1979.

City of Anaheim, Minutes of the Planning Commission Meetings: February 14, 1977; October 25, 1977; November 21, 1977; June 19, 1978; November 20, 1978; December 4, 1978.

City of Anaheim, Planning Department. (1979). "Dwelling unit and population estimates: Anaheim, California," July.

City of Anaheim, Planning Department Staff Memos: October 26, 1977; November 21, 1977; November 20, 1978; December 4, 1978.

City of Anaheim, Planning Division. (1979). "Canyon general plan," July.

City of Anaheim, Planning Division. (1977). "Canyon area general plan," March 8.

City of Anaheim, Planning Division. (1976). "Canyon area general plan land use decision model findings." December 7.

City of Anaheim, Planning Division. (1977). "1976 Anaheim census," January.

City of Anaheim and Ultrasystems, Inc. (1977). *User's manual on economic and environmental growth impact analyses: Computerized/manual methodology for use by local government jurisdictions,* June 30.

City Planning Commission. (1953). *Tulsa's future and you.* Tulsa, OK: Office of City Planning Commission.

City of San Diego. (1967). *Progress guide and general plan for the city of San Diego.* San Diego, CA: General Plan Advisory Committee, July.

City of San Diego, (1975). *North City West: Community plan.* San Diego, CA: Planning Department.

City of San Diego and Marcou, O'Leary and Associates. (1977). *Growth management: Fiscal impact study* (Vol. 1 analysis). Washington, DC: Marcou, O'Leary and Associates.

CRP (Coalition for Responsible Planning). (1977). A North City view of growth management. San Diego, CA (Mimeo).

Coopers and Lybrand. (1976). *Financial disclosure practices of the American cities.* New York: Coopers and Lybrand.

County of Orange. (1973). "Grant Application for H.U.D. Funding (701 Comprehensive Planning Assistance) for the Environmental Cost/Benefit Joint Study," September 28.

County of Orange, Cities of Anaheim, Orange, and Yorba Linda. (1975). "Preliminary Grant Application, Comprehensive Planning Assistance (701), Office of Planning and Research, for the Joint Environmental Cost/Benefit Study—Phase III," January 17.

County of Orange, Cities of Anaheim, Orange, and Yorba Linda. (1976). *Land use decision model* (Vol. 1: Description and use of the model). June 30.

Crecine, J. P. (1964). *Governmental problem-solving: A computer simulation of municipal budgeting.* New York: Rand-McNally.

Crenson, M. A. (1971). *The un-politics of air pollution.* Baltimore: The Johns Hopkins Press.

Curry, D. (1970/71). Irvine: The case for a new kind of planning. *Cry California* *6*(1), 18–40.

Cyert, R., and March, J. G. (1963). *A behavioral theory of the firm.* Englewood Cliffs, NJ: Prentice-Hall.

Dahl, R. A. (1961). *Who governs?* New Haven, CT: Yale University Press.

Dames and Moore. (1978). "Draft Environmental Impact Report for Santa Ana Canyon Annexation #7 to City of Anaheim." Prepared by LAFCO, October, (Job #06076–015–02).

Danziger, J. N. (1979a). The "skill bureaucracy" and intraorganizational control: The case of the data processing unit. *Sociology of Work and Occupations* *16*(2), 204–226.

Danziger, J. N. (1979b). The use of automated information in local government: A critical assessment. *American Behavioral Scientist* *22*(3), 363–392.

Danziger, J. N., and Dutton, W. H. (1977). Technological innovation and local government. *Policy and Politics* *6*(1), 27–49.

Danziger, J. N., Dutton, W. H., Kling, R., and Kraemer, K. L. (1982). *Computers and politics: High technology in American local governments*. New York: Columbia University Press.

Decision Sciences Corporation. (1980). *Fiscal impact analysis systems: Executive introduction to the fiscal impact analysis system*. Jenkintown, PA: Decision Sciences Corporation.

DeFleur, M. L., and Ball-Rokeach, S. (1982). *Theories of mass communication* (4th ed.). New York: Longman.

Department of Community Development. (1977). *General Plan Amendment No. 4, Workbook*. Irvine, CA: City of Irvine, May 3.

Downs, A. (1967). A realistic look at the payoffs from urban data systems. *Public Administration Review 27*(3), 204–210.

Drake, A. W. (Ed.). (1972). *Analysis of public systems*. Cambridge, MA: MIT Press.

Dutton, W. H. (1981). The rejection of an innovation: The political environment of a computer-based model. *Systems, Objectives, Solutions 1*(4), 179–201.

Dutton, W. H. (1982a). Computer models in the policy-making process. *Information Age 4*(2), 86–94.

Dutton, W. H. Politics, planning, and modeling. (1982b). *International Journal of Policy Analysis and Information Systems 6*(1), 65–89.

Dutton, W. H. (forthcoming) Decision making in the information age. In Brenda Dervin and Melvin Voight, eds. *Progress in Communication Sciences, Volume V*. Norwood, NJ: Ablex Publishing Corporation.

Dutton, W. H., Danziger, J. N., and Kraemer, K. L. (1980). Did the policy fail? The selective use of automated information in the policy making process. *In* D. Mann and H. Ingram (Eds.), *Why policies succeed or fail,* 163–184. Beverly Hills, CA: Sage Publications.

Dutton, W. H., and Hollis, M. S. (1980). Fiscal impact budgeting systems. *In* K. L. Kraemer and J. L. King (Eds.), *Computers in local government urban and regional planning,* Chapter 2.9.1. Pennsauken, NJ: Auerbach Publishers, Inc.

Dutton, W. H., Hollis, M. S., and Kraemer, K. L. (1978). "Fiscal Impact Budgeting Systems: A Behavioral Assessment." Unsolicited proposal to the National Science Foundation, Appendix C. Irvine, CA: Public Policy Research Organization, University of California.

Dutton, W. H., and Kraemer, K. L. (1977). Technology and urban management: The power payoffs of computing. *Administration and Society 9*(3), 304–340.

Dutton, W. H., and Kraemer, K. L. (1978). *The automation of bias: Computers and local government budgeting*. Public Policy Research Organization, University of California, Irvine, December.

Dutton, W. H., and Kraemer, K. L. (1980). Automating bias. *Society 17*(2), 36–41.

Economic Research and Analysis Program. (1978). "The Fiscal Impact of Managing Growth: Current Policies vs. Greater In-fill." Report prepared by Bruce Herring, Paul Mutascio, Claire Steinberger and supervised by Geoffrey Holt of the Economic Research and Analysis Program of the Financial Management Department. San Diego, CA: City of San Diego, July 31.

Editors. (1977). A system that's hard to beat. *New Worlds of Irvine 8*(4), 59–67.

Ellul, J. (1964). *The technological society*. J. Wilkinson, Trans. New York: Knopf/Vintage.

Eveland, J., Rogers, E. M., and Klepper, C. (1977). *The innovation process in public organizations*. Ann Arbor: University of Michigan, Department of Journalism.

Fallows, S. (forthcoming). The politics of innovation: Use of micro-simulation models for partisan analysis. *In* K. L. Kraemer, S. Dickhoven, S. Fallows and J. L. King, *Computers, planning models, and policy making: Implementation of high technology in federal agencies*. Irvine, CA: Public Policy Research Organization, University of California.

Financial Management Department. (1979). "The Fiscal Impact of North City West Development on Del Mar." Report prepared by Roy Callahan, Robert Dye, Bruce Herring, and Claire Steinberger and supervised by Connie Jamison. San Diego, CA: City of San Diego, September 25.

Fisher, R., and Ury, W., with Patton, B. (1981). *Getting to yes*. Boston, MA: Houghton Mifflin Company.

Foster, C. S., and Weddell, R. P. (1978). "*Cost/Revenue Analysis: North City West First Neighborhood*." Report prepared for the North City West Property Owners Association. La Jolla, CA: Copley International Corporation, December 12.

Fowler, E. P. (1971). Transportation models and muddles. *In* A. Lupo, F. Colcord, and E. P. Fowler (Eds.), *Rites of way*. Boston, MA: Little Brown, 139–159.

Fowler, J. P., Deputy City Manager. (1979). Report to the Honorable Mayor and City Council from the City Manager, City of San Diego, September 25.

Freedman, D. (1981). Some pitfalls in large econometric models: A case study. *The Journal of Business of the University of Chicago 54*(3), 479–500.

Freilich, R. H. (1974). Development timing, moratoria, and controlling growth. *Proceedings of the Southwestern Legal Foundation,* Institute on Planning, Zoning, and Eminent Domain, 147–219.

Freilich, R. H., and Leitner, M. (1977). *Growth guidance system for the City of Tulsa, Oklahoma*. Tulsa, OK: Tulsa Metropolitan Area Planning Council.

Freilich, R. H., and Ragsdale Jr., J. W. (1974). Timing and sequential controls. *Minnesota Law Review 58*(6), 1009–1090.

Freilich, R. H., and Stuhler, E. O. (1977). *The statutory authority for a growth system*. Tulsa, OK: Tulsa Metropolitan Area Planning Council.

Freilich, R. H., and Stuhler, E. O. (1979). *Flood plain regulations*. Tulsa, OK: Tulsa Metropolitan Area Planning Council.

Freilich, R. H., and Stuhler, E. O. (1981). *The land use awakening*. American Bar Association, ABA Press.

Frieden, B. J. (1979). *The environmental protection hustle*. Cambridge, MA: The MIT Press.

Gaffney, M. (1978). Appendix A. *In* W. H. Dutton, M. H. Hollis, and K. L. Kraemer, "Fiscal Impact Budgeting Systems." Unsolicited proposal to the National Science Foundation. Irvine, CA: Public Policy Research Organization, University of California, Irvine.

Gale, D. (1973). *The municipal impact evaluation system: Computer-assisted cost/revenue analysis of urban development*. Chicago, IL: American Society of Planning Officials.

Gilbert, E. (1961). *The university town in England and West Germany*. Chicago, IL: Department of Geography, University of Chicago.

Greenberger, M. (1983). *Caught unawares: The energy decade in retrospect*. Cambridge, MA: Ballinger Publishing Company.

Greenberger, M., Crenson, M. A., and Crissey, B. L. (1976). *Models in the policy process: Public decision making in the computer era*. New York: Russell Sage Foundation.

Greenberger, M., Crenson, M. A., and Crissey, B. L. (1976). Modeling and the political process. *Computers and Society* 7(1), 3–14.

Greider, W. (1981). The education of David Stockman. *The Atlantic Monthly, 248*(6), 27–54.

Griffin, N. (1974). IRVINE: The genesis of a new community. Washington DC: Urban Land Institute Special Report.

Hafter Jr., H. H. (1976). "Growth management: A study of San Diego's policy and its effect on North City." Master's thesis prepared for the School of Public Administration and Urban Studies, San Diego State University.

Hagman, D. G. (1981). "Santa Monica's call preserve." *Los Angeles Times,* June 14, Part VIII.

Hale, G. E., and Douglass, S. R. (1977). The politics of budget execution. *Administration and Society* 9(3), 367–378.

Hamburg, J. R., and Creighton, R. L. (1959). Predicting Chicago's land use pattern. *Journal of the American Institute of Planners 25*(May), 67–72.

Hansen, W. G. (1959). How accessibility shapes land use. *Journal of the American Institute of Planners 25*(May), 73–76.

Hayes, E. C. (1972). *Power structure and urban policy*. New York: McGraw-Hill Book Company.

Hiltz, S. R., and Turoff, M. (1978). *The network nation*. Reading, MA: Addison-Wesley.

Hogan, M. (1980). "Pete Wilson," *California Business* (February), 35–36, 56.

Hollis, M. S. (1980). "Microanalysis of Decision-Making with a Large-Scale Fiscal Impact Model." (Paper presented at the National Meeting of the American Institute of Decision Sciences, Las Vegas, NV.)

Hollis, M. S. (1978). "Methodological Issues in the Evaluation of Fiscal Impact Budgeting Simulation Models." (Paper presented at the Joint National Meeting of The Operations Research Society of America/The Institute of Management Sciences).

Hunter, F. (1956). *Community power structure*. Chapel Hill, NC: University of North Carolina Press.

Huysmans, J. H. B. M. (1970). *The implementation of operations research*. New York: John Wiley and Sons.

Integrated Planning Office. (1979). "Memo to Board of Supervisors regarding 'Review of City of San Diego Growth Management Plan.' " San Diego, CA: February 16.

Irvine Student Coalition. (undated). ISC Handbook. Irvine, CA.

Kahn, H. (1982). *The coming boom*. New York: Simon and Schuster.

Katz, E. (1980). On conceptualizing media effect. Los Angeles, CA: Annenberg School of Communications, USC. (Mimeo)

Keen, P. (1977). Implementation research in OR/MS and MIS: Description versus prescription. Stanford, CA: Graduate School of Business, Stanford University.

Keen, P. G. W., and Morton, M. S. S. (1978). *Decision support systems: An organizational perspective*. Reading, MA: Addison-Wesley.

King, J. (1983). Successful implementation of large-scale decision support systems. *Systems, Objectives, Solutions, 3*(4), (November), 183–205.

King, J. L. (1984). Ideology and use of large-scale decision support systems in national decision making. *Systems, Objectives, Solutions, 4*(2), pp. 81–104.

Kirlin, J., and Chapman, J. (1980). An active approach to revenue generation. *The Urban Interest 2*(2), 83–91.

Kling, R. (1978). Information systems as social resources in policy making. *Proceedings of the ACM National Conference* (December), 664–674.

Kling, R. (1980). Social analyses of computing. *Computing Surveys 12*(1), 61–110.

Komsky, S. (1983). The utilization of computer-based models in local government. *Systems, Objectives, Solutions, 3*(2), 95–103.

Kovaric, P. (1982). "Acceptance of Modeling and DSS in Policy Making and Organizations." Los Angeles, CA: Annenberg School, unpublished mimeo.

Kraemer, K. L. (1973). *Policy analysis in local government: A systems approach to decision-making*. Washington, DC: ICMA.

Kraemer, K. L. (1977). Local government, information systems, and technology transfer. *Public Administration Review 37* (4), 368–382.

Kraemer, K. L. (1979). *Comparative study of strategies for successful transfer of planning models in German and American governments*. Irvine, CA: Public Policy Research Organization, University of California.

Kraemer, K. L. (1981). The politics of model implementation. *Systems, Objectives, Solutions 1*(4), 161–178.

Kraemer, K. L., Danziger, J. N., and Dutton, W. H. (1979). Automated information systems and urban decision making. *Urban Systems 3*(4), 177–190.

Kraemer, K. L., and Dutton, W. H. (1979). The interests served by technological reform. *Administration and Society 2*(1), 80–106.

Kraemer, K. L., Dutton, W. H., and Matthews, J. (1975). Municipal computers. *Urban Data Service Reports, 7*(11).

Kraemer, K. L., Dutton, W. H., and Northrop, A. (1981). *The management of information systems*. New York: Columbia University Press.

Lambright, W. H. (1976). *Governing science and technology*. New York: Oxford University Press.

Lambright, W. H. (1977). *Adoption and utilization of urban technology: A decision-making study*. Syracuse, NY: Syracuse Research Corporation.

Lambright, W. H. (1979). *Technology Transfer to Cities*. Syracuse, NY: Maxwell School of Public Affairs, University of Syracuse.

Laudon, K. C. (1974). *Computers and bureaucratic reform: The political functions of urban information systems*. New York: John Wiley & Sons.

Laudon, K. C. (1977). *Communications technology and democratic participation*. New York: Praeger Publishers.

League of Women Voters of Anaheim. (1978). "Know Your City: Anaheim, California," June.

Lee, D. B., Jr. (1973). Requiem for large-scale models. *Journal of the American Institute of Planners, 39*(2), 136–78.

Lindblom, C. E. (1968). *The policymaking process*. Englewood Cliffs, NJ: Prentice-Hall, Inc.

Lindblom, C. E. (1980). *The policymaking process*, (2nd ed.). Englewood Cliffs, NJ: Prentice-Hall, Inc.

Lindblom, C. E., and Cohen, D. K. (1979). Usable knowledge: Social science and social problem solving. New Haven, CT: Yale University Press.

Lippman, W. ([1922]. 1965.). *Public opinion*. New York: The Free Press.

Livingston and Blayney. (1969–71). *Foothills environmental design study:* Reports 1 and 2 (1969), Report 3 (1970), Report 4 (1971), and Final Report (1971). Palo Alto, California.

Lockard, D. (1971). *The perverted priorities of American politics*. New York: The Macmillan Company.

Lorsch, N. W., and Morse, J. J. (1974). *Organizations and their members: A contingency approach*. New York: Harper & Row.

Lowi, T. J. (1981). The political impact of information technology. *In* J. Forrester (Ed.), *The microelectronics revolution*, Cambridge, MA: MIT Press, 453–472.

Lowry, I. (1967). "Seven Models of Urban Development: A Structural Comparison." RAND Paper P-3673, The Rand Corporation, Santa Monica, CA.

Lucado, P. A. (1979a). "A case analysis of combining land use planning and economics." A project presented to the Faculty of California State University, Fullerton, in partial fulfillment of requirements for the degree of Master of Arts in Geography.

Lucado, P. A. (1979b). "Fiscal impact considerations for a proposed regional shopping center in the Santa Ana Canyon." A project presented to the Faculty of California State University, Fullerton, in partial fulfillment of requirements for the degree of Master of Arts in Geography.

Lucas, H. C. (1973). *Why information systems fail*. New York: Columbia University Press.

Lupo, A., Colcord, F., and Fowler, E. P. (1971). *Rites of way: The politics of transportation in Boston and the U.S. city*. Boston, MA: Little, Brown and Company.

Magnuson, E., Beckworth, D., and Brew, D. (1981). A visit to the woodshed. *Time*, (November 23), 10–13.

Malone, E. (1976). Orange County Environmental Management Agency. "Report on the history and current status of the joint environmental cost/benefit study." Prepared for the Orange County Board of Supervisors, November.

Margolis, J. (1956). On municipal land policy for fiscal gains. *National Tax Journal* 9(3), 247–257.

Margolis, J. (1957). Municipal fiscal structure in a metropolitan region. *The Journal of Political Economy 45*(3), 225–235.

Matthews, J., Dutton, W. H., and Kraemer, K. L. (1976). County computers: Growth, usage and management. *In The county yearbook,* 133–149. Washington, DC: International City Management Association.

Meltsner, A. J. (1976). *Policy analysts in the bureaucracy.* Los Angeles, CA: University of California Press.

Mendelson, H. (1982). Presentation at the Annenberg School of Communications, January 9.

Meyerson, M., and Banfield, E. C. (1955). *Politics, planning and the public interest.* Glencoe, IL: The Free Press.

Mitchel, R. B., and Rapkin, C. (1965). *Urban traffic: A function of land use.* New York: Columbia University Press.

Marshall, Kaplan, Gans and Kahn. (1976). *The fiscal and economic analysis of general plan options.* San Francisco, CA: Marshall, Kaplan, Gans and Kahn, November 15.

Moritz, M. (1981). "A dip into a think tank." *Time* (November 30), 65.

Morse, P. M., (Ed.). (1977). *Operations research for public systems.* Cambridge, MA: MIT Press.

Morton, M. S., and Huff, S. (1980). The impact of computers on planning and decision-making. *In* H. T. Smith and T. R. G. Green (Eds.), *Human interaction with computers,* 177–202. New York: Academic Press.

Moss, M. (1980). *Telecommunications and productivity.* Reading, MA: Addison-Wesley.

Mowshowitz, A. (1977). "Computers and the Mechanization of Judgment." (Paper delivered at the National Symposium for Philosophy and Computer Technology, SUNY at Albany, New York, March 21–22.)

Nakamura, R., and Smallwood, F. (1980). *The politics of policy implementation.* New York: St. Martin's Press.

National Committee on Governmental Accounting. (1978). *Governmental accounting, auditing and financial reporting.* Chicago, IL: Municipal Finance Officers Association.

Naylor, T., Glass, H. E., Wall, J., and Milstein, D. N. *Simplan: A computer based planning system for government.* Durham, NC: Duke University Press, 1977.

Nora, S., and Minc, A. (1980). *The computerization of society.* Cambridge, MA: The MIT Press.

Oettinger, A. (1971). Communications in the national decision-making process. *In* M. Greenberger (Ed.), *Computers, communications and the public interest,* 73–114. Baltimore, MD: Johns Hopkins University Press.

Pack, H., and Pack, J. R. (1977a). The resurrection of the urban development model. *Policy Analysis 3*(3), 407–427.

Pack, H., and Pack, J. R. (1977b). Urban land-use models: The determinants of adoption and use. *Policy Sciences 8*(1), 79–101.

Pack, J. R. (1973). *The use of urban models.* Philadelphia, PA: School of Urban and Public Policy, University of Pennsylvania.

Pereira, W. L. and Associates. (1959). *A university campus and community study: Phase one*. Los Angeles, CA: W. L. Pereira and Associates.

Pereira, W. L. and Associates. (1960). *Second phase report: A university campus and community study*. Los Angeles, CA: W. L. Pereira and Associates.

Pereira, W. L. and Luckman, C. (1958). *Campus site selection study*. Los Angeles, CA: Pereira and Luckman.

Perry, J. L. and Kraemer, K. L. (1979). *Technological innovation in American local governments*. New York: Pergamon Press.

Peterson, J. E., Spain, C. L., and Laffey, M. F. (1978). *State and local government financial management*. Washington, DC: Government Finance Research Center, Municipal Finance Officers Association.

Porat, M. (1977). *The information economy: Definition and measurement*. Washington, DC: U.S. Department of Commerce.

Pressman, J., and Wildavsky, A. (1973). *Implementation*. Berkeley, CA: University of California Press.

Price, D. K. (1965). *The scientific estate*. Cambridge, MA: Harvard University Press.

Redford, E. S. (1969). *Democracy in the administrative state*. New York: Oxford University Press.

Regional Environmental Consultants. (1979). *Environmental impact report: Carmel Valley—North City West*. San Diego, CA: RECON, Regional Environmental Consultants.

Rice, R. E., and Rogers, E. M. (1980). Reinvention in the innovation process. *Knowledge 1*(4), 499–514.

Robertson, J. (1980). A brief historical summary of Tulsa's growth planning strategies. Unpublished planning research paper. Tulsa, OK: Tulsa Metropolitan Area Planning Commission.

Rogers, E. M., and Shoemaker, F. F. (1971). *Communication of innovations,* (2nd ed.). New York: The Free Press.

Roth, R. F., Gass, S. I., and Lemoine, A. J. (1979). Some considerations for improving federal modeling. *In* B. P. Zeigler. (Ed.), *Methodology in systems modeling and simulation,* 166–175. Amsterdam: North Holland Publishing Company.

Sayre, W. S., and Kaufman, H. (1960). *Governing New York City: Politics in the metropolis*. New York: W. W. Norton & Company, Inc.

Schaff, D. (1977). Computer models do it better. *New Worlds of Irvine 8*(4), pp. 59, 67–68.

Schattschneider, E. E. (1960). *The semi-sovereign people: A realist's view of democracy in America*. New York: Holt, Rinehart and Winston.

Schiller, H. I. (1981). *Who knows: Information in the age of the Fortune 500*. Norwood, NJ: Ablex Publishing Company.

Schroeder, L. (1982). Local government multi-year budgetary forecasting: Some administrative and political issues. *Public Administrative Review 42*(2), 121–127.

Segilman, D. (1981). In partial defense of David Stockman. *Fortune 104*(12) (December 14), 89–90.

Shefter, M. (1977). New York City's fiscal crisis: The politics of inflation and retrenchment. *The Public Interest* No. 48, 98–127.

Shibutani, T. (1967). *Improvised news.* Indianapolis, IN: Bobbs-Merrill.

Simon, H. A. (1960). *The new science of management decision.* New York: Harper and Row.

Simon, H. A. (1971). Designing organizations for an information-rich world. *In* M. Greenberger (Ed.), *Computers, communications and the public interest,* 37–72. Baltimore, MD: Johns Hopkins University Press.

Simon, H. A. (1973). Applying information technology to organizational design. *Public Administration Review 33*(3), 268–278.

Simon, H. A. (1975). *Models of man.* New York: John Wiley.

Simon, H. A. (1977). *The new science of management decision.* Englewood Cliffs, NJ: Prentice-Hall.

Smollar, D. (1979). "Board fears retaliation on North City West," *Los Angeles Times,* (February 14), Part II.

State of California. Office of Planning and Research. (1974). *Growth strategy for California.* Sacramento, CA.

State of California. Office of Planning and Research. (1974). *Urban growth strategy for California.* Sacramento, CA.

Suss, W. H. (1980). "Data Oriented Design: An Approach to Bridging the Means-End Gap in Planning Models." Jenkintown, PA: Decision Sciences Corporation. (Mimeo)

Tannenbaum, P. H. (1977). The indexing process in communication. *Public Opinion Quarterly 19,* 292–302.

"The Stockman Papers." (1981). *New Republic,* (December 2), 5.

Tornatsky, L. G., Roitman, D., Boylan, M., Carpenter, J., Eveland, J. D., Hetzner, W. A., Lucas, B. G., and Schneider, J. (1980). "Innovation Processes and their Management: A Conceptual, Empirical, and Policy Review of Innovation Process Research." Washington, DC: Division of Policy Research and Analysis, National Science Foundation, March 21. (Mimeo)

TMAPC (Tulsa Metropolitan Area Planning Commission). (1965). *Metropolitan land use.* Tulsa, OK: City of Tulsa.

TMAPC (Tulsa Metropolitan Area Planning Commission). (1967). *Zoning policy statement.* Tulsa, OK: City of Tulsa.

TMAPC (Tulsa Metropolitan Area Planning Commission). (1973). *Growth policy.* Tulsa, OK: City of Tulsa.

Tulsa Metropolitan Area Planning Commission. (1974). *Vision 2000: Phase two.* Tulsa, OK: City of Tulsa.

Tulsa Tribune. June 15, 1977.

Tulsa World. Editorials. April 14, 1977; January 15, 1977.

Turner, G. R., and Associates. (1972). *Alternatives for urban growth and form.* Washington, DC: Department of Housing and Urban Development.

Turner, G. R., and Associates. (1973). *Balanced metropolitan growth.* Tulsa, OK: Turner and Associates.

Ultrasystems, Inc. (1980). ". . . A company profile." Ultrasystems, Inc., Irvine, California.

Ultrasystems, Inc. (Date unknown). "How to use the models: Local government fiscal impact model."

Ultrasystems, Inc. (1980). "1980 annual report." Ultrasystems, Inc., Irvine, California.

Voorhees, A. M. (1955). A general theory of traffic movement. *Institute of Traffic Engineers, Proceedings 25,* 45–46.

Watzlawick, P. (1976). *How real is real? Confusion, disinformation, communication.* New York: Random House/Vintage Books.

Weimer, D. L. (1980). CIMS implementation: A demonstration of predictive analysis. *Public Administration Review 40*(3), 231–240.

Weimer, D. L. (forthcoming). *The strategic petroleum reserve: Planning, implementation and analysis.*

Weizenbaum, J. (1976). *Computer power and human reason.* San Francisco, CA: W. H. Freeman and Company.

Weiss, C. H. (Ed.). (1977). *Using social research in public policy making.* Lexington, MA: Lexington Books.

Whisler, T. L. (1967). The impact of information technology on organizational control. *In* C. A. Meyers (Ed.), *The impact of computers on management,* 16–60. Cambridge, MA: MIT Press.

Wildavsky, A. (1957). *The politics of the budgetary process.* Boston, MA: Little-Brown.

Williams, F. (1982). *The communications revolution.* Beverly Hills, CA: Sage Publications.

Williams, S., (1978). "Request for Proposal: Fiscal Impact Analysis." Tulsa, OK: Growth Guidance System, January 6.

Winner, L. (1977). *Autonomous technology.* Cambridge, MA: MIT Press.

Wise, H. (1956). *Sketch plan for Tulsa and five mile perimeter area.* Tulsa, OK: Harold F. Wise Associates.

Wright, B., Hall, Jr., J. R., and Hatry, H. P. (1978). *An examination of productivity-related findings from the "Four-City" projects and the RAND and PTI fire deployment analysis approaches.* Washington, DC: The Urban Institute.

Yin, R. K. (1981). Life histories of innovations: How new practices become routinized. *Public Administration Review 41*(1), 21–28.

Yin, R. K., and Quick, S. K. (1979). Routinization I: Thinking about routinization. Santa Monica, CA: The Rand Corporation. (Mimeo)

Yin, R. K., Heald, K., Vogel, M., Fleischauer, P., and Vladeck, B. (1976). "A Review of Case Studies of Technological Innovations in State and Local Services." Santa Monica, CA: RAND Corporation. (Report R-1870/NSF), February.

Zientara, M. (1979). "Technique aids forecasting of political crises." *Computerworld* (June 4), 30.

Zovanyi, G. (1970). "North City: A metropolis the size of Long Beach right next door." *San Diego Magazine* (August), 42–45.

Author Index

Italics indicate bibliographic citations.

Subject Index

www.ingramcontent.com/pod-product-compliance
Lightning Source LLC
LaVergne TN
LVHW100256210926
848480LV00003B/941
* 9 7 9 8 9 9 4 2 1 7 0 4 7 *